New Perspectives
on Personality Development
in College Students

Florence B. Brawer

Foreword by C. Robert Pace

NEW
PERSPECTIVES
ON
PERSONALITY
DEVELOPMENT
IN
COLLEGE
STUDENTS

 Jossey-Bass Publishers
San Francisco • Washington • London • 1973

NEW PERSPECTIVES ON PERSONALITY DEVELOPMENT IN COLLEGE STUDENTS
by Florence B. Brawer

Copyright © 1973 by: Jossey-Bass, Inc., Publishers
615 Montgomery Street
San Francisco, California 94111

&

Jossey-Bass Limited
3 Henrietta Street
London WC2E 8LU

Library of Congress Catalogue Card Number LC 73-7150

International Standard Book Number ISBN 0-87589-189-6

Manufactured in the United States of America

JACKET DESIGN BY WILLI BAUM

FIRST EDITION

Code 7331

The Jossey-Bass Series in
Higher Education
and Behavioral Science

Portions of this work were provided by

ERIC
Clearinghouse for Junior Colleges
University of California, Los Angeles

ARTHUR M. COHEN, *director*

*The ERIC (Educational Resources Information Center)
program is sponsored by the
United States Department of Health, Education, and Welfare,
National Institute of Education.
The points of view expressed here do not necessarily represent
official National Institute of Education position or policy.*

Foreword

Following the conventions of experimental science is not the only road to knowledge and understanding. Breaking complex phenomena down into smaller segments, measuring and analyzing each piece or variable, often results in losing the very phenomena one wants to study. Like Humpty Dumpty all the pieces cannot be put together again. The study of environments, the concept of an ecosystem, the view of Earth from outer space all testify to the new meaning one can grasp by trying to comprehend the whole directly. At least in some of its manifestations science itself is becoming more holistic, less atomistic.

Florence Brawer's book, as I see it, is her personal exploration of ways of thinking about college students as persons, that is, as dynamic, holistic, individual beings. In this sense, her direction of thought and her persuasion are in line with the global directions of science. But she is not really a scientist; she is what I would call a clinical humanist trying to make the best of a bad scene in educational and psychological testing, especially as used with students not previously inclined to go to college (much of the community college population) who often believe tests are used against them rather than for them.

Although she classifies entering students in the community colleges as being high, medium, or low on a "measure" she labels functional potential, she does not classify them in the spirit of, or with the customary evidence of, a psychometrician. Rather, she does so as a case in point, an example, an idea that might in the future be found to have some utility. In fact, to take up the psychometrician's burden for a sentence, if all we knew about entering students in the community colleges was whether they were high, medium, or low on functional potential, we would know far less about them than we already know from many other extant measurements. But to say this is to miss the point of what the author is trying to do. She is not trying to sell a new measure; she is trying to infuse a new spirit into the thinking of community college staff members and others concerned with higher education. She is trying to show that one can and should look at responses to questionnaire items in relation to concepts about personality—concepts of development, of maturity, of ego strength, or, in her terms, of functional potential. How nice it would be if all questionnaire makers tried to get so much out of what they have asked! And how much junk might be eliminated!

For the practitioner in higher education, the value of *New Perspectives on Personality Development in College Students* may well be that it constantly makes him contend with theories of personality, to think about his students as real people, and to attach faces and histories and feelings to test scores or numbers. What might this mean in practice? The Carnegie Commission on Higher Education has tried to make a case for a three-year degree, which, they argue, can be attained by breaking something called a lockstep, or the notion that a degree means four years of work. Their advocacy is primarily on economic grounds (three years are cheaper than four) and secondarily on educational grounds. If the Commission had thought primarily of the student as a person, with awareness of the concepts of development, maturity, ego strength, and functional potential, it might have guessed that, with increased flexibility in timing, some students (perhaps a majority) may want to take longer and, in relation to their functional potential, probably should take longer rather than shorter periods of time to complete a degree program.

Our judgments are influenced by the concepts and values

that we hold in our consciousness. If education is to be more human-ized and less mechanized, more individualized and less regimented, then the psychological concepts and values that Florence Brawer discusses in this book need to be held clearly in the minds of the decision-makers.

C. ROBERT PACE
Professor of Higher Education
University of California, Los Angeles

Preface

I suppose that almost every person holds within him certain myths or beliefs about his fellow men and about life—ideas that have been a part of his thinking and feeling for as long as he can remember. These are the kinds of emotionally laden "certainties" that form the basis for much of our sense of self, our views of society, and our positive or negative stereotypes of others. They vary in type and in the intensity with which they are held, but they are nonetheless important to their beholder.

One of the beliefs that I hold closely—one that stems from my parents, Sali W. and Henry J. Blum, and that I have passed on to my children—is that people are people. Everyone comprises many strengths and weaknesses; a group of individuals representing a given society or subculture has both positive and negative components. For me, this belief leads to the accompanying conviction that the more one expresses one side overtly, the more the other side lies covered and unconscious—an idea expressed better and in greater depth by Jung, whose thoughts about opposites and their compensatory roles are incorporated in his classification of psychological types.

Further extended, this idea suggests that the positive and

the negative, the "good" and the "bad," the conscious and the unconscious, cross over party lines, go beyond socioeconomic barriers,
and pass through cultural domains. One can like and admire and
feel an affinity for a totally different person who comes from a different cultural group with a different life style. And conversely, a
person can be neutral toward, even dislike, someone who, at least
on the surface, is much like himself or herself. The acceptance of
others unlike oneself is particularly evident today, when the young
especially are leading the way in knocking down some of the fences
that had existed previously.

Feeling so strongly about this people-are-people idea, I set
out to find different ways to look at individuals functioning in
groups. Many of my thoughts were developed through work with
Bruno Klopfer, who, in spending a great part of his life interpreting responses to the Rorschach ink blots, covered the gamut of human strengths, pathology, and potential. Later, working with C.
Robert Pace as my major professor, I developed a word-association
technique to assess ego strength. Other ideas are reported in a variety of papers in which I attempt to conceptually synthesize notions of the functioning person. And still other ideas, prejudices,
and expressions of values and belief systems are merged into a book
that Arthur M. Cohen and I wrote about the community college
instructor—his identity, development, and professional maturity.

*New Perspectives on Personality Development in College
Students* represents another step along the path. It presents a conceptual model and an approach to human assessment that are nontraditional and are unique for the population (Community College
students) involved—a procedure that cuts across many of the educational and ethnic and socioeconomic boundaries previously erected.
It is my way of negating the generalized but narrow suggestion that
innate biological differences among people make some inferior to
others. It is my way of looking at each person in terms of his
strengths and weaknesses, of reinforcing the view that individuals
differ in their abilities to function according to set patterns in various situations. And it is my attempt to show that since the potential
—if not the actual—functioning level of a person may cut across
traditional barriers, each person must be seen as an individual and

be given a chance on the basis of who *he* is—not because he comes from a special place or represents particular people. This applies to all groups—social, religious, cultural, as well as male and female. And it applies to students who, despite much misunderstanding and stereotyping, are people, too.

New Perspectives on Personality Development in College Students furthers personality theory and reports research to support that theoretical structure. Institutional planners and researchers, whose studies may provide the bases upon which plans are formulated, should find this material useful. Guidance counselors, curriculum planners, professors of higher education, graduate students in the behavioral sciences, university and college researchers, and faculty members should also be able to utilize some of the ideas presented here. In general, the book is addressed to anyone who wishes to understand students. It does not offer precise directions for curriculum revision or exact techniques for conducting programs and classes, but it does describe different ways of looking at community college students. Understanding any group seems a prerequisite to the establishment of goals and the means for effecting them.

I would like to look at people on a more horizontal plane than the one I present here. That is, although conscious of the desire to refute certain traditions, I still find myself rating functional potential—the central concept running through most of the material presented here—in terms of one, two, three or high, medium, and low. I would prefer to say that a person who is a high (three) on functional potential may be a low on some other equally important dimension. But this is a direction that remains to be pursued with other data and, possibly, with other populations. I am most aware of my failure to further extend the strength/weakness hypothesis and would someday hope to redress this deficiency.

To advance such understanding, it is encouraging to have a concept or construct or idea or even a myth, if you will, by which people can be examined—something that cuts across many of the prejudices manifested in traditional assessment procedures. My approach bears some promise for appraising people and for devising different curricular schemes that might be implemented in new academic and experiential situations. It offers some alternative ways of thinking about career education and personal development. I am aware of my proselytizing, that I am openly attempting to convert the reader; I hope the person who reads here my rationale, presentation of data, and ideas for further directions will end believing as strongly as I do that people are people.

Chapter One offers theoretical formulations based on empirical data. Chapter Two describes three concepts basic to the central construct, which is described in Chapter Three, and Chapter Four discusses the six major components constituting this concept. Chapter Five presents the paradigm of the study through which many of the ideas described in the first four chapters were tested —the Project for the Design, Development, and Dissemination of Research Models for Junior Colleges, usually referred to as the 3-D Project—and discusses the sample institutions—Urban, Suburban, and Rural—which were used for this study of community college freshmen. In Chapters Six through Eleven, I present theoretical structures, related research, and data gathered on incoming freshmen. Most of this material relates functional potential scores to demographic information, a multiphasic technique for assessing college students, two value scales, other selected variables, and attrition. Chapter Twelve is a synthesis of the findings; it presents ways in which my theories and results may be used as a basis for planning curriculums and instituting changes in higher education. A list of items included in the several independent variables is found in the Appendix.

Many people provided a variety of services for assembling this book. I am especially indebted to the students who were subjects and to the community college presidents and deans who so graciously participated in the 3-D Project.

Many other people contributed to various phases of this project. Kent Dallett, Daniel Fader, and Margaret McClean offered critical comments on a preliminary paper that laid the groundwork for much of my thinking on functional potential. Nicholas E. Brink and Taka Ashigaga did some data analysis, while most of the statistical work was done by Thomas B. Farver, who, in his own intuitive, creative, and patient way, provided much help in transforming raw data into interpretable forms. The ERIC Clearinghouse for Junior Colleges staff was most helpful in the manuscript preparation. Special thanks go to Marcia Boyer, Lorel Bratton, Kary Mercer, Helen Schwartz, and Elaine Sturdivant.

John Lombardi and Leslie Purdy, also of the ERIC staff, read the complete manuscript and offered many valuable comments. Norma J. Feshbach and Louise L. Tyler critiqued the chapter on development. Robert F. Suczek's evaluation of the entire manuscript did much to clarify my own thinking. Milton Rokeach gave special permission to use his value scales and offered useful comments about an earlier presentation of the values material. To all these people I express my sincere thanks.

I am particularly grateful for the constant assistance of Arthur M. Cohen in the early conception of the project, the collection and analyses of data, and the final writing. His encouragement, critical analyses, and participation aided me throughout the development of the book.

This book is lovingly dedicated to my children, Anne and Michael.

Los Angeles   FLORENCE B. BRAWER
September 1973

Contents

New Perspectives
on Personality Development
in College Students

Chapter 1

The Framework

Until the 1960s, higher education knew little about its people. The few early attempts to examine college students stood isolated—occasional cultivated areas dotting the vast and fallow landscapes. And the examination eventually generated by those behavioral scientists who initiated the study of college populations was rather slow in coming. Despite this lag, however, once research on college students began, it began with a special intensity and dedication. Where else were such ready groups available for examination? Who else could compete in terms of accessibility and interest? If most studies merely repeated a handful of original investigations, this lack of creativity was not questioned. The search for models, guidelines, and unique types progressed in earnest and, accordingly, the literature grew. Even though most of these data tend to be parochial, indigenous to the schools that spawned them, and focused on students in select liberal arts colleges or in a limited number of multiversities, we can now draw fairly accurate profiles of people who attended our nation's institutions of higher education in the mid-1900s.

Sometimes yesterday's facts become tomorrow's myths. One of the few certainties about life is that it is an ongoing, changing, hopefully progressing process—in other words, while in many ways it remains uncertain and ambiguous, it is always moving. Thus, data gathered in the past soon become obsolete. We can extrapolate information about the elite who attended colleges during the surge of aristocratic mimicry in the 19th and early 20th centuries and we can make other assumptions about the bright youngsters who went on to higher education during the 1940s and 1950s, at the height of the meritocracy (Cross, 1971). Yet, the information available is not always systematically formulated or appropriate for changing populations. The outlook and aspirations of youth today are simply not those of an earlier day. Berkeley, the Kennedys, and Martin Luther King *did* happen. They *were* watersheds. Looking inward, mind-expansion, astrology, are all real. Whether or not any one of these proves a fad is of no moment—it is *real* now. Tomorrow's reality is for tomorrow.

We are in a new era. Students who enter college today do not belong solely to a landed gentry or an affluent sector of society. Many are from lower socio-economic backgrounds but are highly motivated and intellectually oriented. Others are less well prepared academically and often immature members of the middle class. And tomorrow's college-going populations will likely number as many "new" students—young adults who, in previous years, would not have seriously considered college attendance for themselves— as students similar to those of an earlier day. If present trends continue, this change will hold for the greater number of post-secondary institutions. At the same time, in part because of the national thrust toward assisting potentially able new students and broadening the enrollment patterns in more traditional schools, the community college will undoubtedly find that the majority of its students *both* represent lower socioeconomic levels and have lower scores on the types of intellectual and academic achievement tests generally employed than students in four-year colleges and universities.

What do we know, then, about these students? In what ways are they like the more traditional college-going populations of previous years? How do they differ? What can our studies of these men and women tell us about education and contemporary society? And what future goals and programs will the new research suggest?

In 1968, already aware of the limited research on community college students but anticipating changes and new trends, Cross noted that "we possess only traditional measures to describe a student who does not fit the tradition" (p. 53). Although the research has now become more systemized and broader, if not greater in depth, the traditional measures of ability and previous academic performance are still used. Helpful in sorting, if not in educating, yesterday's students, they are too limited now. They present only narrow facets of the multidimensional man, and they fail to account for changing times, changing emphases, and changing populations —limitations unfortunate for all students in higher education.

The problem is most acute, however, in the community college, this new force called upon to enroll all types of students. The few studies that examine community college students typically see them in terms of academic goals—vocational/technical or transfer, of grade point averages and/or scores on academic achievement tests, and of socioeconomic status. This information, however, is too narrow, too limited, too dependent upon older and traditional measures. Available data also do not account for the different emphases and outlooks of new students who see higher education as the logical extension of secondary school as well as the expected step to preparing for either a vocation or further academic study.

Whereas not so long ago we could say that there was very little research about junior college students and still less about faculties and administrative staffs in these institutions, some material is now available. But when community college faculty are appraised —and such examinations account for only a handful of reports beyond the normative data gathered by single institutions—they most often are viewed in terms of academic degrees, previous experience or, occasionally, a compilation of complaints about teaching conditions, evaluation, or job stability. And the institutions that house these students and faculty members generally are assessed chiefly in terms of their functions—student personnel, remedial, transfer/ technical—as if these functions existed apart from the people themselves.

Very little consideration has been given to the institution as a viable center of human interaction. Only occasional reference is made to either the student or the instructor as a dynamic, whole person. We know much about the ways people differ in academic performances and on measures of achievement, and we have an excess of information about academic dropouts—all gathered in sincere attempts to understand behavior. But we have very little insight into the dynamics of the people who have been our ready subjects, their total personality configurations, their value systems, and the personal as well as academic/vocational goals they erect for themselves.

This book attempts to redress some of these omissions. It presents an operational model of the person together with data by means of which that model is verified. The theoretical base of this paradigm is founded on concepts of ego- functioning—concepts that appear to persist at all economic, cultural, and educational levels—which I pull together and define as functional potential. The information derived from responses to a survey that puts the model to use will, hopefully, prove helpful to people studying themselves as well as to others who would understand them.

The 3-D study reported here is the abbreviation for "The Project for the Design, Development, and Dissemination of Research Models for Junior Colleges." Its purpose was to look at freshmen entering three diverse but proximate California community colleges—urban, suburban and rural. Beneath this examination and the basic model is the assumption that, despite all the catalog pronouncements, despite the evinced ideals and goals and the avowed institutional purposes, any institution is understandable as a viable organization only in terms of its people. If we look at them, understand their belief systems, goals, peculiar traits, and unique characteristics, we are in a position to adjudge what the institution itself is about and how it can be improved.

The 3-D Project differs in several ways from previous research on college students; indeed, much of it differs from most attempts to understand students at any educational level. It views freshmen in three California community colleges on the basis of a construct called functional potential. This construct is based on notions of development, maturity, and ego strength and does not look to socio-economic data, grade point averages, measures of achievement, or intellectual disposition. The data derived from this study do not provide answers to institutional questions concerning new curricula, innovational approaches to education, appropriate objectives. They do, however, provide information that may eventually help to create answers and directions or, at least, to conduct further study based on different perceptions of college populations.

Each person is a many-faceted being, not a uni-dimensional object. This way of viewing people is important for self-understanding, for school planning, and for research into human functioning. If evaluation is to be useful for more than limited prediction, it cannot depend simply on measures of achievement or on a single affective or cognitive dimension. If this approach is to be useful both for the individual who wants to better understand himself from a comfortable and realistic perspective and for the observer who attempts to understand another's frame of reference, then its theoretical basis must be conceptually strong, consistent, and sufficiently comprehensive to cover pertinent facts about the person.

Although I can be rightfully accused of trying to bring the reader "up from Genesis," I feel that some historical background is useful in setting the framework for this book. Man's early attempts to understand his fellows may be seen in the theories of individual functioning advanced by classical scholars—Hippocrates, Plato, Aristotle; in the typologies initiated by Galen and amplified by Carl Jung, Ernst Kretschmer, E. Spranger, and W. H. Sheldon; in the penetrating fictions of Shakespeare and Dostoevskii; and in the pioneering efforts of Francis Galton and James Cattell who, in their studies of individual differences, furnished the bases for subsequent work in the field of mental measurement.

In part as a result of these efforts, a number of people deeply concerned with reliably predicting human performance published manuscripts that now stand out as truly pioneering ventures (Cattell, 1890, Galton, 1883; Whipple, 1910). They gave a certain respectability to psychological variability as a field for scientific investigation and, concomitantly, stimulated an interest in differential psychology and directed attention toward measurement in that field. From these beginnings, a vast body of literature grew, dealing with the theoretical foundations of personality and the measurable differences in human beings.

Two special fields of study eventually emerged. One isolated and quantified information in order to establish discriminate variables such as "intelligence," "dexterity" and achievement in specialized areas. The other, adopting a holistic and dynamic approach, viewed the total personality from a phenomenological viewpoint, as more than the sum of many parts. Although for many years the two approaches functioned in isolation, independent of each other, the accuracy of one method depends upon comprehension of the other. And, in spite of frequent protestations to the contrary, both techniques have the same end—the better understanding of man.

The quantitative approach began with Binet's examinations of French school children and the publication of his scale for assessing intelligence (1905) and with Münsterberg's (1908) report of the use of psychological testing in business and industry. After World War I, psychological assessment entered its boom years. More people became aware of the national needs for general testing and selection programs. Subsequently, the measurement of human differences was augmented by vocational guidance efforts during the Depression; the intensive activities of the Office of Strategic Services in World War II; the expanded activities of the Veterans Administration, working in conjunction with schools and colleges to test and counsel armed service veterans; and, perhaps most important, the development of new statistical procedures. The main criticism that may be leveled against these efforts is that, in so measuring specifics, they often neglected the totality of the person. The examination of variables in isolation may fit into stringent research paradigms, but the extent to which the findings can be applied is minimal.

At the same time these situation-specific tests were being developed, personologists were looking at people in different ways and exploring new approaches to their appraisal—projective techniques, for example. Considerable progress was made along these lines when explorations of the unconscious were linked to the dynamics of observable behavior and when the clinical observations of Jean Charcot and Pierre Janet were further enhanced by the uncoverings of the depth psychologists and the empirical findings of the experimentalists. Personality theory has provided many insights into human functioning. Several people have contributed to this understanding, either by originating theories of personality or enhancing theories that had been developed by others: Sigmund Freud and Carl Jung's analytic principles; the social-psychological orientations of Alfred Adler, Erich Fromm, Karen Horney, and Harry Stack Sullivan; the personalistic psychologies of William Stern and William James; the gestalt tradition established by Leo Wertheimer, Kurt Koffka, and Wolfgang Kohler; and the humanistic approaches advanced by such men as Abraham Maslow, Carl Rogers, and Nevitt Sanford.

Most personality theorists tend to view the individual in a holistic manner but they often differ markedly among themselves in the degree to which they do so. Most are concerned with unconscious dynamics as well as with observable behavior. Some attempt to systematically measure the effectiveness of their theories by developing quantitative ways of prediction, while others depend almost exclusively on clinical intuitive feelings and insights. Conceptions of human functioning based on hunches about unconscious dynamics and motivation do not readily lend themselves to objective analysis, however, and attempts are now being made to integrate these various approaches. The scientific origins of human investigation have given rise to two closely related but independent fields of study— the isolated dimensions of the individual and the phenomenological whole. Although some behavioral scientists still tend to isolate specific variables, most recognize the totality of the person and the concomitant need to see the individual as he relates to his inner self and to the world about him. Thus, the two approaches are merging into a more holistic view of man, a view that is stressed here because it is basic to the assessment procedures discussed in later portions of this book.

In *Self and Society*, Sanford builds a strong case for such a holistic posture, pointing out that "few psychologists care to deny, on principle, the holistic premise. It seems to be almost universally understood and agreed that the way a stimulus is perceived depends on the context in which it exists at the moment; that whether or not an ideal will be assimilated by a cognitive system depends on the degree of that idea's consistency with ideas already present there; that the meaning of a particular act depends on its place in a larger pattern of striving. It can be said with perfect safety that all personality theories are holistic in the sense that they are concerned with the relations of particular processes to larger personality functions" (Sanford, 1966, p. 12).

Yet, while stressing the need to adopt this sort of approach, Sanford also acknowledges the concomitant need to intensively study abstracted part-functions and to reconcile the person/societal nature of any interaction. Not only must the individual be seen as something other than the sum total of his parts but because "There are things about personality that do not become apparent until the individual is seen in the context of the social group" (1966, p. 14), he must also be viewed from the perspective of the society in which he is functioning.

Adopting this type of global perspective is consistent with the ideals of humanistic psychology originally proposed by Maslow (1962) in his conception of that system. This emphasis approaches the person as an individual who is both unique and peculiar, a single member of a class. As Buhler explains, "One of the most generally agreed upon aspects of humanistic psychology is that we strive to find access to the study and understanding of the person as a whole. Ultimately, this was, or is, of course a goal for all psychology. But up to recently there were and still are prevalent attempts to construct the total person out of innumerable details of information which, in the tradition, are gathered preferably from experiments or else out of observations geared to the study of specific functions and behaviors. Furthermore, in following the example set by modern science, the individual was always studied as a member of a group, and the study of one individual alone was not considered to be an object of science" (Buhler, 1971, p. 378).

Getting to know the person in such a thorough way suggests some awareness of his entire life history. Whatever the period of time, however, and no matter how accurate the history, such examination always comprises so many variables that it represents a most difficult clinical exercise. In non-clinical situations, an even more formidable task is posed. Thus, although few psychologists will deny the desirability of maintaining the holistic premise, they find that when it comes to research, empirical methods and the total view are often incompatible. It is possible to ferret out an operationally measurable functioning core on the basis of information covering various segments of the person's life—past and present—but this requires a perceptive sensitivity, a willingness to adopt a phenomenological approach, and an acceptance of his experiential world.

The holistic or organismic theory of personality thus points to the integration, consistency, and unity of the normal person. It starts with a view of man as an organized system whose various dimensions can never be abstracted from the whole because, by studying segments of behavior in isolation, he can never be understood. Further, this theory assumes a potentiality for growth, thereby reinforcing the positive side of man's nature. In other words, a person functions at many levels—physiologically and psychologically. He can survive on a mere subsistence basis. He can live adequately but hardly beyond an average, matter-of-fact existence rate, or he can strive for optimal functioning—operating at nearly greatest potential and approaching that state of integration we sometimes refer to as actualization or self-realization or individuation. Whatever the level, ideally, over a period of time, the individual continues to move ahead.

Although the actual interpretation of this approach will always vary with the individual theorist, the organismic view is very much in evidence—in the works of many gestaltists and, especially, in the writings of such humanistic psychologists as Buhler, Maslow, Murray, Rogers, and Sanford. Rogers appears both to echo the sentiments of earlier organismic protagonists and to express the thinking of his contemporaries by maintaining that "the more fully the individual is understood and accepted, the more he tends to drop the false fronts with which he has been meeting life, and the more he tends to move in a direction which is forward" (1961, p. 27).

In addition to supporting the holistic view of man, one must also adopt a certain "systematic eclecticism," as Allport advocates. When faced with the problem of fitting all evidence into a theory, or of repressing those portions that do not fit, "only three possibilities [appear] before us: a) We can resort to this strategy of denial which includes, of course, the verbal slight-of-hand by which we take into camp evidence that does not fit. b) We can be piecemeal eclectics and take all theories of learning into our jackdaw nest. c) Or finally, we can struggle on for a comprehensive view that will find a place for all valid data: subjective and objective, machine-

like and social, peripheral and propriate. And these same three possibilities confront us not only in respect to the problems of learning,
but in all our fields of inquiry; perception, emotion, conflict, cognition, conscience, and all the rest" (1968, p. 8).

While no theory of personality can be—or, indeed, should
be—exactly like any other theory, three discussed at length in this
book—developmental, maturity, and ego strengths—hold certain
things in common. Theories of development, for example, make
some attempt to predict behavior, just as do basic assumptions of
maturity and ego strength. The prognoses will vary but one of the
prime reasons for understanding the individual is to foresee the
kinds of experiences he may encounter and to anticipate his ability
to deal with them. Additionally, all three positions look at people
in terms of the whole. Certain systems may examine minute variables or isolate singular situations but, to a greater or lesser extent,
all acknowledge that pieces of people, facets of personality, acts of
behavior, must eventually be seen as parts of the whole. Therefore,
our preceding notes about complexity and holism act as a foundation for all theories of development, maturity, and ego strength.
But as with Sanford, I must admit to putting the case for holism
as strongly as possible. We cannot "do without the intensive study
of abstracted part-function . . . [But if] we must abstract parts
from wholes, let us be fully aware of the fact that we *are* abstract-
ing; and let us devote as much energy to finding out how special
bits of knowledge fit in the larger picture as we do to analyzing
wholes in the conventional scientific way" (Sanford, 1966, pp. 14–
15). Accordingly, of the various theories about man that have been
expounded through the years, I emphasize certain ones, either because they appear more meaningful (undoubtedly, in that they fit
my own biases) than others or because they seem to be most pertinent to the student populations with whom the major portion of
this book is concerned.

In our attempt to picture a person we must consider many
variables and synthesize them into a distinguishable pattern or patterns. We must first describe the characteristics that represent him,
then offer alternative ways of perceiving him, and, finally, select one
model that fits from the standpoints of accurate representation, ease

of understanding, and comprehensiveness. Indeed, many possible profiles may be exacted in pictures or in words. No one way may be better than any other. But because choices are almost endless, the problem becomes one of selecting one pattern or model rather than in attempting to devise yet another.

Behind any "theory of personality must be a set of assumptions relevant to human behavior with the necessary empirical definitions" (Hall and Lindzey, 1957, p. 5). My attempt to present a structure of personality that is based on a particular approach to human understanding is no exception. Thus certain assumptions run throughout this book, stemming from the belief that the person can be fully understood only if he is seen as a total organism who functions in diverse and complex ways, both inter- and intrapersonally. Operating under these premises but also believing that no *one* way of looking at people meets *all* criteria, I chose an eclectic approach in developing the rationale for the 3-D Project, thereby selecting ideas from several personality theorists. The way in which the theories are drawn together and a few of the constructs may be unique but I borrow heavily from several people—especially dynamic psychologists who are so strongly committed to the idea of the unconscious and humanists who look upon the person as a totality.

The structural pattern or model of the person evolving from these basic beliefs represents an individual's phenomenological world and includes important conceptual variables. It is hoped that the concepts comprising this conceptual synthesis are broad enough to apply to large populations of college students and at the same time, specific enough to represent an individual student if such an in depth explanation were desired. One way of matching this particular approach against the criteria of accuracy, usefulness, appropriateness, and general applicability is to ask if the synthesis leads to better understanding of groups of people as well as individuals in multi-dimensional ways. If this is so, it will be adjudged at least partially successful.

Eleven major categories that constitute the personality pattern used are described here. These are basic to the design of the 3-D project, and each includes other variables, the most important of which are also described. Functional potential, the primary variable, is presented first. Otherwise, the eleven categories are in alphabetical order rather than in order of importance.

Functional Potential, like most of the variables in this system, is a hypothetical construct built upon psychodynamic principles of human functioning. It describes the degree to which a subject incorporates various characteristics, offering a picture of the functioning individual in terms of the personal dynamics basic to his behavior and life style. At this point in time, it seems to be the most important and central variable within the personality structure, thus assuming the most emphasis in the structural model presented in this book. Functional potential is comprised of six fundamental traits called modes: *Relatedness/Aloofness* indicates the degree to which an individual invests himself in involvement with others, his sense of belonging or, at the other end of the continuum, his feelings of alienation. *Identity/Amorphism* describes the sense of certainty about self that may be equated with feelings of wholeness, sameness, directedness, or at the opposite pole, diffuseness and uncertainty of direction. *Flexibility/Rigidity* measures the openness and closedness of belief systems (Rokeach, 1960) and authoritarianism (Adorno, Frenkel-Brunswick, Levinson, and Sanford, 1950), including the individual's cognitive and affective manner of approach. *Independence/Dependence* suggests autonomy, the readiness to act on one's own, but does not imply separation or alienation from others. *Progression/Regression* assesses an orientation toward optimism, which involves such related traits as activity/passivity, fluidity/immobilization, and flow/fixedness. *Delay of Gratification/Impulse-Expression* is best seen in mature individuals who both have access to their more archaic impulses and are able to exercise secondary controls when appropriate for the situation encountered.

An indefinite number of variables are subsumed in the category of *dependent variables.* For the 3-D project, the dependent variables were School Withdrawal and School Persistence, with less attention paid to Transfer to Another School and to Securing an Associate Degree.

Demographic Variables represents absolute and easily quantifiable dimensions—age, sex, place of birth, educational attainment.

The Environment includes data about outside forces that impinge upon a person. These may be type of school, work setting, place of residence. For the 3-D project, one of the three sample schools represents the environment dimension for each subject.

Group Cohesion is not a pure or basic component because it is based on a projective device that assesses the individual's perceptions of his closeness to others, his feelings of relatedness to specific reference groups.

Multiphasic Characteristics, like the Group Cohesion score that is derived from a particular technique measuring a personality trait, are derived from special inventories. In the 3-D project, the technique employed was the Omnibus Personality Inventory (Heist and Yonge, 1962), which was used for two purposes: to gain insight into characteristics not assessed by other devices and to provide a measure of concurrent validity with the functional potential score.

Five variables constitute *Orientations* and all have something to say about the person's approach to the world. They represent a cross between his values, interests, and general move toward certain vocations and avocations. These Orientations approach the Freudian notion of cathexes as driving forces or the Jungian concept of libido as a source of psychic energy: The *Ideas* Orientation represents a concern with the world of cognition, an intellectual approach to life and work. The *Esthetics* Orientation suggests a concentration on the world of beauty—art, sculpture—either in an active, doing sense or as an appreciation that leads to spectator involvement. The *Others* Orientation includes both social and political concerns, the individual who is oriented in this direction expressing an interest in others. The *Practical* Orientation represents a concern with business expediency, the world of practicality. The *Motor* Orientation covers athletics, mechanical work, farming—any endeavor that involves kinesthetic or physical functioning.

Like Group Cohesion and Multiphasic Characteristics, the *School Directedness* category represents a compilation of data—in this case, selected items from the survey used in the 3-D project, which reflect the student's attitudes about school. Indicators of this variable are the courses the person selects, the major he declares, the number of hours he is enrolled in school.

Significant Others constitutes a separate category since no one lives in the world alone. For the college student, the most significant others are family, peers, faculty; for the non-student, work colleagues and others would replace student peers and faculty.

Unconscious Dynamics represents yet another category. How does one assess, let alone understand, the unconscious? Dreams, active imaginations, hallucinations, have all been used as inroads to those deeper portions of the self that play such a major role in the person's behavior. These Unconscious Dynamics cannot be measured directly but we should be aware of their intensity and consider them in any appraisal of a person.

Values and attitudes comprise the individual's belief system. They may be assessed in a number of ways; in the case of the 3-D project, the two lists of values developed by Rokeach (1968) (Terminal—Freedom, Wisdom, for example, and Instrumental—Ambitious, Loving) were used as further inputs to our student data.

These eleven major categories, representing some of the most basic characteristics of the person and influences acting upon him, are here conceived in terms of various patterns. One way of integrating the several variables is in terms of a clothesline. In this model, less holistic than desirable, functional potential becomes the line and the other components are garments hanging from it. Each separate component consistently touches the line but only affects another component when they are in close contact—in a basket prior to or after hanging, when a wind blows them together.

Somewhat similar to the above design is a pattern representing a tree with several branches growing out of the trunk. Here the trunk of the tree represents the basic concept, functional potential and the various other dimensions of the individual are the branches. The model also might be interpreted as a marble cake with various dimensions interacting with others at certain points or in certain spaces, all existing at the same time but differing in intensity and spatial arrangements. Or, perhaps the dark or chocolate areas of the cake represent that series of dimensions while the lighter parts act as other dimensions. In such a view, functional potential applies consistently, and any one of the other variables exists to a lesser extent.

Other models might be suggested, perhaps as many as metaphoric language or fantasy allows. The model that seems most graphic is given in Figure 1. Like the clothesline or the tree, however, this pattern also suffers from the fact that points of interaction are spatial, and actual contacts between certain variables are not demonstrable. While the core concept of functional potential

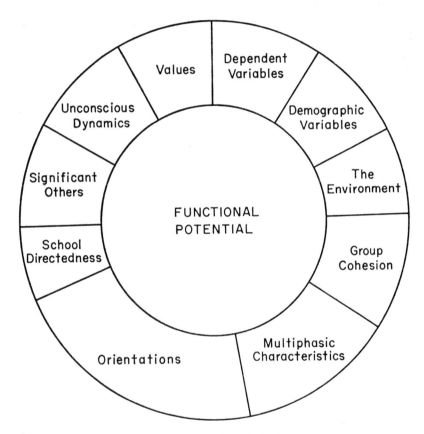

FIGURE 1.   A Model of the Person.

touches upon all other variables, any one of the others may be only proximate to the remaining dimensions.

Perhaps the important point to remember is that whatever model is selected as representative of the personality structure, each implies a holistic, integrated pattern—complex, sometimes difficult to understand, but actually mirroring the person as an individual.

Schools and other social institutions must be aware of the variations on the theme—the facts that individual differences do exist and that the ways in which the person's many variables are synthesized may also vary. Colleges as social institutions must both tolerate and understand these differences, for heterogeneity stimulates interest and verve and sometimes serendipitous events, and homogeneity breeds dullness and inflexibility. Recognizing the differences, then, is prerequisite to planning programs, ascertaining goals, and thinking about the ways in which the person and the institution might mesh so that each will be served.

This model, then, has many parts, each one representing important aspects of the person. Functional potential is at its core, based on three constructs which represent its foundation stones, development, maturity and ego strength. These are discussed in succeeding chapters.

Chapter 2

Development, Maturity, and Ego Strength

> All the world's a stage,
> And all the men and women merely players:
> They have their exits and their entrances;
> And one man in his time plays many parts,
> His acts being seven ages.

Concern about the stages delineating man's span of years did not initiate with Jacque's soliloquy—nor will it end tomorrow. The many schemes that more or less systematically chronicle life's moves from infancy to senility attest to man's interest in pattern and order. Concern with developmental hierarchies and maturity is reflected in sometimes elaborate rites of passage performed by various cultures at different points in time. Early hieroglyphics and subsequent written reports alike proclaim the importance of key periods —the beginning of pubescence, for example, when both primitive groups and formal religious orders prepared definitive rituals in order to formally acknowledge the "coming of age." These ceremonies are intended to teach the novitiate the privileges and responsibilities that accompany his new position. And, while they do not always guarantee an easy transition into the ensuing period of development, they do provide a certain structure that suggests to the candidate a feeling of community: "It is right that you are here now in this phase of your life; others have shared the same experiences. You are one of us."

Development

Interest in developmental processes extends far beyond the cultural rite of passage. In the twentieth century, in fact, several scientists have devoted themselves to devising schemes that would systematically reflect the ways people develop. Although functional potential does not fit into a developmental pattern, primarily because I do not specify a hierarchical arrangement of tasks to be achieved or processes to be followed, it may be clarified with an understanding of developmental levels. The material discussed here may be of special interest to educators without a background in psychology.

Of those dealing with individual development, Freud, with his emphasis on the psychosexual or instinctual stages, stands out as a landmark. He saw the child as passing through a series of dynamically differentiated levels, from the pregenital stage to the so-called latency period and on to adolescence and adulthood. For Freud and his followers, development is an ebb and flow process in which dynamic and quiescent periods alternate.

In cognitive rather than psychosexual theories—for example, Werner (1948)—personality is also viewed in terms of successive developmental stage. In the global phase, equated with a primordial type of organization, everything is homogeneous. Conversely, the differentiated stage is characterized by heterogeneity and independence; the individual's responses are specific rather than general. And during integration, the final stage, the parts move together to form an interdependent system. The individual's behavior is organized and his response to his environment is not random but total and integrated.

The hierarchies posed by such men as Freud and Werner generally are limited to discrete, albeit, pervasive, elements. Other people look at personality in terms of broad development, encompassing cognitive, affective, and physiological dimensions. "Development" previously seemed to be equated with experiences of early childhood, but in recent years some behaviorial scientists have been concerned with development during the college years. Development, then, implies either movement or progression within a particular stage or changes that result from the resolution of conflicts and the mastery of specific tasks. In many cases, however, especially when students drop out of school or, at best, stop in/stop out, development during the college years is seldom apparent and, at best, difficult to assess. This is especially true in community colleges, where most of the students remain but a few months. In such cases, it seems more useful to talk about developmental levels at the time of college entrance (as I do later) than to discuss changes in development.

When we consider adolescent or post-adolescent development, certain authorities crop up again and again. For example, Erik Erikson's (1959; 1963) hierarchy of psychosocial development —worth considering in an attempt to understand any age level—has had a particularly significant impact on educators and psychologists who study the development of college students. At each phase in the life cycle, there are "phase specific developmental tasks" to be mastered, and, since "the human cycle and man's institutions have evolved together" (Erikson, 1963, p. 250), every stage relates to a basic element of society. In addition, each stage represents further developments of the ego that may be characterized in terms of polarities. Constantinople explains that the ego qualities or basic attitudes postulated by Erikson ". . . develop as a result of the interaction between the developing potentialities of the individual and the pressures and sanctions of the social environment. At each of [the] eight hypothesized ages from infancy to adulthood, a particular crisis evolves which leads to a developmental task which must be mastered. The relative success or lack of success in the resolution of each crisis leaves the individual with a residual attitude or orientation toward himself and the world which will help to determine his relative success in the later stages" (1969, p. 358).

The first of Erikson's levels, basic trust vs. basic mistrust, marks the infant's early social achievements and implies "not only that one has learned to rely on the sameness and continuity of the outer providers, but also that one may trust oneself" (Erikson, 1963, p. 248). Here the ego's first task becomes the establishment of effective patterns that solve the conflict of trust versus mistrust. This level is followed by autonomy vs. shame and doubt, and initiative vs. guilt. Finding its institutional counterpart in the principle of law and order, autonomy "becomes decisive for the ratio of love and hate, cooperation and willfulness, freedom of self-expression and its suppression. From a sense of self-control without loss of self-esteem comes a lasting sense of good will and pride; from a sense of loss of self-control and of foreign overcontrol comes a . . . propensity for doubt and shame" (p. 254). The child, identifying with the parent of the same sex, furthers his independence while continuing to look to significant adults for guidance.

Moving into the latency and adolescent period, industry vs. inferiority represents that stage wherein "the normally advanced child forgets, or rather sublimates, the necessity to 'make' people by direct attack or to become papa and mama in a hurry; he now learns to win recognition by producing things" (p. 259). Writing about the identity vs. role confusion of adolescence, Erikson makes one of his most significant pronouncements, one that has stimulated much thought and, occasionally, some action by those who are especially concerned with the development of college students: "The adolescent mind is essentially a mind of the moratorium, a psychosocial stage between morality learned by the child, and the ethics to be developed by the adult. It is an ideological outlook of a society that speaks most clearly to the adolescent who is eager to be affirmed by his peers, and is ready to be confirmed by rituals, creeds, and programs which at the same time define what is evil, uncanny, and inimical" (pp. 262–263).

During the next stage, intimacy vs. isolation, the young adult is "eager and willing to fuse his identity with that of others . . . for intimacy, . . . the capacity to commit himself to concrete affiliations and partnerships" (p. 263). The seventh stage, generativity vs. stagnation, exhibits "primarily the concern in establishing and guiding the next generation . . . (p. 267).

Finally, then, man arrives at integrity vs. despair, marked by "the ego's accrued assurance of its proclivity for order and meaning," "the acceptance of one's one and only life cycle as something that had to be," "a comradeship with the ordering ways of distant times and different pursuits." And here man, whose "cultural entity develops the particular style of integrity suggested by its historical place" (p. 269) . . . "knows well that his individual life is the accidental coincidence of but one life cycle with but one segment of history; and that for him all human integrity stands or falls with one style of integrity of which he partakes . . ." (p. 267).

These eight hypothetical stages represent special concerns with basic attitudes that result from the interaction of the individual with his social environment. Moving from infancy to adulthood, the particular crisis that evolves at each stage leads to a task that, if mastered, can facilitate future development. It is possible, too, that if a later stage is successfully handled, an earlier stage can be resolved more satisfactorily. Thus, as with Maslow's hierarchy of needs, Shakespeare's stages of man, and Freud's psychosexual scheme of development, growth at any level beyond the first is facilitated if tasks at previous stages have been performed. Then, at the end of each major crisis, the person develops a sense of self-esteem because he "is learning affective steps toward a tangible future, . . . is developing a defined personality within a social reality which one understands" (Erikson, 1959, p. 89).

Several modifications of the stage theory have been developed, with Constantinople's (1969) way of assessing personality development particularly pertinent to the focus of this book. This scheme and other systems that are at least partially based on Erikson's psychosocial stages (Loevinger and Wessler, 1970; Prelinger and Zimet, 1964; for example) all mark a departure from earlier psychoanalytic and behavioral theories that hold that, for the most part, personality is formed in early childhood. All these approaches are built on certain premises that stem from ego, psychological, and cognitive theories of personality development. And all hold in common certain concepts of personality structure that perceive people as moving through a "sequence of qualitatively different stages or levels of structural development" (Sullivan, McCullough, and Stager, 1970, p. 400). Adapting this "classical" approach, Loevinger (1966) deals with ego development; Harvey, Hunt, and Schroder (1961) consider conceptual-systems development; and Kohlberg (1958) concerns himself with the articulation of Jean Piaget's (1969) theory of moral judgment.

In each case, the problem of individual differences is approached in essentially the same way—that is, every person is seen as possessing certain dominant characteristics at any given time. Yet, individuals "may pass through stages at different rates and ultimately may achieve different structural levels (Emmerich, 1968). Harvey, Hunt, and Schroeder's conceptual-systems viewpoint, which might be seen as another extension of Erikson's work, assumes that, under optimal conditions, the normal course of development is characterized in terms of specific stages that lead to flexible orientations toward both the environment and the interpersonal world. Loevinger's theory postulates a stage or hierarchical paradigm that covers ego development from birth to maturity and involves seven sequences—symbiotic, impulse ridden, opportunistic, conformist, conscientious, autonomous, and integrated—with several transitional points also delineated. In Kohlberg's theory, there are three levels and six stages of moral development, also described in hierarchically ordered sequences.

The different theories include varying numbers of stages and an assortment of labels but all are hierarchical and display some overlapping content areas. For example, moral development is treated by Loevinger as one aspect of the larger area of ego development while Kohlberg feels that ego development is really a mediator between moral judgment and moral conduct. In fact, all systematic or formalized stage theories of development share common assumptions. Variations occur in the definitions of different phases and point out nuances in each, but many classical developmental theories designate the steps, describe the tasks to be mastered, and operationalize the criteria in order to assess the attainment level. In this sense, development is a typology based on hierarchical order.

At the same time, there are certain theoretical approaches that do not employ the concept of stages to interpret development. These theories tend to lean heavily on environmental influences, regarding behavior as continuous. Other interpretations integrate stage and nonstage theories and employ the critical period notion

(Scott, 1958) as a means of interpreting or satisfying both approaches. This notion emphasizes the fact that during certain periods of development the organism is especially receptive to particular environmental conditions and that, in fact, certain interventions are important to the whole growth process. Something more than mere stages is implied, therefore, and those who favor the critical period notion stress the changes that occur within a particular period (for example, at college entrance) although they may well acknowledge previous levels and they will certainly recognize subsequent steps.

Whatever the special concerns and however a theory of personality enables one to understand the several stages of growth that mark man's lifetime, most people agree that social institutions—especially schools and colleges—are important to the development of integration of personality. The relationship of schools and development has become a basis for study of students at different educational levels. Isolating specific elements, a number of investigators compare their college student populations on such variables as cognitive ability and socio-economic status (Berdie and Hood, 1965; Schoenfeldt, 1966); motivation (Douvan and Kaye, 1962); interest (Abe and others, 1965; Cooley, 1966); academic achievement (Fishman, 1962; Holland and Richards, 1965); vocational development (Davis, 1965; Flanagan, 1966); and a general category called personality development (Freedman, 1960; R. Heath, 1964; Plant, 1962; and Telford, 1966). Others are concerned with the interrelationship of academic development and family background, social class, abilities, and motivation (Brown, 1960; D. Heath, 1958; Murphy and Rauschenberg, 1960; Sanford, 1959; Thistlewaite, 1959). Again it must be pointed out that whatever the particular theories to which these investigators may adhere, each examines intrastage differences, similarities, and change, viewing development in the college student as a multi-faceted process.

Among those concerned with intrastage development, Sanford (1962; 1967) has been most instrumental in stressing its holistic aspect and suggesting that colleges must affect changes in their students along affective as well as cognitive lines. With Freedman (1967), he indicates ways in which postsecondary institutions can stimulate personality change by challenging the student to reevaluate himself and, further, by allowing him the experience of such reevalution. Believing that all dimensions of personality are important and that the institution must be personalized, Sanford argues that one of society's basic concerns must be the fullest development of the individual. He writes that goals "must be stated not only in terms of what is to be modified, corrected, or prevented, but also in terms of what is to be built up. Schools, colleges, correctional institutions, and mental hospitals as well as child guidance clinics and various programs for youth should be conceived, first of all, as institutions for human development" (Sanford, 1966, p. x).

The developmental model that Sanford formulates as a guide for these institutions both supplements and incorporates the traditional medical model (concerned with the cause and cure of disease) with the educational model (typically focused on cognitive processes). Integrating two basic approaches and viewing the subject—as either an individual or member of a group—from a holistic perspective, it is hoped that this approach will encourage each person to develop to his greatest potential.

Reviewing the different approaches to development discussed here, several appear pertinent to the functional potential construct. There is an obvious connection between Freud's psychosexual stages and the functional potential construct of delay of gratification/impulse expression. Werner's emphasis on the integrative ability of the mature individual is picked up in the way in which various dimensions of functional potential are added together to form a total score. Emmerich, and others, suggest that people pass through similar stages at various rates and Erikson suggests a way of dealing with adolescent development. Functional potential offers a means of assessment through its attention to the level of individual development and the related concepts of maturity and ego strength discussed in the following section.

Maturity

Together with development maturity is one of the psychological constructs that we have generated as a way of understanding people in our society. It is an especially appropriate concept to apply to college populations. As Katz points out, "By the time a student reaches college, he is usually chronologically and physiologically an adult. It is primarily in his psychological and social growth that he is considered an adolescent or in transition to adulthood. Many writers in the educational and psychological fields have recently been listing the numerous tasks that college students must master if they are to be considered successful in their maturation; for example, achieving independence, dealing with authority, handling ambiguity, developing with regard to sexual matters, attaining prestige, and developing value systems" (1968, p. 345).

Who is a mature person? How do people mature? Is it the accrued experiences of childhood and adolescence that establish the mature person? And conversely, does the inability to integrate past and present and prepare for the future imply immaturity? These questions are indirectly but essentially related to understanding and facilitating individual development.

Because the term *maturity* is used in so many contexts, a consistent definition is difficult. For example, people often assume that adulthood is tantamount to maturity. If maturity is something one attains at a prescribed age merely because he has experienced certain rites of passage, it tells us more about chronology than development. This quantitative measure is easily apprehended but defines maturity in the same sense that twelve defines a dozen.

In the classical literature of developmental psychology, maturity—like childhood, adolescence, and old age—is a discrete stage in the growth process; once again, age is the determinant. Such a view, as Sanford argues, does not allow the individual to become more mature as he grows older because "old age" takes over at a certain point. "In the common-sense view, adopted by many psychologists, maturity is simply the predominance of the efficient, the discriminating, the differentiated, and realistic over the primitive, the impulsive, the passionate" (Sanford, 1966, p. 32). This definition seems broad enough to serve as a basis for understanding this period of development and is one to which I subscribe, but further discussion seems warranted if we are to relate the concept to college students.

Sanford (1966) also points out the importance of differentiating mental health, maturity, and maximum development—concepts that are independently variable and not necessarily positively correlated in large samples. Mental health is a way of meeting and dealing with life's problems. It is the potential for coping with, rather than the absence of, strain. Stability, on the other hand, may be due to an absence of strain. "A person might be so well adjusted to his environment, or his environment might be so simple or so protective of the individual, that he was not called upon to manage any severe strains. He might have all the health he needed in the circumstances, or even all he would need for any forseeable future, but still be relatively lacking in what it takes to deal with a variety of severe strains" (Sanford, 1966, p. 30). The ability to cope depends on environmental conditions as well as past experiences. Necessity is to invention as challenge is to development.

D. Heath addresses a confusion in terms by pointing out that the mature person and the normal person are not necessarily the same inasmuch as the term *normal* should be restricted to behavior that would typify most people in a given situation. Further, the normal person is not necessarily an adjusted person since "adjusted assumes the psychological worth of the sociocultural milieu to which the individual adjusts and ignores the legitimate internal demands and structure of the person himself" (1965, p. 4).

The mature person, according to Heath, is a judicious and realistic individual who has a reflective sense of values, respects the values of others and finds an underlying meaning to life that he maintains with integrity. These characteristics, however, do not imply a static existence, for the mature person is adaptable—open to new experiences and continued growth and able to tolerate and control most tensions. The accumulative and relatively resilient integration that is growth (Bloom, 1964) is accompanied by an innate drive toward self-actualization (Maslow, 1954). The mature person is not just a mirror of his environment but balances and accommodates the demands of others with his own autocentric demands. Maturity increases awareness until the individual symbolically represents and coordinates a great variety of the dimensions of both his external and internal worlds. And finally, "not immediately controlled . . . by his immediate environment or his motivational state or by his earlier childhood history . . . man becomes less reactive and more self-active" (D. Heath, 1965, pp. 28–31).

Maturity does not imply an absence of conflict or severe

adjustment problems. Rather, the factors that differentiate maturity from immaturity are the controls used to master problems or develop a particular life style (Barron, 1954; 1963), with the individual's unique response to problems providing a way to distinguish between these concepts (Frankenstein and others, 1957). And the conflicts—inner and outer—that the person weathers lead to inner unity, good judgment, and especially an increase in his capacity to "do well,"—a relative quality that ranges from doing good to "not much more than just getting along" (Erikson, 1959, p. 51).

What predisposes one person to fall behind, never maturing on other than physiological or chronological levels while another rallies in response to challenges and becomes better for them? Sanford says that "a young person can establish a suitable ego identity only after attaining adequate independence from his parents; and only after his identity is established can he lose himself in a relationship of genuine intimacy. Readiness in itself, though, is not sufficient cause of development: the personality will not automatically proceed from one "life crisis" to the next, according to a plan of nature. What the state of readiness means, essentially, is that the individual is now open to new kinds of stimuli and prepared to deal with them in an adaptive way" (1968, p. 861).

Schools, Sanford continues, can encourage such readiness by presenting challenging stimuli that do not discourage and that may be confronted in a variety of ways. A structure which allows that flexibility appears to be essential for human growth and development. Just as they promote academic goals, schools and colleges must also implicate themselves in the moral and social development of their students. Arguing for the creation of "an appropriate curriculum for fostering psychosocial maturity," Greenberger and Sørenson point out that "the periodic assessment of achievement now furnishes information about how well individual students are learning academic subject matter in comparison with other students. . . . Eventually, periodic assessment of maturity . . . could yield information on a [person's] psychosocial development" (1971, p. 28). A potential maturity scale which builds on psychological standards of maturity, involves the development of favorable attitudes—toward self and others—and assumes a system of value-guiding behavior has been devised by Greenberger and others (1971).

Whatever the definition or method of promoting the concept in practical usage, maturity is a term that must be seriously considered by those who wish to influence educational systems. Just as an integrated or holistic approach that includes a variety of dimensions is prerequisite to considering developmental levels in human behavior, it is also necessary in merging understanding of individual functioning with notions of schooling and academic objectives.

The way that the person has dealt with previous experiences and the manner in which he copes with challenges that invariably confront him as he moves through life determine his development as an adult. Mastery of experiences, particularly extreme difficulties, is equivalent to maturity and is of special importance to those responsible for planning school and college curriculums. Even the most flexible person must acknowledge the importance of some structure, and the most rigid must see the need to bend with the times, the people, the conditions. There must always be a viable link beween the situation one encounters and his personal development. Merely because the person is of sufficient age to be considered an adult does not—for me, at least—suggest maturity. Under the normal conditions assumed here, the individual remains in one phase or stage and then moves up, step by step—a progression that implies a readiness to go on. The fact that different people show similar changes at different ages, however, leads one to acknowledge the importance of individual rates of development. And these differences must be taken into account in any attempt to understand the process of development—whether it be in childhood, in what we typically consider the college years, in adulthood, or in old age.

Ego Strength

For years, people have been concerned with all aspects of ego functioning: ego strength, ego weakness, ego development—all referring to variations in degree—have been postulated to help understand the person. *Ego* refers to the *I*. It is that portion of the individual's awareness which mediates between his internal impulses and external realities. While the origin of the concept is frequently attributed to Freud, it actually may be found in the writings of the ancient Greeks, Hebrews, and Hindus, and within the psychoanalytic framework, ego is "analogous to what it was in philosophy in earlier usage: a selective, integrating, coherent, and persistent agency central to personality formation" (Erikson, 1964, p. 147).

The *Psychiatric Dictionary* defines ego strength as the "effectiveness with which the ego discharges its various functions. A strong ego will not only mediate between id, superego, and reality and integrate these various functions, but further it will do so with enough flexibility so that energy will remain for creativity and other needs. This is in contrast to the rigid personality in which ego functions are maintained, but only at the cost of impoverishment of the personality" (Hinsie and Campbell, 1960, p. 257). While this definition is adequate as far as it goes, it does not differentiate subordinate and subtle variations within the construct.

Schafer (1958) describes the strong ego as an entity that freely uses its energies to effectively control, defend against, modify, and discharge tension in accordance with adaptive, reality-oriented pursuits. The secondary processes (reality oriented) predominate over the primary (pleasure oriented). Again, recurrent themes are emphasized—control, modification and discharge of archaic impulses or tensions, reality-orientation, and the freeing of energy. Defense mechanisms, developed as reactions against instinctive impulses, play an important role in the strength-weakness balance. Klopfer (1962) suggests that the ego's potency is dependent not only upon the organism but also its exposure to experience. Creative individuals are seen as those "gifted normals" who are able to tolerate a number of critical experiences; that is, in difficult situations they are able to maintain ego defenses so that available energy (libido) may be used positively. They differ from those who mobize so many defenses to avoid emotional entanglements that they diminish their own energy.

I continue to believe that ego strength is positively related to coping mechanisms, experiences, and creative expression and negatively related to defense mechanism. With ES representing ego strength; DM representing defense mechanism; CM representing coping mechanisms; E, experience; and CE, creative expression, these relationships may be expressed in the following formula:

$ES = \dfrac{CM}{DM} \times E \times CE$ (Brawer, 1967, p. 16).

Central to the degree of strength manifested by the ego is the manner in which it reconciles the archaic or primitive impulses of the inner world with the reality of the external environment. Thus, ego strength is related to the utilization of libidinal forces (psychic energy), to the mechanisms of defense and coping, and to experiences and stresses that result, at the one extreme, in creative organization and, at the other, in neurotic crippling. Accordingly, ego strength might be understood in terms of the ability to handle stress creatively rather than defensively, to tolerate incongruent or opposing internal forces, and to cope with the experiences that allow the organism to both test and utilize its strengh.

Although one of the most amazing things about the ego is its relative stability, accounting for this stability typically is not seen as a major theoretical task in ego theory. Indeed, few people delve into the question. Of those who do consider the issue of stability, Sullivan (1953) formulates a theory of ego stability; Loevinger and Wessler (1970) suggest that the ego maintains its stability, its identity, and its coherence by selecting out observations that are inconsistent with its current state; and White (1958) includes the stabilization of ego identity as one of his four major "growth trends"— the others being the deepening of interests, the freeing of personal relationships, and the harmonizing of values.

Sanford adds a fifth dimension: general development and strengthening of the ego. He writes that the stabilization of ego identity implies "a certain level of strength and development within the ego, as well as the individual's ability to incorporate in his ego some of his more persistent and central personality needs." Replacing "old defense mechanisms with adaptive devices that spring from the ego and are better attuned to reality" encourages freedom of personal relationships, and integrating the superego with the ego leads to the humanizing of values "which in turn depends on development in the ego itself. The direction of ego growth is toward increased ability to plan realistically, to set goals, to make decisions, and to persist in one's chosen course; toward increasing self-awareness, breadth of consciousness, at homeness with one's inner life, awareness of some of the diversity of human values and of the complexity of human experience; toward increasing realism and objectivity and command of feelings" (Sanford, 1966, p. 278).

Erikson interweaves ego development with his eight stages of man, pointing out that "a weak ego does not gain substantial strength from being persistently bolstered. A strong ego, secured in its identity by a strong society, does not need, and in fact is immune to any attempt at artificial inflation. Its tendency is toward the testing of what feels real, the mastery of that which works, the understanding of that which proves necessary, the enjoyment of the vital, and the extermination of the morbid" (Erikson, 1959, p. 47).

D. Heath (1965) maintains that certain concepts emanating from psychoanalytic ego psychology and Piaget's (1947) theory of intelligence and adaptation are the most comprehensive and important theories of development yet enunciated. Both theories describe similar developmental trends in the maturing person. For psychoanalytic ego psychology, the task is to explain the development of and interaction between internal structures (for example, regulatory ego defenses, controls, id) and external demands (partially internalized in the superego). The mature person has successfully reconciled these frequently conflicting demands, is highly differentiated and (ego) organized, is able to control as well as regress when necessary, and has an autonomous cognitive structure.

In spite of much discussion about the ego's functions, when we look at the interpretations offered by depth psychologists, a consistent, fundamental rationale appears to be lacking. This is partially due to the fact that although ego strength is often acknowledged to be central to personality structure, it is a center that is not directly measurable. Because the subordinate manifestations of this construct can be observed, however, they become the objective criteria for judging the relative strengths and weaknesses of the basic element.

My own definition, which is central to the material that follows, measures ego strength by the *extent to which the ego functions in its relationship to both outside reality and the larger self.* The following dimensions, any or all of which are present, to varying degrees, within the individual, comprise the over-all area of ego-function: the ability to rebound, to emerge from challenging experiences; the ability to delay gratification; the ability to tolerate internal and external ambiguity and conflict; the ability to accept complexity; a capacity for flexibility rather than constriction and/or authoritarianism; a capacity for reality testing; energy, creativity, and intelligence; and, at the highest level, the ability to relate to the unconscious, to become subservient to the Self, and to tolerate regression when necessary to meet the demands of the Self. This is at the highest level of development.

Despite the importance of ego strength as a source of understanding people, however, the construct is seldom used in assessing students or institutional impact on their developmental processes. Although there are a few exceptions—for example, some material reported on the Omnibus Personality Inventory (Heist and Yonge, 1962) alludes to ego functioning, and the Adaptive-Flexibility Inventory (Brawer, 1967) has been used to assess ego functioning in college freshmen—the importance of ego strength remains more appreciated in the treatment room than the classroom. Ego functioning cannot be separated from physiological, cognitive, conative, or affective developmental processes, however, and schools should encourage growth by allowing the student to experience success in increasingly difficult situations and by providing tasks that are not so threatening, authoritarian-bound, or over-protected that he must fall back on archaic defenses. As Sanford maintains, anything that frees "the individual from the necessity of defensive operations favors the development of the ego" (1966, pp. 288–289). And while ego development "depends partially on the ability to symbolize abstractly the events and objects of one's experience . . . for the young person whose experiences are primarily verbal or otherwise symbolic, first hand encounters with concrete materials and objects are also required" (Chickering, 1969, p. 27).

Development, maturity, and ego strength all feed into functional potential, a term developed to avoid some of the ambiguity noted in these three constructs. The advantage of operationally defining a new term is that one can accept or reject portions of other theories and other concepts. Functional potential, discussed in the following chapter, is my attempt to look at the person in a holistic or global fashion, to see the individual as an integration of many parts. It postulates three levels of development and isolates certain features that may be equated with maturity. And although it draws heavily on many of the ideas formulated by ego psychologists, it does not describe a hierarchy of development but focuses on development in college students.

Chapter 3

Functional Potential: The Core Concept

Functional potential is a hypothetical construct built upon psycho-dynamic principles which describes the degree to which a person is able to tolerate ambiguity, delay gratification, exhibit adaptive flexibility, demonstrate goal directedness, relate to self and others, and have a clear sense of personal identity. It views the individual in terms of the personal dynamics that are basic to his behavior and life-style. Functional potential is the way the person demonstrates what he is about. It provides both a conceptual foundation upon which the observer may build descriptions of an individual's be-havior and a set of dimensions by which the individual may under-stand himself. It is through the various components of functional potential—components representing the most fundamental and dy-namic portions of any personality configuration—that the person's reactions to himself and others become evident. If proven valid and reliable over time and with different populations, this comprehen-sive yet simple system will be useful for assessing developmental levels of college students whether they fit old stereotypes or are what we now perceive as nontraditional, or "new."

Functional potential, as I have noted, was developed within the context of maturity, development, and ego strength, but with certain notable differences. For example, although the concepts of age and growth that are often implied by maturity are not suggested here, the individual who is well integrated and operating at a high level of functional potential is a mature person—whether he is six, sixteen, or sixty. Similarly, the functional-potential level at which he operates may be equated with specific stages of development. Yet, no definite hierarchical steps are designated here but rather, three general stages—high, medium, and low.

There are other lines of affinity as well as other points of departure. Basically, functional potential is tied more closely to notions of ego psychology than maturity or even most developmental theories, although *ego strength* and *ego functioning* are terms that have heretofore been used chiefly in clinical settings. Rarely have they been used to understand normal behavior, especially in academic settings. On the other hand, I conceive of functional potential as chiefly applicable to populations who function adequately if not optimally. And finally, although all the traditional components of ego strength are not included in this construct, functional potential accurately reflects individual ego organization on a quantitative level and operationally describes the extent to which pertinent variables are ego-syntonic. Because this construct expresses individuals' abilities, those who demonstrate high capability are presumed to have maximum chance for personal satisfaction; that is, achievement for their own benefit within their own environment. However, although functional potential is a core dimension, the degree to which its dimensions express themselves varies with the individual.

Scores attained for the six modes comprising the central construct are totaled and the individual is ranked either high, medium, or low. This method reflects Allport's "personal disposition" theory that every individual possesses systems of action tendencies that are integrated to "comprise the molar units of the total structure of personality." These units are dynamic in their motive power and functionally autonomous. Like Allport's traits, the modes have more than nominal existence; are more generalized than a habit;

empirical; only relatively independent of other traits; not synony-
mous with moral or social judgment; may be perceived in light of
the personality which contains them or in the light of their distribution in the population at large; and, finally, are independent in that
acts and habits inconsistent with a trait do not prove the nonex-
istence of the trait (Allport, 1937, p. 289).

    As the variable representing what I believe is the truly viable
core of the human personality, functional potential is very much
"alive," dynamically representing the person. Although differences
exist in the degree to which its component parts—the modes—are
demonstrated in behavior, functional potential is an enduring tendency. In fact, longitudinal studies might well reveal that a high level
of functional potential depends on early feelings of warmth, security,
and closeness. One's environment plays a part, as do one's interpersonal and educational experiences, but these only build upon—or
negate—the experiences of the infant and very young child. Accordingly, the salient dimensions of every individual that reflect his
basic functional potential are essential to understanding human
functioning.

    The modes (relatedness/aloofness; identity/amorphism;
flexibility/rigidity; independence/dependence; progression/regres-
sion, and delay of gratification/impulse expression) will be described in detail in the following chapter. I discuss elsewhere
(Brawer, 1970) six auxiliary modes: satisfaction/dissatisfaction,
sensory relatedness/sensory deprivation, intensity/placidity, humor/
seriousness, sense of reality/lack of reality; intuition/factualism. All
these dimensions are relevant to the person's manner of functioning,
but, with the exception of sense of reality/lack of reality, they appear less consequential than the major six. While the exception is
extremely important, measuring an individual's reality testing is
difficult in a paper and pencil survey and, when dealing with "normal" populations, it is almost automatically assumed that the characteristic is adequately represented. Thus, it is not included in the
discussion of the major modes; items to measure reality testing have
not been included in the Freshman Survey, from which the data
pertinent to our 3-D project were obtained; and it was not used in
arriving at the total functional-potential score.

    The dichotomous pairs do not imply an either/or condition

but a continuum, the terms on the left side of the pair tending toward the positive and those on the right toward the negative. (This is reminiscent of Jung's (1933) theory of opposites, which suggests the presence of equally extreme but unconscious and diametrically opposed traits.) While the person who functions best usually tends toward the left dimension in the mode pairs, he demonstrates optimal functioning only when he also demonstrates some of the opposed behavior. In the case of flexibility/rigidity, for example, flexibility is desirable, but if there is too little central structure, flexibility is only indecisive chaos. Finally, and again consistent with Jung's conceptual framework, the ability to express contradictory mode characteristics—and to tolerate the resultant ambiguity—may correlate positively with the highest stages of development. The fact that a particular mode (behavior) is not readily apparent, however, does not imply its absence. Indeed, a person's unconscious forces are often instrumental in determining his behavior. It is the degree to which a trait is demonstrated that allows the individual to be described along any particular dimension. And it is the tendency toward one side or the other that helps delineate personality.

Needs are also relevant to functional potential. For example, four mode pairs approximate needs which Fromm (1955) believed arose from the conditions of man's existence. He postulated that the need for relatedness was caused when man, becoming man, was torn from the animal's primary union with nature. The degree to which one feels or expresses this need may be seen in the relatedness/aloofness mode. Man's urge for transcendence—his need to rise above his animal nature—relates to his ability to delay expression of primary impulses (delay of gratification/impulse expression). His most satisfying and healthiest feelings derive from his positive relationships (relatedness/aloofness), but he also needs some ties with his natural roots, a sense of personal identity, and a sense of his uniqueness (identity/amorphism) that can be obtained either through his own creative efforts or by his identification with others. His need for a frame of reference may be primarily rational, irrational, or combine elements of both.

Horney describes anxiety as "the feeling a child has of being isolated and helpless in a potentially hostile world. A wide range of adverse factors in the environment can produce this insecurity . . .

direct or indirect dimensions, indifference, erratic behavior, lack of respect for the . . . [needs of the individual], lack of real guidance, disparaging attitudes, too much admiration or the absence of it, lack of reliable warmth, having to take sides of parental disagreements, too much or too little responsibility, overprotection, isolation from other children, injustice, discrimination, unkept promises, hostile atmosphere, and so on" (1945, p. 41). The individual reacts to these conditions of insecurity and hostility by expressing one or more of ten needs from one of three postures: moving *toward* people (the need for love); moving *away from* people (the need for independence); or moving *against* people (the need for power). Each of these stances represents a basic "set" toward oneself and toward others and, since the sets are not mutually exclusive, the normal person is able to resolve his need-conflicts by integrating the three.

In terms of Murray's (1938) need-structuring, a need produces an activity that the organism maintains until he or the environmental situation, or both, has been sufficiently altered to reduce it. Some needs are accompanied by particular emotions and are frequently associated with particular acts which produce the desired end. From Murray's long list of needs, those especially relevant to the modes are affiliation, aggression, autonomy, nurturance, play, rejection, and succorance.

Just as no discussion of functional potential would be complete without some reference to needs, any such reference must include Maslow, whose hierarchy of needs is a valuable contribution to understanding the individual: physiological needs for food, safety, protection, and care; psychological needs for gregariousness, love relations, respect, status, self-respect, and self-actualization; cognitive needs for knowledge and understanding; and aesthetic needs for beauty, symmetry, simplicity, completion, and order. According to Maslow, human motivation is based on the hierarchical arrangement of these and other needs. When needs with the highest priority are satisfied, the next in the hierarchical scheme emerge and press for satisfaction. For example, although hunger and thirst always take precedence over the desire for approval or recognition, these preempt the need for beauty. Consistent with his "Man is good" ideal, Maslow believes that the person becomes antisocial only when society denies him the fulfillment of his inborn needs.

The relationship of needs and certain modes is apparent. The modes, however, are dichotomous and do not operate in the hierarchical manner that Maslow attributes to needs. It is not necessary for one mode to be demonstrated before another can be expressed. In other words, we here perceive a kaleidoscope rather than vertical lines or pyramids.

Because they appear to be more meaningful when taken as a whole—grouped together to represent the totality of the person rather than singular parts—the six modes are added together to form an aggregate score. This total is called functional potential, the core of our paradigm of personal functioning. To arrive at this score, the respondent's reactions to Freshman Survey items assessing each of the six Modes are all added together. Depending upon the way his scores fare in terms of the total group responses, the person is then placed into the high, medium or low functional potential group. Thus, strength in any one of the six modes may compensate for a deficiency in the others.

Chapter 4

Characterizing
the Modes

In this chapter, the basic structure of functional potential is amplified by a detailed analysis of the modes which play such an important role in this model of the person and the way in which the subject population has been examined. The disparate treatment given
to the six modes suggests my interests and biases and, indeed, I feel
that certain modes warrant greater attention because they are fundamental. The attention given to relatedness/aloofness and iden-
tity/amorphism—the characteristics central to functional potential
and therefore discussed most extensively—probably will not be questioned by students of human functioning. Personal prejudices may
be evident in other areas, however.

Although the modes are not directly related to specific stages
of growth, there are periods when one mode may appear dominant
—for example, in early childhood controls are externally mandated
rather than self-determined and impulses are readily expressed. Accordingly, a particular developmental phase may suggest the need
to express certain modes over others. And although each pair is dis-

cussed separately, it should be remembered that it is the six modes together that define the individual personality. In this way, it is hoped that the reader will get a "feel" for the people examined and will better understand what it means to operate at one of the three levels of functional potential, designated as high, medium, and low.

Relatedness/Aloofness

Like all elements of functional potential, relatedness/aloofness is expressed as one unit containing two opposites. The paired terms refer to the extent to which these qualities are present and do not necessarily describe behavior or even attitudes of introversion or extraversion. The strength of either trait is measured by responses to items assessing this mode. The idiosyncratic degree of relatedness/aloofness possessed by the individual is dependent upon his primary experiences. These characteristics are fundamental, maintained with a fair amount of consistency, and continue throughout life as keys to personality functioning. Most people experience elements of both affiliation and detachment. If early life has greatly deprived them of close attachments, however, and if their needs for security were not met during infancy and early childhood, they likely will be unable to relate in more than a limited fashion to either themselves or others.

The extent to which an individual can allow himself to become involved with others approximates, but cannot be equated with, Jung's (1923) "feeling" function. However, the opposite of the ability to feel is not the ability to think. In fact, it is likely that the affiliated individual is well integrated at several levels of functioning.

In the normally functioning person, aloofness may be a protective screen that prevents or at least alleviates personal hurt. At its negative extreme, the same attitude may be apprehended clinically in the classic schizophrenic or autistic child who is so removed from human contact that no rapport can exist. The distantiated, alienated person, having failed in early attempts to find warm, satisfying relationships, expresses his disappointment and hurt in terms of isolation and rejection of ties. Here, of course, is the "lone wolf" syndrome. Such aloofness, alienation, or separation is a movement *away* from others while relatedness or affiliation is a movement *toward* people (Horney, 1945). People are affiliated or distantiated to varying degrees, but the extremely alienated person will not allow himself to feel with or be related to anyone—not even himself. Conversely, the extremely affiliated person is unable to cut himself off from others, even when it might be to his advantage. Both extremes are pathological—the one leading to separation and the other to symbiotic dependencies. A little of both seems essential for optimal functioning.

The notion of relatedness/aloofness is evident in much of Fromm's writing, and he argues that man has two choices in a basically rootless world: he can unite himself with other people in the spirit of love and shared work, or he can find security by submitting and conforming to society.

Keniston (1968) attributes personal alienation to contemporary developmental patterns, and Goodman (1960) describes the detachment and invulnerability adopted by youth to cope with a mechanized and emotionally meaningless environment. This detachment from and disillusionment with the adult world is comprehensible in terms of the "phenomenology of unrestrained change" (Keniston, 1968, p. 48). Young people seem extremely aware of differences between their world and that of their parents. Perceiving the social changes being enacted around them, they sense that their parents are poor or, at best, irrelevant models for the lives they themselves will lead. The disillusionment resulting from this lack of positive models might be better understood if it were expressed in terms of overt antagonism.

Another aspect of this disinvolvement is a diffuse sense of powerlessness. Such feelings, which tend to be self-fulfilling, may be expressed in the crucial need of young people for privacy. Such professions may veil a deep need for relatedness that previously has been denied and is the source of much disappointment. A posture and the real thing are, of course, very different, and the person who invests a great deal of libido in defensive maneuvers often may be likely to discard his own mask if he feels someone will respond. If early relationships have not contained many elements of emotional and physical closeness, if the "terry cloth" needs postulated by Harlow (1958) have not been met, then distantiation becomes a very basic part of the person—and much searching-in-depth would be necessary for any transformation to occur eventually. If the posture is built upon suppression rather than a fundamental repression and if, further, considerable effort is made toward affecting alienation, the person is in a position to be swayed, to show his needs for others and his desire to relate.

Despite my own strong feelings that people functioning at either extreme of this continuum probably exhibit considerable consistency over both time and place, it is necessary to think of relatedness/aloofness in terms of specific situations and periods. As the individual moves toward greater flexibility, for example, he concomitantly develops increased capacity to relate to people around him. At the same time, as many behavioral scientists recognize, there are typical adolescent tendencies toward introversion and less outer-directed activities in favor of deeper relationships with fewer people. Indeed, as Chickering (1971) suggests, "the relatively greater importance of the group during early adolescence is consonant with the proposition that during later adolescence and early adulthood, increased maturity of interpersonal relationships involves increased 'introversion,' at least as that tendency is reflected by less need to be a 'joiner' and by less need for association with more than a few close friends" (p. 102).

"Disengagement from parents, the development of self-direction, formerly was called *adolescent rebellion;* now the term is *alienation.* Of course it never was the case that all adolescents were rebellious and now not all are alienated. Both terms oversimplify and exaggerate; they only suit the most visible minority. Yet the shift in terms does reflect a shifting stance of adolescent toward adult" (p. 59).

Erikson talks about the eagerness of the young adult who, emerging from that developmental stage in which the central theme is the search for identity, is "ready for intimacy . . . to commit himself to concrete affiliations and partnerships and to develop the ethical strength to abide by such commitments, even though they may call for significant sacrifices and compromises. . . . The avoidance of such experiences because of a fear of ego loss may lead to a deep sense of isolation and consequent self-absorption. The counterpart of intimacy is distantiation, to destroy those forces and people whose essence is dangerous to one's own" (1963, p. 264). As the person moves into later adolescence he develops the need to involve himself with others. The individual who does not know "what he is about" cannot cope with interpersonal intimacy. He isolates himself or finds stereotypical and cold, formal, interpersonal relations. The more certain he becomes of his identity, however, the more he can allow himself to seek friendships and love.

These positions are substantiated by some empirical evidence. Tolor and LeBlanc (1971), investigating the relationship between alienation and such personality variables as anxiety, hostility, and depression in college students, report that "the experience of estrangement is a pervasive syndrome which involves a composite of perceptions regarding social institutions and events, and expectancy that external factors over which one has little control will determine one's successes and failures" (p. 444).

Much has been written about the early developmental patterns of the disengaged person, of his environment's impact, and his family's influence on his sense of identity and relatedness. Just as one's family is most important in developing basic personality characteristics, the person's sense of family cohesiveness, coupled with his deep awareness of their feelings, thoughts, and attitudes, contribute much to his sense of security. Equally important in studies of both clinical and normal populations, the sense of family may provide cues for understanding man's relationships to himself and others.

In my earlier thinking (Brawer, 1970), the family was seen as a separate area for study, an approach that was consistent with the work of many investigators who treated the family as an independent variable and thus isolated it from the person's own characteristics. While the primary group is considered to be a major link between society and the individual, it is seen as something *apart* from the person. Accordingly, a distinction is made between innate and adopted characteristics—a distinction that is almost impossible to maintain once the person has gained some kind of sophistication and independence. While it is, of course, a simple matter to distinguish demographic information (and such separations are maintained in this project), it appears both expedient and sensible here to incorporate nondemographic family-related variables into the relatedness/aloofness mode.

Positively or negatively, obviously or subtly, images of family cohesiveness and awareness of family feelings are tied to the individual and to the way he addresses himself and others. Because the sense of family cohesiveness, the general feelings of protectiveness, and the closeness experienced in the primary family are allied to one's feelings of relatedness, this mode includes both the person's recollection of early family life and family relationships and his current feelings regarding parents and siblings. Incorporated in our measurement are such questions as: Does the person feel close to his family? Does he undersand how his mother or father feels about his work? Is he aware of his parents' ambitions for him?

From the theoretical positions outlined and the empirical findings cited, it is clear that relatedness/aloofness plays a major role in the larger construct of functional potential. It is particularly important in the transition from adolescence to adulthood and therefore essential to understanding college students. Both this mode and identity/amorphism, discussed next, are pivot points in the individual's personality constellation. They account for many of the behavioral variations exhibited in diverse populations.

Identity/Amorphism

Identity/amorphism refers to the sense of self that is equated with feelings of wholeness, sameness, "I am-ness," and directedness. It suggests that the person honestly can say, "I know who I am and have a fair notion of where I am going." In our context, identity is not considered a substitute for but an integral part of the ego. "Identity involves a drawing together, a crystallization of being. It allows the individual to preserve his sense of self despite the vicissitudes of life that are yet to come" (Lidz, 1968, p. 344). The "process of formulating an independent identity encompasses both earlier stages of development and future processes, integrating all one's experiences into a holistic pattern" (Cohen and Brawer, 1971, p. 2).

The search for identity is especially marked during adolescence, but the seeds that encourage such a quest must be planted when the child is first able to recognize the differences between "you," "they," and "me." In fact, as Erikson notes, "While the end of adolescence . . . is the stage of an overt identity *crisis*, identity *formation* neither begins nor ends with adolescence: it is a lifelong development largely unconscious to the individual and to his society. Its roots go back all the way to the first self-recognition: in the baby's earliest exchange of smiles there is something of a *self-realization coupled with a mutual recognition*" (1959, pp. 113–116). The identity/amorphism mode is closely allied with the total growth process since the self-actualized, individuated person is forever digging deeper into his inner self in order to discover new dimensions.

Erikson, whose work has initiated so much contemporary thinking about the search for identity, characterizes our present youth culture as a psychosocial "moratorium" on adulthood that provides the young with opportunities to develop their identities as adults. This involves the gradual integration of all identifications and the merger of old experiences with present functioning and future planning. According to Erikson (1964, pp. 91–92, 95–96):

[*It involves*] *a progressive continuity between* . . . *the long years of childhood* . . . *and the anticipated future; between that which he conceives himself to be and that which he perceives others to see in him and to expect of him. Individually speaking, identity includes, but is more than the sum of, all the successive identifications of* . . . *earlier years.* . . . *The adolescent search for a new and yet a reliable identity can perhaps best be seen in the persistent endeavor to define, to over define, and to redefine oneself and each other in often ruthless comparison; while the search for reliable alignments can be seen in the restless testing of the newest in possibilities and the oldest in values.*

The key problem of identity, then, is . . . *the capacity of the ego to sustain sameness and continuity in the face of changing fate.*

In societies where roles are sufficiently stable and openly acknowledged, children are able to move into their work roles with relative ease. In such cultures, the main problem for young adults may be the development of socialized behavior and the integration of value systems rather than the development of self. This is in contrast to rapidly changing and more acculturated societies in which the prime problem for youth becomes identity formation. As Keniston points out, "The youth culture . . . provides not only an opportunity to postpone adulthood, but also a more positive chance to develop a sense of identity which will resolve the discontinuity between childhood and adulthood, on the one hand, and bridge the gap between the generations, on the other" (1968, p. 54). When this sense of identity is not developed beyond a minimal level, the personal referent is unstable and amorphous.

Identity/amorphism includes the sense of goal directedness. In the latter part of the twentieth century, a tendency to social amorphism is evident in uncertainty about personal, national, and international goals, rights of law and judgment, and life styles. Doubt has replaced the simple assurance, felt by people in less technological societies, that old habits and styles of conduct will be perpetuated. Along these lines, Klapp recounts a telling story: "As a professor of philosophy once confessed to me, in talking about the meaning of life with a Minnesota farmer, 'As I looked him in the eye I felt ashamed that he knew exactly where he stood but I didn't' " (1969, p. 4).

The relation between identity and goal directedness has been documented by some investigations of college students. R. Heath's (1959) in-depth study of a small group of Princeton undergraduates isolated a few men who had a high level of "integrative ego functioning." Over a period of years, these "reasonable adventurers," as he called them, were found to be oriented toward the future, intrinsically involved in liberal arts subjects, close to their peers, objective toward self, certain of values and orientation, tolerant of ambiguity, curious, and endowed with a sense of humor. Similarly, the Haverford students whom D. Heath (1965) described as most mature showed a high relationship between "stability of self-organization" and motivation, academic achievement, imagination, openness, and social interest.

Such investigations provide information about the theoretical, the conceptual, and the ideal, but to understand the identity/

amorphism concept we should examine motivation and goals. Chickering, who sees the establishment of identity as a major vector of development, observes, "Many young adults are all dressed up and don't know where to go; they have energy but no destination. The dilemma is not just 'Who am I?' but 'Where am I going?' Development of purpose occurs as these questions are answered with increasing clarity and conviction in three domains: avocational and recreational interests, vocational plans and aspirations, and general life-style considerations" (1971, p. 15).

Unfortunately, however, the tie between identity and occupational role is not considered in the majority of studies of goals and vocational directions and, in fact, there are few attempts to tie even vocational guidance to the fundamental issues of self-awareness. Studies frequently provide information about life goals as if they existed apart from the individual, not as intrinsic qualities but extrinsic measures. Goals and expectations are formulated, of course, in terms of the future and require a perspective different from that which typifies other analyses.

Whether goals are immediate or long term, temporary or enduring, they are definitely tied to one's self-concept. In the college population, a sense of goal directedness represents the degree to which the person is able to designate academic, vocational, and personal goals; consider the way his future (for example, the next five years) will accommodate these goals and the relation between his plans and his past performances, abilities, and interests.

The individual who has a high degree of self-directedness or a considerably secure identity is able to ask himself about his goals with the expectation of reasonable—if not immediate—answers. Conversely, the person who has a low degree of directedness and is close to the amorphism side of this mode can only ask, if he asks at all, "What should I be asking myself?" Certain cues to the sense of being are apparent in such statements as "I'm sure I will," "I haven't the slightest idea of what I will do," "I plan to be . . . ," and "I couldn't care less."

Academic institutions can play a major role in the development of goal directedness and, consequently, the strengthening of identity. Indeed, since one of their potential functions is to allow— better yet, to stimulate—individual development in terms of identity, academic institutions should encourage their students to define academic and vocational directions. Personal goals may be more difficult to delineate than either academic or vocational goals because, while they are more pervasive and basic, they are often less conscious. All goals include both affective and cognitive dimensions, and attitudes, values, special views of society and self, environmental perceptions, and the very "I-ness" of the person are as essential to goal formulation as the more intellectual variables.

As complex as relatedness/aloofness, identity/amorphism includes the person's feelings about his past experiences, awareness of the way he functions, the ability to look ahead, and the way in which he sets goals for himself. Identity also relates closely to sense of reality, tendencies to plan, and a clear-cut notion of role in a changing, confusing world. When we consider the mature individual, we find that the search for identity is an on-going, life-long process. At the same time, however, striving for individuation or self-actualization is a far cry from amorphism, and the critical search for ego identity that characterizes much of the adolescent's thinking, acting, and incessant probing becomes, with time, a sophisticated, knowing, and rewarding process.

Flexibility/Rigidity

In education and psychology, as well as in many social situations, a considerable amount of attention centers on the antithetical notions of flexibility and rigidity. Flexibility may be equated with the ability to change directions and, when necessary, to move with a situation or a feeling. Rigidity, on the other hand, relates to authoritarianism, dogmatism, and conventionalism.

Flexibility is the ability to tolerate diversity among people as well as situations. Chickering says it well: "By increased tolerance we mean not simply an improved capacity for teeth gritting and tongue biting in the face of those who differ, nor the development of callouses and screening devices that shield us from, or obscure, the values and behaviors of others that might threaten our own sheltered and carefully protected structure. Instead we refer to an increasing openness and acceptance of diversity, which allows our own sensitivities to expand and which increases the range of alternatives for satisfying exchanges and for close and lasting friendships" (1971, p. 94).

Even in the 1957 report that summarized research about the impact of college on students, Jacob states, "Social harmony with *an easy tolerance of diversity pervades the student environment*" (p. 2). Tolerance does seem to increase among college students, but there is some question as to whether this change is due to the college experience or if it is a measure of development. In Plant's (1958) study of students at San Jose State College and their equally qualified peers who were not admitted because of space limitations, for example, increasing liberalism and decreasing dogmatism and ethnocentrism with age occurred in both groups. However, "the changes in students seemed to increase with length of college attendance, so that students who completed four years changed more than those completing two, and that students completing two years changed more than their peers who did not attend at all. So although such changes apparently do occur among all young persons, college attendance seems to amplify or accelerate them" (Chickering, 1971, p. 98).

The rigid person is unable to integrate his archaic urges with a long-range value system or liberate his intellectual potential toward creative achievements that can serve those values. Conversely, the creative personality demonstrates "flexible and constructive use of the imagination to manipulate the possibilities of the reality situation and thus to solve problems and to arrive at fuller satisfaction of needs" (Klopfer and others, 1954, p. 367). Whatever the framework in which one works, flexibility and rigidity are terms frequently associated with discussions of the creative process (Getzels and Jackson, 1962; Guilford, 1956; Koestler, 1970).

MacKinnon, who studied creativity in writers, mathematicians, physical scientists, engineers, architects, and industrial researchers, describes a certain personality lability than can permit complexity and disorder and an ability to achieve some kind of structure out of chaos. Indeed, the "more creative a person is the more he reveals an openness to his own feelings and emotions, a sensitive intellect and understanding self-awareness, and wide-ranging interests. . . . All creative groups we have studied showed a clear preference for the complex and asymmetrical. . . . Creative persons are especially disposed to admit complexity and even disorder into their perceptions without being made anxious by the resulting chaos. It is not so much that they like disorder per se, but that they prefer the richness of the disordered to the stark barrenness of the simple" (MacKinnon, 1962, pp. 488–489).

Comparing elements of creativity and intelligence, Getzels and Jackson (1962) wonder whether heavy reliance on the concept of intelligence (as reflected in intelligence tests) might not be one reason that the understanding of gifted children has slackened. This hypothesis may apply also to the junior college student who falls considerably below his liberal arts or university peers on the usual tests of ability and achievement but, throwing aside the traditional mode of assessment, might reveal other strengths.

Both flexibility and rigidity play central roles in Adorno and others' (1950) major work on the authoritarian personality, in the Rorschach literature of Klopfer and others (1954, 1956, 1970), and in Rokeach's (1960) investigations of open and closed belief systems. In the literature of ego psychology, flexibility is viewed as an important indicator of the individual's basic structure and ego strength (Brawer, 1967). Accordingly, the flexibility/rigidity mode is an essential feature of the larger construct of functional potential.

While they are often conceived to be "personality" or noncognitive variables, flexibility and rigidity have cognitive as well as affective components. They are tied to both the individual's intellectual manner and his affective relationships. The way that any given material is structured, the range or scope of intellectual capacity, the tendency toward a cosmopolitan rather than parochial approach, and the ease with which the person is able to move from one domain to the other are important indicators of these concepts. The observer who attempts to understand an individual along the continuum of flexibility-rigidity might ask such questions as: Is this person tied only to the immediate present or can he look ahead? Can he extend his thinking beyond his own community? his cultural group? If so, to what extent? Can he move in different directions, yet maintain a sound ego stance?

The polarity of this mode as well as the close interrelationships of these constructs do not imply an either/or situation—neither in this mode nor in the other five modes discussed in this chapter. Seldom does any individual stand over to one side, wholly rigid or completely flexible. Indeed, a firm stance at either pole would be undesirable since too much rigidity suggests so great a need for structure that the person cannot move outside the parameters established by previous experiences, while too much flexibility implies a looseness of ego functioning. Here again the degree of flexibility or rigidity manifested by the person becomes an important input in considering his total being, as well as a comparatively direct way of assessing his strengths and weaknesses.

One requirement of a healthy personality is that "its cognitive style be broad, confident, flexible" (Allport, 1961, p. 274). Disordered lives, cognitively crippled, manifest a rigidity that results from personal insecurity in a world of flux. Early experiences have much to do with the degree of rigidity or flexibility that characterizes the person's style of functioning, a tie that strengthens the alliance of this mode to functional potential. Both reality-orientation and flexibility are implied in Kris's notion of "regression in the service of the ego." Emphasizing the ego's capacity to regulate regression under certain conditions, he points out that the organizing functions of the ego "include the . . . voluntary and temporary withdrawal of cathexis from one area or another, in order later to regain improved control" (1951, p. 488). While ego-regressions or the primitivization of ego functions can occur in such weak ego states as intoxication and psychosis, they also occur during creative and inventive periods. Only a strong ego can afford to loosen controls and regress to a more primitive condition, and flexibility becomes an index to ego function—the healthy individual being able to rebound and to tolerate ambiguity, opposite forces, and complexity. "If a subject allows himself to express primary-process thinking, suggesting that his controls over unconscious material are flexible rather than repressive, if he can also use secondary-process associations which suggest good, reality-oriented control . . . and if, further, he is able to employ creative and unusual associations to . . . stimuli . . . he reveals his ability to regress temporarily, confident that he can recoup and return to secondary-level associations . . . [This] is, therefore, indicative of a high level of adaptive-flexibility" (Brawer, 1967, pp. 57–58).

Flexibility/rigidity, so strongly rooted in the basic construct of functional potential, is closely tied to other characteristics. As an example, the autonomy and religious liberalism scales of the Omnibus Personality Inventory together serve "as a dual measure of nonauthoritarian thinking. Persons scoring high on both are cognitively, if not emotionally, released from their own subcultural pasts; they are much less judgmental and exhibit greater independence in their thinking than those scoring below the normative mean" (Heist and Yonge, 1962, p. 43).

Several people have tried to assess systematically flexibility and rigidity. As long ago as 1942, Luchins developed a series of complicated problems in order to study rigidity. Significant differences between rigid and nonrigid students were found in their abilities to recognize a logical hypothesis, a valid experiment supporting the data, and a reasonable interpretation of data. Dressel's (1958) experiments corroborate these differences, suggesting that flexible students show a tendency to see more and closer relationships among interrelated terms. In our own work (Brawer, 1967; Brawer and Cohen, 1966; Cohen and Brawer, 1967), differences in adaptive-flexibility among community college teaching interns correlated highly with their ratings by independent supervisors.

As noted earlier, people are generally familiar with the two basic dimensions of this mode. Both flexibility and rigidity are important variables for understanding creative personalities, mature individuals, and students at all levels of education. If those who are involved with enhancing growth in individuals and society can stimulate flexibility while providing sufficient controls, it eventually may be possible to find better ways of preparing people, vocationally and developmentally.

Independence/Dependence

Because these terms are so commonly used and there is general consensus about their meaning, it is unnecessary to suggest equivalent phrases or define them to the extent that the other modes have been. This discussion, therefore, will be limited to a brief review of their theoretical role, the related literature about college populations, and notes from those ego psychologists who draw heavily upon these dimensions.

Independence, or autonomy (the terms are used interchangeably here), is the power to direct one's affairs. Autonomy suggests an inner control, in which both cognitive and affective traits are equally important. The concept is frequently mentioned in clinical literature and is included in recent studies of students in higher education. Sanford (1962), for example, makes a plea for the kinds of school experiences that will encourage emotional and cognitive development and autonomy in both. Others have followed his lead —both in structured academic settings and in alternative forms of education such as the "free" school that came into vogue in the late 1960s.

The notion of independence, however, is hardly new. Certainly it preceded Freud and his coworkers. Yet it was a neo-Freudian, Hartmann (1961), who stressed the autonomy of the ego and proposed a "conflict-free ego sphere" in favor of the orthodox notion of an ego held at the mercy of archaic forces. Still other ego psychologists, as well as behavioral scientists who concentrate on the developmental implications of the constructs, refer to autonomy as one of the most significant dimensions of human growth. Erikson (1963) includes it in his eight stages of man, noting that "if denied the gradual and well-guided experience of the autonomy of free choice (or if, indeed, weakened by an initial loss of trust) the child will turn against himself all his urge to discriminate and to manipulate. He will overmanipulate himself, he will develop a precocious conscience. Instead of taking possession of things in order to test them by purposeful repetition, he will become obsessed by his own repetitiveness. By such obsessiveness . . . he then learns to repossess the environment and to gain power by stubborn and minute control . . . [which] is the infantile source of later attempts in adult life to govern by the letter, rather than by the spirit" (p. 252).

Loevinger and Wessler (1970) define autonomy as the seventh of eight stages of development.

[It is] marked by heightened sense of individuality and a concern for emotional dependence. The problem of dependence-independence is recurrent throughout ego development. What characterizes this transitional stage is the awareness that even when one is

no longer physically and financially dependent on others, one re-
mains emotionally dependent. Relations with other people, which
have been becoming deeper and more intensive . . . are seen as
partly antagonistic to the striving for achievement. . . . The mor-
alism of lower stages begins to be replaced by an awareness of inner
conflict . . . [and] conflict is part of the human condition.

The autonomous stage is so named partly because one rec-
ognizes other people's need for autonomy . . . [and respects] their
need to find their own way and even make their own mistakes. . . .
The autonomous person has the courage to acknowledge and to
cope with conflict. . . . [He] has a broader scope [and] is con-
cerned with social problems beyond his own intermediate experi-
ence (p. 6).

Autonomy develops along with emotional independence and the
conscious recognition of interdependencies. In fact, "Recognition
and acceptance of interdependence is the capstone of autonomy.
One realizes that parents cannot be dispensed with except at the
price of continuing pain for all; that he cannot be supported indefinitely without working for it; that loving and being loved are
necessarily complementary. Then as interdependence is recognized
and accepted, boundaries of personal choice become clear. One can
become an effective agent for himself" (Chickering, 1971, p. 12).

There is a consensual regard for independence/dependence
as an important intrapersonal psychological dimension. Equally important are the educational and social implications for developing
this characteristic in students who may be operating at various stages
of development. As Sidney Marland points out, it is important to
find ways to encourage all students, from elementary and secondary
schools and community colleges to four-year institutions, to develop
a sense of independence. "So many find themselves aimless, without
purpose, without a sense of career . . . and a sense of controlling
their own lives. And we hold with many of the ablest psychologists
that one of the great solutions to our education for the disadvan-
taged will be when these people, especially in our inner cities and
rural depressed areas, begin to feel and generally know that they
can have a control over their own lives" (Marland, 1971, p. 9).

Several studies (Chickering, 1971; Lehmann and Dressel,
1962; Rowe, 1964; Webb and Crowder, 1961; Webster, Sanford,

and Freedman, 1957) concur in the finding that, with few exceptions, college seniors are more independent and autonomous than freshmen. The difference is not always large, however, and in only a few studies does it achieve statistical significance. In many of these investigations, the criterion of autonomy is the degree to which one develops a critical attitude toward authority figures, satisfaction from one's behavior, or the ability for independent decision-making. Some researchers regard autonomy as part of the total developmental pattern and one important measure of maturity (Heath, 1965; R. W. White, 1952; and Sanford, 1956).

Finally, it is necessary to allude briefly to the concept of authoritarianism, a cluster of personality traits predisposing a person to dogmatism and punitive moralism as well as denial of some of his own impulses and needs (particularly the need for dependence). The authoritarian personality projects the unacceptable characteristics of his own nature onto those outgroups against which he is prejudiced. Katz reports that "the achievement of greater autonomy and a clearer ego identity, the development of more integration, and control of the impulses are major developmental tasks achieved in varying degrees in [that phase of the life cycle known as late adolescence. Data compiled by Katz and others] suggest that even students who remain relatively high in authoritarianism progress in these directions, although somewhat less, to be sure, than others do. What has been referred to as external supcrego can thus be said to become weaker during the college years, even for those whose authoritarianism otherwise changes relatively little, while the cognitive attitudes change less" (1968, p. 384).

As conceived in this model, independence does not imply separatedness or alienation. In fact, it may be that those who are most independent are also most aware of their dependencies. Perhaps only the person who is secure enough to recognize his dependency needs can be truly independent.

Progression/Regression

This mode may best be understood in terms of the person's attitudes regarding life's flow. It is at the basis of his perception that the glass is either half-full or half-empty and his tendency to move either forward or backward. Progression/regression also encompasses such human manifestations as negativism/positivism, activity/passivity, fluidity/immobilization, and flow/fixedness.

Each person interprets these concepts in a somewhat different way. Rogers, for example, maintains that: "Life, at its best, is a flowing, changing process in which nothing is fixed. . . . When life is richest and most rewarding it is a flowing process. To experience this is both fascinating and a little frightening. I find I am at my best when I can let the flow of my experience carry me, in a direction which appears to be forward, toward goals of which I am but dimly aware. In this floating with the complex stream of my experiencing, and in trying to understand its ever changing complexity, it should be evident that there are no fixed points. When I am thus able to be in process, it is clear that there can be no closed system of beliefs, no unchanging set of principles which I hold. Life is guided by a changing understanding of an interpretation of my experience. It is always in process of becoming" (1961, p. 27).

This existential view of the well-functioning individual is based on the fundamental and allegedly empirically-based assumption that man has a natural tendency to actualize himself, to meet his potentialities. Together with his desire to integrate his experiences, he feels the urge to expand, to develop, to mature, and to express all his capacities. The person who is on his way to "becoming" responds to change and complexity, trusts and accepts himself and others, and is open to experience. Rogers maintains that these are the directions in which all people will move when there is true psychological freedom. For Rogers, as well as for Goldstein (1939) and Maslow (1954), the total individual reacts as an organized whole to the phenomenal field. The proposition that "the organism has one basic tendency and striving—to actualize, maintain, and enhance the experiencing organism" (Rogers, 1951, p. 487) is also consistent with ideas expressed by Syngg and Combs (1949), Angyal (1941), and Maslow (1954). As the individual matures, he becomes more differentiated, socialized, and autonomous.

Also noting the tendency to a forward movement, Hall and Lindzey stress the ebb and flow aspect of human functioning. "Self-actualization is not accomplished without struggle and pain, but the person engaged in the struggle stands the pain because the creative urge to grow is so strong. The child learns to walk in spite of his initial tumbles, the adolescent learns to dance in spite of his awkwardness and embarrassment" (1957, p. 481). Rogers (1951) also observes "that the forward-moving tendency can only operate when the choices are *clearly perceived and adequately symbolized*. A person cannot actualize himself unless he is able to discriminate between progressive and regressive ways of behaving. There is no inner voice that tells him which is the path of progress, no organismic necessity that thrusts him forward. He has to know before he can choose, but when he does know he always chooses to grow rather than to regress."

Jung (1933) maintains that there is progressive and regressive movement in all human developmental processes. When there is progression, the ego is satisfactorily adjusting to the needs of the unconscious and the demands placed upon it by external situations. Even opposing forces are coordinated, enabling a harmonious flow of psychical processes. Conversely, when the libido, or psychic energy, is interrupted in its forward movement, there is regression. As opposed to the traditional Freudian view that repression implies negative force, Jungian theory holds that it frequently enables the ego to find a way around certain obstacles so that progression may occur more rapidly and explicitly.

Adler's concept of superiority is analogous to Jung's ideas about the self and Goldstein's and Maslow's self-actualization principle, "the great upward drive." "I began to see clearly in every psychological phenomenon the striving for superiority. It runs parallel to physical growth and is an intrinsic necessity of life itself. It lies at the root of all solutions of life's problems and is manifested in the way in which we meet these problems. All our functions follow its direction. They strive for conquest, security, increase, either in the right or in the wrong direction. The impetus from minus to plus never ends. The urge from below to above never ceases. Whatever premises all our philosophers and psychologists dream of—self-preservation, pleasure principle, equalization—all these are but vague representations, attempts to express the great upward drive" (1930, p. 398).

These tendencies are evident in research with both clinical and academic populations. Rogers and his coworkers have conducted several experiments that substantiate their position, and several developmental psychologists hold similar ideas. Chickering (1965, 1967), for example, notes that seniors have been rated higher than freshmen on such dimensions as goal directedness, full involvement, personal stability and integration, and "venturing" (openness to new experience and willingness to confront questions, discover new possibilities, and initiate things). These changes, seen as indicators of increased maturity, offer empirical support for the notion of progressive movement.

Progression, then, represents general or specific movement forward. On the other hand, reconciling both Freudian and Jungian theory, although regression may recoup energy for later forward thrusts, it is here seen as a static or even a depressive condition. Whether regression is temporary or permanent can be established only by longitudinal examination.

Delay of Gratification/Impulse Expression

Institutions reflect cultural attitudes toward specific behaviors. In a period when religious feelings are dominant, schools are concerned with students' morals. When people recoil from totalitarianism, democracy and ethnic toleration are proper subjects for study. Now we are in a time when it is acknowledged that all people possess some measure of hostility—whether or not openly expressed. Primitive or impulsive forces are seen to affect both the individual and the culture. Whatever direction these archaic forces take, both their expression and control are perceived as significantly important to warrant the attention of many scientists. Different disciplines offer different formulas for understanding these phenomena but there appears to be a consensus that they are essential and dynamic features of every personality. Indeed, expression and control are tied so directly to the broader construct of ego strength that they are essential components of functional potential.

Of the several scholars who have been concerned with these variables, a few are cited here because they offer interesting variations on a familiar theme. Maslow (1954) describes self-actualized individuals as those who have the capacity to appreciate good times and to capture "peak experiences" of living. While they exhibit a freshness of spirit and an appreciation for life that is revealed by their responsiveness and spontaneity, they are also able to plan ahead and delay immediate gratification in order to attain future goals. Kris's (1952) postulation of "regression in the service of the ego" has already been alluded to and implies a balance between expression and delay. Actualized people are able to tolerate both the expression and withdrawal of impulses, often in rapid sequence.

Stressing the attraction of opposing forces, Klopfer points out that although the avenues through which drive impulses express themselves are controlled by the ego, the ego does not control the productive energy itself. He writes that phenomenologically, when the individual has reached the state of self-realization, his unconscious and archaic forces "are no longer a threat that has to be neutralized; they have become, instead, a source of creative self-expression. The drive impulses reflecting archaic forces are not only accepted here but are recognized as an essential part of the Self; namely, as the part of the Self which is the essential source of productivity even though, and because, it is outside the realm of conscious ego control. . . . This self-realization may express itself in "Leistung" (productive achievement) or mature love, and it may also express itself in a comfortable relationship to one's Self, which makes the individual a 'Rock of Gibraltar' in his social setting. . . . To sum up: Instead of speaking of a regression in the service of the ego, we could speak of the ego functioning in the service of self-realization" (1954, p. 568).

Delay of gratification is related to a number of other variables. The choice of delayed reinforcement has been found to increase with age and intelligence (Mischel and Metzner, 1962), to differentiate between degrees of pathology (Shybut, 1966), and to be affected by family and cultural patterns (Mischel, 1961). When delay of gratification is measured in terms of the person's choice of a large, delayed reward or an immediate, small reward, two factors seem to be operating: a relatively enduring and generalized personality or motivational characteristic, which may be called ego strength, and an individual reinforcement expectation, which may be called trust. Studying the relationships of this construct to social-economic variables, Shipe and Lazare (1969) found no support for the thesis that lower class five- and six-year-olds are less able to delay gratification than other children of the same age, or that these children are less willing to trust adults.

Although "we should recognize . . . that actual behavior is usually more restrained and conservative than responses to questionnaires and personality inventories" (Chickering, 1971, p. 45), we find fairly consistent changes in impulse expression through various phases of development. Basically, most theorists and researchers recognize aggression and hate as the two major impulses requiring management. They also recognize, however, that "before emotional control can become effective, emotions have to be experienced, to be felt and perceived for what they are. Biological forces provoke sexual desire. Contact with a broadened life space provokes hostility toward parents and toward more generalized authority. Until lust and hate are admitted as legitimate emotions, as legitimate as love and admiration, their motive power is not likely to be harnessed to productive ends. Further, problems of control are aggravated because such feelings as lust and hate may be expressed in unrecognized ways or with unexpected intensity, triggering unanticipated consequences" (Chickering, 1971, p. 11).

It is generally accepted that the inability to manage emotions hampers learning. The underachiever may not lack intellectual power but ability to control his emotions, and his underachievement may prevail until he reaches a higher level of integration or development. Chickering maintains that, in this area, control means receptivity to new experiences which encourage development, while lack of control restricts new stimuli, hampers processing, and interferes with the development of sensitivity and flexibility. "We do not propose that college students manage their emotions as sixty-year-olds do" but "develop increasing capacity for passion and commitment accompanied by increasing capacity . . . [for] intelligent behavior. . . . Increased awareness of emotions and increased ability to manage them effectively are, therefore, developmental tasks central to social concerns as well as to full and rich individual development" (1971, p. 53).

Other behavioral scientists also believe that delay/impulse responses change with developmental level. Of the five genotypes by which D. Heath (1965) defines the maturing person, for example, one factor—"increased stability of organization"—refers to increased identity maintenance and lessened impulsive behavior. On the whole, the seniors in Heath's small group of students—as well as those at a number of other schools—appear to be less restrained and more impulsive than freshmen. Sanford explains this apparently curious phenomenon when he notes that as the individual grows older "there is a sharp increase in the ratio of ego to impulse. And this . . . expresses a most important fact about the freshman's stage of development. The maximum crisis of adolescence is over, and controlling mechanisms are again in the ascendancy. But the controls developed for the purpose of inhibiting impulse are still unseasoned and uncertain; they are likely to operate in a rigid manner, that is, to be rather overdone as if the danger of their giving way . . . were still very real" (1962, p. 260). Awareness of these impulses and the readiness to acknowledge their expression, then, suggest a level of development usually not attained by freshmen.

Some of these controls lead to authoritarian behavior, one facet of flexibility/rigidity. The satisfactory integration of flexibility and control calls for a strongly defined ego structure which is sometimes beyond the typical adolescent or young adult. And the increased impulse expression represented by college seniors suggests a genuine freedom manifested by flexible rather than rigid control. In other words, seniors seem to have developed "a higher degree of socialized expression of impulses" (Feldman and Newcomb, 1969, p. 349) than freshmen, although differences exist among the disciplines (students in the humanities and social sciences generally exhibit such expression more consistently than natural science and engineering students).

Notwithstanding these studies, however, impulse expression and the concomitant ability to postpone gratification are investigated more often in the psychological and psychoanalytic than the educational literature. Nevertheless, since it appears that these dimensions are essential to not only functional potential but the whole question of motivation and choice, it seems important to investigate their relation to students at different school levels.

The line between delay of gratification and impulse expression is thin but must be fluid. The mature individual must be able to exercise both control and spontaneity and must have the capacity to achieve and maintain a balance between the poles. This particular mode is not so much a continuum as it is two competing forces. Perhaps maturity is most firmly established when the individual is reconciled to this ebb-and-flow nature and is not unduly concerned with his abilities to either delay gratification or express the primary forces that inevitably besiege him.

The descriptions of the modes are predicated on the concept that ego strength is a basic dimension of the individual and on my own variation on this theme—functional potential. Although the modes are depicted as somewhat discrete dimensions, their overlap is evidence that they are directly related to the core of the individual and express his being in all of its manifestations. The modes are the basis for interpreting inventory information about students and staffs in three community colleges, and it is expected that, with more study, some may be revised or deleted and others may be suggested. At this point, however, each mode appears to represent an important dimension of the individual. Their use in the functional potential score and as a basis for grouping students is reported in the following chapters.

Chapter 5

Theory Into Study

Ideas about the ways people grow have been with us for a long time—undoubtedly long before they were formalized in writing. Elements of concern about human development and human differences are found in classical documents as well as in the recent literature of behavioral scientists. And in the years since the first depth psychologists presented their views on dynamics and action, interest has increased in the ways that people think, act, believe—and why.

There is a basic consensus regarding certain patterns in development and certain measures of differences. It generally is accepted, for example, that people develop at different rates, that society is the better for such diversity, and, lately, that educational institutions must heed these variations in growth. Slowly, attention is being given to structuring academic programs on the basis of behavior theories, and some schools and colleges are already convinced that they must tailor their curriculums to recognize and reconcile these factors rather than, as earlier, to change their students so they would fit into established patterns.

It seems important to use approaches that look at students along dimensions other than intelligence or academic achievement.

In emphazing dimensions of ego functioning as a vehicle for looking at those often-studied, seldom fully understood student subjects, I feel that individual strengths should be encouraged, that weaknesses should not be maximized, and that assessment procedures should be clinically sound, intuitive, global, and feasible in terms of administration and ease of scoring. A desire to find a means of assessment that is somewhat objective, fair, and based upon sound clinical knowledge as well as an understanding of human growth patterns, resulted in the formulation of functional potential as a core construct. Data are presented throughout this book to show how this major variable may be put into practice with normal adolescent and adult populations, how other information can be employed to establish its construct validity, and how the three levels postulated in this concept relate to other pertinent information.

Although a construct and, in that sense, artificial, functional potential is predicated on the assumption that no typology, no system of classification, is ever wholly discrete. People reach different levels of development and move in different directions; this diversity is evident in all strata of society, in all situations in which man interacts with his fellows. Within the small sample selected for this study, some interesting variations are evident in terms of developmental levels, attitudes and values, orientations toward life goals, and those characteristics generally labelled "demographic." This diversity seems to extend beyond the rather narrow confines of the geographical areas of the subject schools. Indeed, the freshmen who were studied in the 3-D project appear to be fairly representative of beginning students in many post-secondary educational institutions. A number fall short of the four-year college norms on conventional or traditional measures of achievement and aptitude, but some are close to their peers at academically prestigious schools.

Does functional potential relate to demographic traits and other personality characteristics; is it valid for predicting persistence/dropout? As background for the answers to these questions, I first describe the methodology of the study.

The subjects for the 3-D project were 1876 men and women tested during their first week as community college freshmen. (These students are more fully described in subsequent chapters.) This population was drawn from the freshman classes of three community colleges in southern California, selected because, while proximate, they appeared to represent three distinct types of institutions—urban, suburban, and rural—and were thought to represent similar institutions throughout the country. (The three schools are described in more detail later in the chapter.)

The information reported stems from two major sources. The Omnibus Personality Inventory (Heist and Yonge, 1962) is a polyphasic technique designed especially to assess characteristics of normal college populations. (In Chapter Twelve I discuss the fourteen scales comprising this inventory and the results and responses obtained from our community college sample.) The second instrument, the freshman survey, is a paper and pencil inventory, including items from which functional potential scores were derived, which provided the primary source of data for the 3-D project. The freshman survey actually is a mini-battery of tests designed to obtain a variety of data about students—information that is demographic or actuarial in nature, that is idiographic and thus not typically found in cumulative records, and that reflects potentials for growth rather than measures of intelligence. Prior to developing the freshman survey, certain basic assumptions were established:

(1) Community/junior colleges generally are believed to consist of heterogeneous faculties and to serve heterogeneous student bodies. While this may be challenged, for purposes of this study the two-year college is seen as an institution that embraces a varied population.

(2) School files are replete with data about students, faculty, and administrators, as well as such institutional "facts" as number of books in the library and test tubes in the labs. However, because it covers only a narrow spectrum, the information contained in these files is not helpful in answering many questions about human functioning.

(3) Nondemographic data—values, attitudes, potential for growth and development—are essential to fully characterize the individual.

(4) Useful instruments are designed with an understanding of the particular populations that they will assess as well as the theoretical constructs guiding them. (This is true of the OPI—devel-

oped for the study of college students—but few other published inventories are geared to such nonclinical populations.)

(5) Data derived from any instrument designed to serve a large population should be easily translated into numbers for machine scoring.

(6) Instruments should be developed and administered in such a way that they create a climate of good will; do not further feelings of animosity, activism, inadequacy, and the like; and encourage the respondents to express their feelings, ideas, and attitudes honestly.

(7) Projective techniques tend to lessen superficial responses. Subtle or ambiguous items built into the questionnaire stimulate responses that may not be obtained otherwise and may not have been made conscious previously by the subject.

(8) Although sensitivity and respect for the feelings of others are exercised, it is always possible that any instrument designed to elicit basic attitudes and feelings may prove threatening to the respondent. No one should be urged to participate in a study if he feels uncomfortable in so doing.

The freshman survey was designed to obtain base-line information of a demographic nature; data regarding attitudes, feelings, and values as well as goal directedness; and more subtle and subjective information than that typically elicited from subjects in school settings. Some items were designed in such a way that they tend to force a response choice while portions of the Inventory scale statements according to particular hierarchical orders. Still other items were formulated in such a way that the subject was free to respond to the extent he felt most comfortable. But most important, as a basis for assessing functional potential, the freshman survey is an information source that can be objectively scored and statistically interpreted.

Responses to the Survey generally fall into one of four categories: academic (information and attitudes about schools, goals, and experiences); personal (sense of identity and strength, affiliation or alienation to self and others, esthetic feelings and values); social (views about significant others and goals pertaining to personal relationships); vocational (attitudes and goals). The Terminal

Values and Instrumental Values Scales (Rokeach, 1968) also were included in the Inventory (for a fuller report of responses to the two scales by the entering freshmen as well as faculties of the three schools, see Brawer, 1971). Other sections of the freshman survey include an abbreviated version of Pace's College and University Environment Scale (1969), selected items developed for inventories used in various other projects, and a short, specially designed projective technique.

During their first week as college freshmen, in the fall of 1969, the subjects for the 3-D project attended large group orientation sessions at which the two inventories were administered. Most of the students were able to complete the forms in less than the 140 minutes allowed. Although all 1876 students in the initial testing did not respond to all items in the two surveys (thus accounting for some disparity in numbers), the final sample for the different variables comes close to the original population.

At the end of their second semester as freshmen, all students in the initial testing group who were still in school were asked to participate in a second testing session at each of the three colleges. Unfortunately, the original sample was reduced markedly—because controls were not always executed, because of attrition, or because the students had other interests. Except for some comparisons between the OPI and the functional potential groups, this second sample was considered too small for the analysis that had been anticipated in the original design. Limited follow-up information is available for the original student group regarding the OPI responses, drop/persist figures, and, more sporadically, transfers to other schools. Results of the information gathered from both instruments—the OPI and the freshman survey—together with the statistical tests used to interpret responses, are found throughout the chapters that follow.

Because the three schools examined in the 3-D project were selected for what was seen as diversity, it is important to understand the institutions themselves as well as characteristics of other colleges. Accordingly, the schools are discussed here.

In initiating the 3-D project, it appeared more important to address the notion of diversity/conformity by examining ostensible variations in community colleges within a narrow geographic area than to draw comparisons across different areas and thereby test regional impact. This choice is somewhat consistent with Lombardi's thesis (1971) that every educational institution has something in common with others of its type, independent of locale: community colleges attract similar students and faculty. More than a theoretical issue is at stake here. Diversity and conformity must be considered in terms of impact, effect, and, ultimately, funding, program planning, and selection. If schools vary and the populations remain constant along certain dimensions, then the impact of a school or group of schools can be evaluated on the basis of its differential effects on its students. If schools are very much alike and the student bodies vary, it probably does not matter so much which school the individual attends since whatever changes occur in him will be due to factors other than the school. If both schools and populations are differentiated in certain respects, however, interesting multivariant studies can be conducted on types of people, programs, and environments. Less provocative from an investigative standpoint are similar schools with similar populations. Here too, however, effects are probably due to individual and idiosyncratic rather than institutional factors.

The basic questions regarding institutional effectiveness relate to the role of the institution in stimulating change in the individual. Is it more important, for example, that the person is enrolled in a community/junior college rather than in a university, or that his parents had hundreds of books in their home, that they encouraged him to attend college, that his best friend was a college student, or that he was a member of a particular ethnic group? Does the academic institution have a greater effect than his ethnic affiliation upon the individual's eventual earning capacity? Does the college help create a climate wherein the student is encouraged to explore worlds of art, or does his instinctive appreciation of a leaf or a flower enable a positive response to esthetics? Do educational institutions or Mrs. Jones's Cadillac stimulate the desire for material goals? Do religious experiences or religious courses affect moral conceptions? Which aspects of the individual are most affected by exposure to colleges or other academic institutions? Which are affected by other institutions, group affiliations, interpersonal relations (teachers, peers, parents, friends, authority figures), personal experiences with family, work, school, people? The three colleges finally selected are located within ninety miles of Los Angeles and hereafter will be designated as Urban, Suburban, and Rural. Despite some obvious superficial differences, there was no assumption that the three community colleges were significantly different or similar, and the study attempted to locate and define the characteristics that might differentiate among or relate the schools.

Urban College is a large school in an industrial community of 250,000 people. Its district covers an area slightly less than thirty square miles which, at the time the school was established in 1927, was sparsely settled. Now this may be described as "inner city area." There are six feeder high schools in the area, each one serving approximately 41,000 people. Like many other colleges located in densely populated areas, this school has more or less successfully weathered a number of modifications, not the least of which has been a changed ethnic composition that reflects a changing community. At one time a "rah-rah" school, Urban College boasted a nationally recognized football team. It took pride in the number of its graduates who went on to four-year colleges and universities and it was viewed with respect by its supporting community. Representing a primarily white, middle-class population, it acted as an agent of upward mobility at a time when "going to college" meant a step up the ladder for many of its students and, less directly but perhaps as importantly, for their parents.

The decline of its dominance in athletics coincided with the change in ethnic composition of its community and student body. The white businessmen who financially supported the athletic program left this urban community and were replaced by others who showed less interest in the teams. A second contributing cause was the organization of colleges in nearby preponderantly white communities. One of these new colleges stressed athletics and attracted the high school athletes who formerly would have attended Urban College. Urban College, on the other hand, could not recruit athletes from the new district. Finally, the athletic conference declared nonresident and out-of-state students ineligible to play during their first year of college attendance.

The population has seen a shift in numbers, too. Now, at a time when postsecondary schooling is more expected than unique, when the enrollments in most institutions of higher learning have markedly increased from the 1920s, Urban College has few students in relation to its district population. In fact, in some courses that are necessary for state certification, fewer than ten students are enrolled. In the late sixties and early seventies, enrollment distribution by class was approximately 75 percent freshmen and 25 percent sophomores (or students who had completed more than two semesters). Of the full-time students in 1969, freshman males comprised 57 percent of the total class and sophomore males comprised 62 percent. Female students predominated among the part-time day students, representing 61 percent of the freshman and 39 percent of the sophomore classes. Among the 1969 graduates (333), 56 percent were males.

In recent years, because of low enrollment figures, few new faculty members have been employed. The instructors who have been at Urban College for a decade or more have seen the character of their school change markedly. The student population has moved from primarily white to approximately 39 percent white, 49 percent black, 8 percent Spanish surname, and 4 percent oriental. Whereas a considerable number of students transferred to universities from this community college in the 1930s, only about 340 now obtain an A.A. degree annually and fewer go on to further schooling—at least immediately after securing the associate degree or obtaining sufficient credits to transfer. Pride in the football team, the school publications, and similar activities has dissipated.

Whatever the problems, Urban College still has its lovely grounds and interesting clustered layout—assets with creative potential. It still has recreational facilities—even a new recreational program—and a few apparently enthusiastic staff members. It is still far from a "has been," but it has seen happier days.

Suburban College is in many ways the antithesis of the inner-city school. It is the junior member of a two-campus, seventy-six square mile district located in a coastal region approximately fifty miles south of central Los Angeles and serves 361,000 people. Eight high-schools feed into this college. Initial planning by the five-member district Board of Trustees began in 1961, and the college opened in September 1966, with an enrollment of two thousand regular day students and over three thousand in the evening college. In

1969–1970, enrollment reached 3,500 day and 4,500 evening students. It is the youngest and fastest growing of the three colleges under study. The college occupies a master-planned campus of 122 acres, smaller than the 160 acres of Rural College but larger than the 83 acres of Urban College. Its size is about average for newer colleges in the state.

The area surrounding the college is composed of conservative, predominantly white, middle- and upper-middle-class families. Scattered among this group are walled tracts of modest homes for lower-middle-class families. Although approximately 10 percent Spanish surname people (mainly Mexican-American) live in the area, they are spread among several barrios, or communities, and the district is predominantly one of "bedroom communities" (most of the population commutes to work).

The economy of the district is largely oil production, manufacturing, construction, communications, financial, and distributive services enterprises. However, the district has only two large companies, and the oil production, once a major economic asset, now is of secondary and diminishing importance. If new industries and businesses move into the area—as they are being encouraged to do—its complexion may change. Conceivably, then, the school will become truly representative of the community, but now it provides a rather sheltered feeling, like a fortress or perhaps a castle that stands aloof from everything around it.

This campus has a certain latitude to develop an educational program for the needs of its students and community. Because of limited facilities, it concentrated in its early years on courses and curriculums that required more in the way of an innovative and imaginative staff than expensive equipment. Its new audiotutorial designs, carrels, and creative laboratory setups, which have become an integral part of the system, are sources of pride to faculty and staff. The technical media are used by students as essential components of, not merely adjuncts to, their courses and the curriculum as a whole. Yet, in spite of its emphasis on media, it is the attitudes of many people at Suburban College that are particularly refreshing. In fact, one probably would be quite accurate in concluding that it is not the innovative equipment but the people who run the school that define its uniqueness. A contagious spirit still exists—

an eagerness and desire to create something new and effective—which, despite all the spirit of advocates of innovation in other institutions, is all too rare.

Although 75 percent of Suburban Colleges' students typically indicate a transfer goal, only about 25 percent actually transfer, 5 percent become occupational majors, and 70 percent are neither. This initial emphasis on transfer, a characteristic of junior college students, concerns the staff of Suburban College just as it concerns the staffs of most junior colleges. In the spring semester of 1969, 37 percent of the students registered in classes failed to complete them. The lowest percentage (31.3) was in physical and recreational education, the highest (40.2) in communications. The median for the seven classifications was 37.7 percent.

This picture of attrition at Suburban College looks similar to that of other community colleges, but different mobility patterns exist. Indeed, one of the greatest differences between most colleges and this institution is that it does not appear to be an agent of upward mobility for its community. Whereas many students in the two other project schools—which typify community colleges in this respect—are the first in their families to go to college, Suburban students frequently have parents who themselves are college graduates. Thus the school performs a different function—it serves to maintain the status quo, to catch students who perhaps couldn't care less about further schooling but who enroll because of parental expectation.

Rural College is notably different from the other two institutions. It is in a rural community that covers 2,500 square miles but has only 60,000 residents. With few students, who typically are drawn from four feeder high-schools, Rural College is fairly new. Whereas Urban College is potentially an agent of upward mobility and Suburban College acts to control downward mobility, this school functions as a more traditional and self-contained college in a rather isolated area. With approximately 40 percent of its students going on to four-year colleges and universities and with few students whose parents have gone to college, it acts as a springboard for socioeconomic movement upward and out, away from the home town.

The communities served by Rural College are small, have a disproportionately large retired population that includes many people on fixed incomes, have relatively few middle-aged families with children of high school and college age, and have not been affected yet by suburbanization. The college was authorized by a four-to-one vote of the electors in the large district that it serves, but, despite this apparently overwhelming support, the district suffered three bond proposal defeats before the voters approved a bond issue, which indicated to the president and other observers that the vote to form a district did not support the conclusion that voters also were willing to pay for a college. In any event, the college was launched in 1962 and in the fall of 1969, with an enrollment of 809 day and 538 evening students, it was the largest of the small colleges in the state. The ethnic composition of the student body is 90 percent white, 6 percent Spanish-surname, 3 percent black, 0.5 percent American Indian, and 0.5 percent oriental, while the ethnic population of the district is 71.3 percent white, 16 percent Spanish-surname, 9 percent black, 2 percent American Indian, and 0.7 percent oriental. This disparity between the district and student populations troubles the administration. Also troublesome, but typical in California colleges, is that no student from a minority group was enrolled in a trade-apprenticeship program.

The administration has concentrated a great deal of attention on and given exceptional support to the development of multimedia instructional programs. It adopted the concept of defined outcomes (in which instructional objectives are stated in terms of expected student operational ability at course completion). A tutorial instruction center contains the instructional materials and audiovisual equipment needed by the student, with a credentialed person available for consultation. The college president has developed materials for sale to other colleges, and in number and quality of equipment and materials, Rural College ranks among the best in the state.

Small group sessions, individual sessions, and general assemblies form the elements of the multimedia instructional program. Emphasis is on the individual and the rate of progress that is best for him. At the same time, the pattern of enrollment is typical of junior colleges: 76 percent freshmen and 24 percent sophomores. This pattern was true of full-time and part-time students. In the fall of 1969 the total enrollment was 1343, of which 809 were day and 538 evening. The graduating class of 1969 numbered 106.

It is interesting that the retention rate in classes taught in the traditional manner was no higher than in multimedia classes. Addressing the problem of high attrition rates, shared by the three schools, many critics charged that the cause lies in an educational program suitable only for students from the middle and upper socioeconomic strata. However, if this charge had merit, the enrollment pattern in the colleges with higher socioeconomic status should reflect the situation and, except for the smaller numbers in remedial courses, it does not. If this exception were overlooked for purposes of gathering information about persistence/withdrawal, then this phenomenon does not differ markedly in our three colleges. At each college, the first semester of a sequential course in any subject has from two to three times the enrollment that the second semester course has. In small colleges, third and fourth semester courses have very small enrollments, and, in many instances, the administration must offer these courses once a year and sometimes combine two of them in order to keep instruction costs within bounds. For students with high aptitude or strong motivation, this situation poses the possibility that they will not be able to complete the transfer requirements or, in many cases, even the two-year technical program because they must wait until required courses are offered.

This comparison of three colleges provides a general background that in some ways is general rather than specific and superficial rather than probing. A depth analysis of any major institution would take reams of paper; and even then only a small part of what makes the place function would become apparent. Possibly more important than the extent to which a school is examined is the way it reflects other institutions that are seemingly similar. School A may not be exactly like School F, but certain characteristics are consistent. Thus, any urban school has much to say to other inner-city institutions, small rural colleges represent others of their kind, and those suburban schools that have recently seen an influx of people into their area bear striking resemblances to other institutions bordering a large city.

❦❦❦❦❦❦❦❦

Chapter 6

Demographic Variables and Functional Potential

Certain demographic variables are typically used to characterize students—age, sex, and ethnic background, among others. These types of data were collected for students in the 3-D population, along with their functional-potential groupings. In this chapter, selected variables for students in the three schools are compared in order to establish relationships among the variables and student profiles. To begin, a brief review of broad-scale related studies is presented as background.

It is easy to document the strong correlations between high school grade point averages and grade point averages earned in college. It is almost equally easy to point out that in the long-run, very little relationship actually exists between academic performances in college and postcollegiate success.

In part because of these kinds of obstacles, the inappropriateness of measuring devices to assess certain variables, and the lack of criteria, attempts to better understand college populations have gradually led to other ways of appraising them. Some demographic and other information appears more pertinent to the person than GPA or achievement scores alone. Accordingly, in addition to reports of previous grades and achievement test scores, The American College Testing Program presents demographic or actuarial data in their profiles of contemporary college-bound students. The typical student was described as being either 17 or 18 years old and a B— student in high school who earned a 19.8 composite score (on a 1-36 scale) on the ACT examination. The typical student indicated that he needed help in "study and math skills," that he expected to apply for financial aid in college, and that he was one of between 100 and 400 students in his high school graduation class. He estimated his parents' annual income at between $7,500 and $10,000, he planned to live in college housing, and he had been employed regularly at a job obtained without parents' help (ACT, 1970, p. 1).

Of the 859,518 students taking the ACT examination, 30 percent of the males and 31 percent of the females said they had been involved in student movements in their high schools. Almost one-fourth of the ACT-tested students designated a special curriculum as the most important factor in selecting a college, while 15 percent of the respondents rated location and 5 percent rated low cost as the prime selection factor. As for grade-point averages in high school, male students reported generally lower averages than female students, even though average scores on academic sections of the ACT test were higher for men than for women. In fact, although females typically appear to earn higher grade point averages than males, male respondents redress the imbalance by scoring higher on achievement tests.

Baird et al (1969) conducted a follow-up ACT survey of 4009 second-year students at 29 two-year colleges. Although most subjects in the repeat group worked for at least part of their two years and most commuted to their campuses, neither working nor commuting had much effect on either their reported experiences or their academic achievement.

Actuarial data gathered by the American Council on Education (Creager, et al, 1969) also provide an interesting basis for comparing students at two- and four-year colleges and at universities. For instance, whereas only 3.2 percent of all junior college freshmen reported an A or A— average in high school, 15 percent of the four-year college students and 19.9 percent of the university students designated these same grade-point averages. On the other hand, grades of C+ and C were reported by 52 percent of the freshmen from junior colleges, 21.1 percent from four-year colleges, and 14.1 percent from universities. Similar differences are apparent in responses to items referring to the highest anticipated degree and to the highest level of schooling attained by the respondents' parents.

Stimulated by Jacob's (1957) impressions regarding the effects of the college experience on important attitudes and values, and by Sanford's (1962) psychological and social interpretations of higher education, a broad range of characteristics have been recently examined. Observations about self-concept; such traits as autonomy, impulse expression, and flexibility; socioeconomic patterns; interests; and major field designations point to considerable differences among student populations. A major portion of the research dealing with college students has been summarized by Feldman and Newcomb (1969), who consider such issues as values and goals; changes in attitudes toward political, economic, social, and religious orientations; authoritarianism; sense of integration or well-being; and masculinity-femininity. Some psychological processes, as well as some expressed concerns about future academic plans and vocational choices, also have been selected as important variables by which to examine students enrolled in higher education. However, the preponderant number of these comparatively more involved studies are devoted to students in four-year colleges and universities rather than to students in a wider range of schools—especially the community college.

The major research syntheses—Hoyt's (1965) examination of college grades and adult achievement and Price, Taylor, Richards and Jacobsen's (1964) report on physicians—suggest that little or no correlation exists between academic achievement and effective functioning after formal education has been completed. At the same time—and despite such caveats as the importance of keeping "in mind that measures of ability can reflect only a part of personality functioning, and that, consequently, they will probably always be insufficient predictors of later intellectual performance" (Webster, Freedman, and Heist, 1962, p. 821)—many studies continue to focus on the prediction of academic success from one level of school-ing to another. Thus, while a student's grades in medical school may have little or nothing to do with his eventual effectiveness as a prac-ticing physician, in most cases a person's high school grades are closely related to his college grades and his undergraduate grades are closely tied to grades earned in graduate school.

In a somewhat comparable vein, when success in school is defined in terms of the almost ubiquitous GPA, it becomes con-nected to such other "hard" facts as the number of books in the home, parental occupation, parental level of completed schooling, and socioeconomic status. If certain conditions remain constant, certain things will happen—factors that higher education and so-ciety as a whole are now being forced to deal with in several areas. The person whose parents are college graduates is more likely to attain a comparable level of schooling than is the person whose par-ents' formal education ended at the twelfth grade. The individual who grows up with a number of books in the home, whose family can afford to send him to college, and whose friends all aspire to college graduation, has a head start in the academic world over the person who claims but a few books at home, who must weigh the economic pros and cons of further schooling, and whose friends "couldn't care less" about post-secondary education.

Drawing a *Statistical Portrait of Higher Education* through his in-depth analysis of several reports, Harris suggests that the fac-tors most important in determining "enrollment in institutions of higher education are occupation and income of parents, aptitude and scholastic record at high school, and environmental conditions, including the size of the town in which the high school attended by the student is located [even though wide variations exist] in some of these factors by type and control of institutions . . . The impor-tance of high school grades is emphasized by a comparison of per-centile rank in high school graduating class and probability of en-tering and of graduating from college" (Harris, 1972, p. 6).

Although higher education's enrollment increment from the 1950's to the 1970's must be taken into account, figures provided by Wolfe (1954) corroborate Harris' point about the importance of high school grades in determining college achievement. Of the high school graduates whose grade-point averages were in the upper

20 percent (or the 81st to 99th percentile), 53 percent entered college. Of these, 82 percent graduated, which represented 43 percent of the total group. Conversely, of the high school graduates who were in the bottom 20 percent of their class, 17 percent entered college and 26 percent of this considerably smaller group graduated —4 percent of this total.

When data about junior college students are included in reports such as Harris', however, the figures become less discrepant— suggesting that while socioeconomic conditions are important considerations, they hardly explain the entire reason for two-year college attendance. Medsker and Tillery (1971), for example, report that 39 percent of the students enrolled in private two-year colleges had fathers who had gone to college and 42 percent reported family incomes as being over $10,000. Among students in public two-year colleges, 34 percent had fathers who had attended college and 40 percent reported family incomes over $10,000. These figures are consistent with Jencks and Riesman's (1968) short but interesting discussion of community colleges but not consistent with Cross' earlier speculation that "perhaps the junior college makes the greatest impact on the youth from middle and lower economic levels because it usually has lower tuition costs than the extension center, or perhaps the image and goals of the junior college have greater relevance for young people of this background" (Cross, 1968, pp. 21–22). In fairness to both these points of view, the inconsistencies in interpretation may be not so much a function of the interpretors as of the sources from which their evidence was drawn.

Despite the pitfalls inherent in looking always to the already tried, certain givens—the GPA, socioeconomic indices, and the number of years parents spent in school—do provide base-line figures by which to examine and compare students at various institutions. Viewing students engaged in the 3-D project along these same lines suggested that in many ways they could be described as nontraditional; we then need to ask whether the same relationships among selected variables exist for them as for the typical student of an earlier era. The following procedure was used to identify three functional potential groups. Each student's total score was derived by summing his six mode scores. The highest possible score was 51 and the lowest was 0. There were eighteen items in the relatedness/

aloofness mode, six in identity/amorphism, eight in flexibility/rigid-
ity, five in independence/dependence, eight in progression/regres-
sion; and six in delay of gratification/impulse expression. The maximum and minimum possible score, determining the range, was
subsequently divided into thirds (low: 0–17; medium: 18–28;
high: 28–51). A student whose total mode score was equal to one
of the scores in the lower one-third of the range of possible scores,
for example, was placed in the low functional potential group. Interestingly, although the freshman survey from which the scores
were derived had not been designed as a parametric instrument,
the scores approximated a normal distribution, those in the low
and high range forming the tails of that distribution. Of the 1876
students in the original sample, 1770 responded to enough items to
warrant their inclusion in the mode tabulation. Of these, 146 (8.2
percent) formed the low functional potential group; 1205 (68.1
percent) fell in the middle range, and 419 (23.7 percent) scored
high.

Age

The χ^2 test for k independent samples was used to test
whether the three functional potential groups differ in demographic
make-up. When the 1770 respondents are divided into four age
groups and compared with the three functional potential groups, a
$\chi^2 (12) = 47.86$, $p < .005$ results. One thousand three hundred
and fourteen students were 18 years or younger; 301 were 19–22
years old; 71 were 23–26; and 84 were 27 years or older. In the 18
and younger group, 6.9 percent fell in the low FP category; 67.0
percent fell in the medium category; and 26.1 percent scored high.
The next age group (19–22) accounts for 15.2 percent low FP; 69.0
percent medium; and 15.8 percent high. The 23–26 year group has
13.9 percent low FP students; 70.9 percent medium; and 15.2 percent high. Finally, students 27 years and older fell into FP groups
in the following percentages: 11.1 percent low; 73.3 percent medium; and 15.6 percent high.

A higher proportion of students from the high FP group belong to the "less than 18" age category than the medium and low
FP groups. The proportion of students from the low FP group who
are 19–24 years of age (33.92 percent) is larger than for the me-
were 19–24 years of age (33.92 percent) was larger than for the

medium (20.72 percent) and high (12.42 percent) FP groups. Forty-two percent of the students in the low FP group were 19 or older, while only 17.6 percent of the high group were 19 or older.

Sex

A comparison of functional potential by sex results in a $\chi^2 (2) = 8.90$, $p < .025$. Of the 1770 subjects, 995 were male and 775 were female. Ten percent of the males and 7.4 percent of the females fall in the low FP group; 68.9 percent of the males and 66.4 percent of the females fall in the medium group; and 21.1 percent of the males and 26.2 percent of the females fall in the high FP group. Males make up a higher percentage of the low FP group than of the medium and high FP groups. The high FP group comes quite close to being evenly divided sexually.

Work

The variable work had a $\chi^2 (10) = 19.26$, $p < .05$. More than half (56.3 percent) of the low FP students indicated they were not working while attending college, which is higher than the proportion from either the medium (47.9 percent) or high (42.0 percent) groups. The high FP group has the highest proportion of students who work 1–10, 11–20, or 21–30 hours per week. These percentages decrease from the high to the low FP groups. However, of those who do work, there is a higher percentage of students from the low FP group than from the other two groups who work more than 40 hours per week.

Military Service

This variable had a $\chi^2 (2) = 10.29$, $p < .01$. A lower percentage of students from the high FP group (3.93 percent) reported that they had been in the military. Of the low and medium FP groups, 8.70 percent and 8.54 percent, respectively, have been in the military. This result is undoubtedly related to the age composition of the groups.

Ethnic Background

This variable, crossed with FP groups, resulted in a $\chi^2 (6) = 14.69$, $p < .025$. The high FP group is composed of a higher percentage of whites (75.7 percent) than are the other two groups—medium (70.6 percent) and low (62.3 percent). As a consequence, there is a high percentage of non-whites in the low FP group—blacks, Mexican-Americans, and Orientals. However, when one looks at the total composition of the ethnic groups in California and in the nation, the differences here do not appear marked. Further, the question must be asked whether these results are really a function of ethnic differences or whether they actually reflect occupational backgrounds of parents and other indices such as the number of books in the home. It appears to me that it is not a question of the relationship of FP to any special ethnic group as much as it is a matter of relating FP to other indicators—especially socioeconomic ones.

Religion

When it came to religious comparisons with functional potential scores, χ^2 was 8.95 with 4 d.f. This was not significant.

Number of Books in Home

This variable had a $\chi^2 (8) = 36.24$, $p < .005$. The major differences noted between the low FP group and the medium and high groups is the higher percentage of students in the low FP group who indicated that they had 0–10 books (15 percent) or 11–25 books (15 percent) at home. These same percentages for the medium group were 3.24 percent and 10.4 percent. The major difference between the medium and high FP groups was in the last category, where 27.3 percent of the high FP group indicated they had more than 200 books at home, as compared with 19.6 percent of the students from the medium FP group and 19.7 percent from the low FP group.

Academic Major

It is interesting to note in Table 1 that all differences are directional. In other words, if the highest proportion of students who indicated an intention to major in a given area (e.g., natural sciences) was from the high FP group, a lower percentage was

Table 1.

ACADEMIC MAJOR AND FUNCTIONAL POTENTIAL GROUPS

Major	Proportion	N	Low F.P.	Medium F.P.	High F.P.
Natural Sciences	High	295	16.0%	16.6%	23.4%
Social Sciences	High	213	11.0%	15.6%	17.9%
Humanities	High	187	13.0%	13.6%	15.2%
Engineering	Low	247	23.0%	20.7%	14.0%
Business	Low	254	23.0%	20.5%	18.5%
Education	Low	168	14.0%	13.1%	11.0%
$N =$		1364	112	929	323

$$\chi^2 (10) = 18.88, \ p. < .05$$

registered from the medium FP group, and a still lower percentage was from the low group.

Thus, with respect to the typical demographic variables, a few significant differences do exist among the three functional potential groups. However, other indicators of diversity cut across many of the usual or established boundary lines. For example, younger students in the three schools combined seem to be higher in FP than older students, although this difference may reflect sample size discrepancy more than age differences. While some differences are tied to ethnic groups, these differences are not large and may reflect other variables (e.g., books in home, which markedly differentiates FP groups).

Students in the Three Colleges

In many ways, all community/junior colleges are alike. Programs are similar and attrition/persistence figures remain constant over a period of years. The students themselves have been characterized as rather homogeneous (Cross, 1969; Cohen and Brawer, 1969) across various dimensions, and they generally fall below the "typical" freshman in the four-year college or university on measures of ability, achievement, and motivation. However, if a college is truly representative of its parent community and if these communities differ in the ways our urban, suburban, and rural schools are assumed to differ, then their student bodies should show accordant differences.

One of the major purposes of the 3-D project was to investigate the differences and similarities among the participating colleges, and the information presented on colleges and faculties partially fulfill this purpose. But, a more interesting and perhaps more appropriate approach to examining diversity and conformity is in terms of the entering students. In this way, input variance can be established before the college has had a chance to have any effect on its students. Possibly, the input—the students as they enter college, the independent variable—is something that changes from year to year or semester to semester; the students of one year may not adequately represent the students of another year. However, if we carry one step further our belief that people are people, interesting in their many complexities, and that a certain amount of diversity among them is the norm rather than the exception, then we can make a fairly sound case for believing that, at least within a circumscribed time period, one year's crop of students is not unlike the previous year's or the ones expected in the future.

These, then, are our general hypotheses regarding diversity and conformity in three community colleges, as measured in terms of their incoming freshmen. It was hypothesized: (1) Differences in the physical and geographical structures of the urban, suburban, and rural schools will be reflected in differences in their student bodies along specific demographic type variables—such as the number of books in the home, the size of the town or city in which the student grew up, etc. (2) Differences suggested by the area differences of the three schools will not be reflected in student differences in ego functioning, as defined in the concept of functional potential.

This section presents functional potential data for the freshman survey respondents and demographic/actuarial types of information for these same cuts—the total group of respondents and subsets divided by schools. Subsequent chapters deal with the students in the three subject colleges as seen in terms of their Omnibus Personality Inventory responses, orientations, values, attrition/persistence, group cohesion, and other data.

Functional Potential Results. The χ^2 test for k independent samples was used to test whether the frequencies of students in the three functional potential groups was the same for the three junior colleges sampled. The resultant χ^2 (4) = 12.08, $p < .01$ suggests that it was not. The 616 students from the urban college included 11.0 percent in the low FP group, 67.8 percent in the medium, and 21.3 percent in the high. Suburban college's 949 participating students were divided into the three functional potential groups as 7.1 percent low, 67.7 percent medium, and 25.2 percent high. The 205 students from the rural college were distributed according to low, medium, and high functional potential as 11.6 percent, 67.9 percent and 20.5 percent.

The significant χ^2 statistic denotes that the actual cell frequencies observed were different from those expected. One way to analyze which cells are contributing to a large χ^2 statistic is to see if there are important differences in the percentage of respondents in each column across the three schools. A close inspection of the first table shows, for example, that the major contribution to the χ^2 is that a lower percentage (7.1 percent) of students at the suburban college belong to the low functional potential group than that of the other two schools. Since there is no difference among the three schools in the percentage of students belonging to the medium group, it necessarily follows that a higher percentage (25.2 percent) of students at this institution make up the high functional potential group than that of the other two schools. In conclusion, the chief differences among the three schools in terms of functional potential are the lower than expected number of suburban college students belonging to the low functional potential group and the larger than expected number belonging to the high functional potential group.

With respect to other information derived from responses to the freshman survey, contingency analyses were used to evaluate the demographic characteristics of the students at the three schools. In the main, the significant results are reported—that is, those analyses yielding χ^2 statistics that are significant.

Age. Although age comparisons with functional potential for the total population is significant at the <.005 level, when students at different age levels were examined in terms of the three colleges, the resultant χ^2 (6) = 6.01 is not significant.

Sex. The proportion of male students at the urban school

is statistically less than at the other two schools. This was seen in a $\chi^2 (2) = 12.24$, $p < .01$. It is interesting to note, however, that this college shows the most balance in terms of sex among the three schools. Of 695 urban students, 50.8 percent were male, while the suburban and rural schools had 58.7 percent and 60.6 percent males among their 956 and 213 students, respectively.

Marital Status. A $\chi^2 (8) = 9.90$ for marital status (single, married, separated, widowed, or divorced) was not significant. A lower percentage of the students at the suburban college than at the other two schools is married. As one moves from the rural environment to suburbia to the city, there is a gradual progression toward marriage's being a factor in students' lives. In other words, there is less tendency for students in a rural setting to consider marriage at this stage in their formal education.

Children. A total of 1834 students responded to the question "Do you have any children?" "Yes" responses came from 10.4 percent at the urban school, 8.0 percent at the suburban, and 4.8 percent at the rural ($\chi^2 (2) = 7.27$, $p < .05$).

Hours Employed. A higher proportion of the students at the urban school do not work at all compared with the other two schools, while the rural students have a higher percentage of students working between 1–10 hours weekly (Table 2).

Table 2.

HOW MANY HOURS ARE YOU EMPLOYED WEEKLY?

School	N	None	1–10	11–20	21–30	31–40	More than 40
				Per Cent			
Urban	683	55.9	6.4	14.6	10.1	2.8	2.8
Suburban	951	41.6	6.1	21.6	18.4	9.7	2.6
Rural	212	44.3	12.3	18.4	15.1	7.1	2.8

$N = 1846$

$$\chi^2 (10) = 57.66, \, p. < .001$$

Number of Schools Attended Before Tenth Grade. Previous to the tenth grade, a high percentage (nearly 60 percent) of students at the suburban college had attended four or more schools. The students at the urban school had the least mobile background before the tenth grade (χ^2 (10) = 237.71, $p < .001$). (These findings might be compared wth a study reported by Cohen and Brawer, which noted that "dropouts tended to have attended more schools prior to the tenth grade than did persisters [$\chi^2 = 12.65$, p $< .01$]" [1970, p. 30]).

Number of Schools Attended from Tenth to Twelfth Grade. The important factor here is the high proportion of urban school students who attended the 10th to 12th grades at the same school (7.7 percent), as compared with the high percentage of students at the rural institution (8.4 percent) who attended two schools in that same time interval. A comparison of number of high schools attended across the three colleges resulted in a χ^2 (10) = 34.27, $p < .001$.

Military and Service Length. With respect to military service and length of service, nonsignificant χ^2 (2) values of 1.56 and 0.71 were observed between schools. The percent responding positively were urban, 6.5 percent out of 690; suburban, 7.9 percent out of 948; and rural, 8.6 percent out of 209.

Part of Country Lived in Longest. A higher proportion of urban college students (8.3 percent) came from the South; a higher percentage of students at the rural college (9.5 percent) came from the Midwest; and a higher percentage of suburban college students (9.1 percent) came from the East (χ^2 (10) = 94.51, $p < .001$).

The high Southern influx at the urban school may be related to the ethnic composition of its student body. The higher percentage of people from the Midwest locating in the rural area appears consistent; and, considering its particular geographical area, middle- and upper-middle class migrants from the East are probably white collar workers who locate in suburbia.

Ethnicity. Responses to a question on ethnic background resulted in a χ^2 (6) = 804.29, $p < .001$. Of the 1802 respondents, urban college had 33.9 percent white students, 53.6 percent black, 8.6 percent other, and 3.9 percent unknown. Suburban college's freshmen respondents included 94.6 percent white, 0.1 percent black, 3.3 percent other, and 1.9 percent unknown. Eighty-four point nine percent of the rural students were white, 5.2 percent black, 8.5 percent other, and 1.4 percent unknown. Thus, the urban school has a high proportion (more than half) of black students, while the suburban school has very few. None of the schools is balanced racially.

Home Town. There was a χ^2 (10) = 165.4, $p < .001$ in response to the question, "Which represents the community you grew up in?" The only real difference is the high proportion of students at the rural school who grew up on a farm (24.0 percent) or in a small town (50.0 percent).

Current Community. Although the question, "Which represents the community you now live in?" resulted in a χ^2 (10) = 635.49, $p < .001$, it was a question poorly adapted for a large, sprawling area like Los Angeles. In many cases there seems to be confusion as to the difference between a city and suburbia. If anything is substantiated by the item, it is that the students from the three proximate schools attend the college in their own community. Thus, in a very real sense, the colleges are commuter schools with very little mobility between school site and home.

Data were also analyzed pertaining to country of father's birth, country of mother's birth, languages spoken in home, and religion in which subject was raised. Nothing here differentiated among the three schools.

Responses to other freshman survey items indicate that the urban school students show the least tendency to disavow their childhood religion, while those at the rural school are most likely to do so. Eighty-four percent of 674 urban students, 80 percent of 926 suburban students, and 76 percent of 206 rural students did not disavow their childhood religion. This gave rise to a χ^2 (2) = 7.70, $p < .05$, indicating a possible difference among schools.

Indicated Major. Responses (χ^2 (10) = 76.4, $p < .001$) to a question regarding designated major indicate a low proportion of rural students majoring in the natural sciences (12.3 percent) and a high proportion majoring in the humanities and arts (22.1 percent) and in education (22.8 percent). A high proportion major in engineering and technical (21.9 percent) and business administration (25.8 percent) at the urban school, whereas the suburban school claims a high proportion in the social sciences (21.1 percent).

Books in Home. A question regarding the number of books in the home netted a χ^2 (8) = 66.98, $p < .001$.

The proportion (27.6 percent) of urban students who had 25 or fewer books in the home was higher than the figures for students at the other schools. Again, as in other studies, this item seems to differentiate among inventory respondents.

Family. More of those who are from the urban school come from what may be regarded as families in which the marital situation is not intact (χ^2 (12) = 57.01, $p < .001$). This is corroborated by the finding that a lower proportion of urban students live with both parents, and a higher percentage of those who do not live with both parents indicate they live with their mother (χ^2 (14) = 57.98, $p < .001$). However, if one combined the two categories—both parents and mother—it is doubtful that a statistical significance would pertain.

School Related Data. Considering the so-called demographic characteristics of the total population and the populations of the three schools separately, some differences are statistically significant. But there are enough similarities among the students that the school attended appears of less importance than the predispositions of the students—their backgrounds and early environments. The results presented next have to do with current questions regarding subjects' enrollment in their community college. Thus, they may be considered more temporal in nature and perhaps of lesser importance in terms of lasting effects on the students.

There is a significant difference among the schools in the number of units carried by the students. This is seen in a χ^2 (2) = 14.80, $p < .001$. Specifically, 92.0 percent of the 213 students at the rural college take 12 or more units, which is higher than the 82.2 percent of 680 and 81.1 percent of 941 students from the urban and suburban schools.

Similarly, there is a significant difference among the three schools in the number of hours students worked, as seen in a χ^2 (10) = 57.66, $p < .001$. A higher proportion of students at the urban school (55.9 percent) indicated they did not work, whereas 41.6 percent of suburban students and 44.3 percent of rural students were not employed. When work hours are divided into units of 1–10 hours per week, 11–20, 21–30, 31–40, and 40 hours or more, responses were distributed as follows: Urban College, 6.4 percent, 14.0 percent, 10.1 percent, 10.1 percent and 21.8 percent; Suburban College, 6.1 percent, 21.6 percent, 18.4 percent, 9.7 percent, and 2.6 percent; Rural College, 12.3 percent, 18.4 percent, 15.1 percent, 7.1 percent, and 2.8 percent.

Summary of Findings

These are our impressions as to the chief contributions of the significant χ^2 values obtained for the variables presented:

1. *Number of units carried by the student:* Higher than expected number of students from the urban college taking 12 or more units.

2. *Age:* No significant χ^2 statistic obtained.

3. *Sex:* Higher percentage of female students at urban college (and hence, a lower than expected percentage of male students). This school comes the closest to achieving a sex balance in the student body.

4. *How many hours are you employed weekly?* A higher than expected number of students at urban college do not work at all. The rural school has the highest percentage of students working 10 or less hours, while the suburban school has a larger than expected number of students working between 11 and 40 hours.

5. *How many schools did you attend before tenth grade?* The main difference here is between the high percentage of urban students attending one or two schools in the stated period and the high percentage of suburban students attending four or more schools in the same period.

6. *How many schools did you attend from tenth to twelfth grade?* Among the contributors (and there do seem to be several) are: (a) high percentage of urban students attending only one school, (b) lower than expected number of urban students attending two schools, (c) lower than expected number of rural students attending three schools.

7. *Geographical:* (a) low percentage of urban students from Midwest; high percentage of rural students from the Midwest; (b)

higher than expected percentage of urban students growing up in the South; (c) higher than expected percentage of suburban students from the East.

8. *Ethnic Background:* Lower than expected percentage of whites at the urban school. Higher percentage of black students at this school. Lower than expected percentage of Mexican-American students at suburban school.

9. *Religion:* No significant results.

10. *Do you have the same religion now?* Lower than expected number of urban students who indicated they had the same religion as their parents. Smaller than expected frequency of rural students who indicated they had the same religion as their parents.

11. *Books:* Higher percentage of urban students indicating they had 25 or fewer books at home. Lower than expected percentage of urban students indicating they had 101 or more books at home.

12. *Major:* Lower than expected percentage of rural students in the natural sciences and business administration. Higher than expected percentage of rural students in education and humanities. Higher than expected percentage of suburban students in the social sciences. Lower than expected percentage of urban students in social sciences and humanities. Higher percentage of urban students in engineering/technology and business administration.

Profile of Urban College Students. (1) Urban college students, like students in the two other sample schools, are likely to be 18 years or less. (2) No sexual differences. (3) A lower proportion of urban students are enrolled in the social sciences and humanities and a higher proportion in the business-related disciplines. (4) More likely to carry 12 or more credit units than the suburban students, but less likely than students from the rural school to carry more than 12 units. (5) More than half (55.9 percent) indicate that they do not work. Of those students who do, most work between one and 20 hours per week. (6) They attended fewer schools than did the other students before the tenth grade—50 percent attended only one or two schools during this period. (7) Between the tenth and twelfth grades, they generally attended two schools. (8) Ethnic background: 53.6 percent black, 33.9 percent are white, and the remainder of the students indicate "other" backgrounds. (9) If these students had not spent most of their life in California, they probably came from the South. (10) Like most students at the other schools, they tend to be Protestant. (11) A higher percentage of students at this school (27.6 percent) than at the other schools indicated they had 25 or fewer books at home. Forty-two percent said they had 26–100 books. (12) A lower percentage of students at this school (67.3 percent) indicated that their parents were married and living together. If the parents are divorced, a lower percentage (1.5 percent) have remarried. Urban students also indicated a higher percentage of parents separated (6.6 percent). (13) A lower percentage of students at this school than at the other two schools live with both parents, and a higher percentage live with their mothers. (14) Functional potential: These students show no striking departure in percentage of students belonging to any of the functional potential groups.

Profile of Suburban College Students. (1) Like students in the two other sample schools, suburban students are likely to be 18 years or less. (2) A bit more likely to be male, though the difference is slight. (3) They tend to be evenly distributed across the six majors. (4) They are more likely to carry less than 12 credit units; are less likely to carry more than 12 units than are students from the urban and rural schools. (5) If they work more than 10 hours per week—as about half the students from this school do—it is likely to be between 21 and 30 hours weekly. (6) They attended more schools than did others before the tenth grade—4, 5, or 6 and over. (7) Between the tenth and twelfth grades, they generally attended two schools, again implying considerable family mobility. (8) Their chances of being white are over 9 out of 10 (94.6 percent). (9) If they had not spent the most time in California, they probably came from the East. (10) Like students at the other schools, they are probably Protestant. (11) There are more books in the home than in the homes of students from other schools (26.6 percent designate over 200 books, and 21.4 percent designate 100–200). (12) In 7+ cases out of 10, their parents are married and living together. If parents are divorced, chances are they have remarried. (13) These students tend to live with both parents. Fewer live alone than at the other schools; if not living with parents, they are more likely to be married and living with spouse. (14) Functional potential: The suburban college has fewer students in the low FP group and more in the high group than the other two schools.

Profile of Rural School Students. (1) Like students in the two other sample schools, rural students are likely to be 18 years or less. (2) No great sexual differences, but less balanced population than the urban college and tendency to have more males. (3) Lower percentage of these students majoring in natural science and business and twice the percentage in humanities and education. (4) More likely to carry more than 12 units than students from the other two schools. (5) A higher number of rural students than students at the other two colleges do not work at all. If they do work, it is likely to be between 11 and 20 hours and less likely to be over 31 hours per week. (6) They attended fewer schools than did the suburban students before the tenth grade. Over 75 percent of the rural students attended more than one school; about 4 out of 10 attended 2 or 3 schools. (7) Over 8 out of 10 students attended two schools during their high school career, implying again a considerable amount of mobility in the family. (8) A preponderance of white students at the rural school (84.9 percent). (9) The length of California residence was the longest for these students, but of those who spent most of their lives elsewhere, the majority came from the Midwest. (10) Like students at the two other schools, they are probably Protestant. (11) The preponderant number (41.0 percent) of students claimed 26–100 books in their home. (12) A higher proportion of rural families are intact than the families of urban students and somewhat higher than those suburban students. (13) Rural students are more likely than urban students to live with both parents, but less likely than the suburban students to do so. Rural students are less likely than urban or suburban students to live with their mothers, and more of those whose families are not intact live with their fathers. (14) Functional potential: No difference at each of the functional potential groups is indicated between the rural and urban schools.

It was hypothesized that differences in the three colleges would relate to differences in actuarial data derived from the freshman survey and that differences in functional potential scores would not relate to the three schools. In fact, as the summary indicates, the differences noted suggest considerable diversity among the schools with regard to student population. These findings, in turn, suggest certain questions. For example, is it the geographic area that attracts families whose children display the characteristics which typify students at Suburban, Urban, or Rural College? Or are these findings haphazard—a function of these data which cannot be replicated in other studies? The functional potential scores of students at the three community colleges, however, tend toward conformity. The low functional potential group at Suburban College was smaller than expected and, because no differences existed in the medium group, there was an accordingly higher percentage in the high group. However, these differences (χ^2 significant at the 0.01 level) were not large. Urban and Rural schools had similar high, medium, and low distributions.

It appears that while certain demographic data differentiate types of school populations, functional potential scores do not. Indeed, it would seem that functional potential cuts across many of the barriers that other assessment methods appear to exaggerate and even encourage. If this is true, functional potential can serve as a better gauge for understanding students than traditional methods of appraisal. If differences cannot be attributed to the type of community college attended, we can deal with students intrainstitutionally, within a precise rather than an extended framework. The advantages of such specificity are obvious.

Chapter 7

Self and School

In the assortment contained in this chapter, the relationships between student characteristics and functional potential are the basic component. The diversity appears in the three variables by which these relationships are examined: school directedness, the impact of significant others on school-related attitudes, and group cohesion. Each of these three themes may be viewed independently of the others since each reflects a different way of looking at college populations. But for all three, the common denominator is the student.

School Directedness

Certain things exist outside the individual which, despite their separateness, play a part in his personal interactions. School, job, recreation, and other people are important to any consideration of the person. What anyone brings to each may be seen from either his own or the situational perspective. And what he derives from his experiences with these external factors must be understood from these perspectives as well; both are stimuli, both are responses.

For years people have studied schools and school personnel, and they now focus also on the impact of schools on various types of students. The purpose here is not to review either schools or their effects but rather to build a rationale for examining students in terms of the way they perceive the academic external. The underlying premise is that, in large measure, the impact of any school experience is largely a function of the way the individual has internalized the concept of "school." The way he approaches and interacts with the academic milieu depends not only on external patterns but also on the way he relates to them and to himself, the degree to which he incorporates outside forces into his own being.

For the student who is enrolled in any postsecondary academic institution, higher education might be viewed in any number of ways: as a base for attaining a liberal education; as vocational preparation; or as an environment for self-examination and the establishment of personal identity.

If a primarily practical person who desires training for a specific trade or a profession finds himself in a school that stresses theoretical learning, the discrepancy may result in disinterest, discontent, and ineffective learning. The same individual in a technically-geared organization fares quite differently. Or, as another example, the highly person-minded individual in a tightly structured, intellectually bent institution may seek answers to his quest for self through nonacademic avenues, while, in a liberal, psychologically determined environment, he may tend not to look elsewhere. Although the disparity between expectation and reality may lead some students to develop previously unexplored capabilities, I believe that people generally function best in environments consistent with their personalities, interests, and abilities.

In spite of contemporary concern for the individual and the appreciation of higher education as a force for personal development, many schools still emphasize academic performance to the exclusion of the overall development that the educational process might facilitate. Some students move toward the traditional educational system, accept its demands, and profit from their exposure to it. Others maintain a noncommittal attitude and, of course, still others move against the school, its personnel, and the system it represents. Such generalizations should not obscure the fact that an individual's attitude toward school largely determines the impact that educational institution has on his development.

In order to assess such attitudes and general academic goals, several items in the freshman survey (see Appendix) related to educational aspirations, vocational goals dependent on varying degrees of academic commitment, and reasons for enrolling in the subject schools. Scores on this school directedness index were related to functional potential scores, a one-way analysis of variance (BMD 07D) resulting in F (2,1873) = 150.43, $p < .001$. Means, standard deviations, and number of students for this analysis were as follows: For the low FP group, the mean was 12.382; SD, 3.607; and N = 170. The medium FP group's mean school directedness score was 14.872; SD, 3.445; and N = 271. And the high FP group's mean was 17.424; SD, 3.5; and N = 435. Thus, it becomes evident that there is a clear positive relationship here between functional potential and school directedness, with the mean scores increasing from the low to high functional potential groups.

Looking at school directedness scores for the three colleges, the significant F score indicated some difference in School Directedness among students at the three schools, with Urban students having higher mean scores (15.54; SD, 3.83) on this variable than those in either the Suburban College (mean, 15.09; SD, 3.61) or the Rural College (mean 14.94; SD, 4.04).

Impact of Significant Others on School Attitudes

It is always difficult to assess direct effects—whether these are the impact of an extrinsic force such as school, the influence of another person, or the result of an important experience. Nevertheless, whatever the effect and however strong the motivational force, we do know that significant others play major roles in the lives of most people. First and most importantly, of course, are one's parents; then, other family members and friends; and finally, people encountered either in school—peers, faculty, friends, other academic personnel—or in other situations where people gather—work, social groups, religious institutions.

Some of the early literature in education dealt with the effects of schools on children and young adults. Later, faculty and other staff members and eventually the entire academic environment were included. Ultimately, answers were sought to such questions as: With what teachers do students best interact? Is there one special instructor who is most effective? Aside from the student himself and the faculty, who else is important in the student's life? And how? What is the influence of peer groups and of family? The questions could go on indefinitely. Their answers swell the educational and psychological literature.

Several items in the freshman survey were designed to assess the extent and type of influence which the respondent felt other individuals (parents, faculty, peer groups, school counselors, and friends) had contributed to his attitudes about education.

A one-way analysis of variance for impact of significant others and functional potential groups resulted in F $(21,1873) = 58.16$, p $< .001$. Here the impact means and standard deviations, with respective numbers of respondents, for the Low FP group were 12.671, 4.270, and 170. For the medium FP group, the impact mean was 14.778, SD, 3.982, and N $= 1271$; and for the 435 high FP subjects, the impact mean was 16.467 with a standard deviation of 435. Again, the results suggest an increasing trend from low to high.

When impact means are seen in terms of the three separate colleges, the one-way analysis of variance does not reveal significant results (F$[2,1873] = 0.21$). Mean impact scores for the three colleges showed no difference among them in regard to impact.

Group Cohesion

Despite the considerable literature about alienation, rebellion, and anomie, ambiguity and contradiction still abound. Indeed, as Dienst remarks in her interesting review of alienation and activisim, the "term alienation has . . . been so widely and indiscriminately used, both in popular and professional literature, that it has come to be either empty of meaning or so freighted with meanings that few can agree on a definition" (1972, p. 1). Further difficulties arise because alienation is seldom considered in terms of activist behavior, even though Marx (1965) and Merton (1957) both suggested that revolution and rebellion indicated an active rather than a passive alienation. Thus, contradiction as well as ambiguity adds to the confusion; "the term has rarely been modified to specify the object of the alienation (estrangement from self or society) or the form of estrangement (passive retreatism or active rebellion)" (Dienst, 1972, p. 1).

The sense of apartness, aloneness, distantiation was discussed in Chapter Six, where the mode form of Relatedness/Aloofness was explained as a way of establishing the degree to which a person was affiliated with others. Without early experiences of physical contact and emotional warmth, a sense of alienation develops as counterreaction to feelings of aloneness and separation. Some experts may disagree with such a simple explanation, and I would understand this discord. At the same time, I firmly believe that if the early "terry cloth needs" (Harlow, 1958; Klopfer, 1954) have not been met, the child feels a sense of separation that is usually irrevocable unless there is appropriate intervention. The earlier that frustration occurs, the deeper and more permanent the sense of alienation. Further, it seems to me that while one cannot be intimately related to or involved with everyone with whom he deals, a basic alienation from self eventually becomes evidenced by a generalized separation from others. Conversely, if the person's basic security needs have been met, he does not need to feel apart from self or others in either reaction or defense. The degree to which one feels a sense of cohesiveness or separatedness represents the extent of these early satisfaction or deprivation experiences.

Although one's sense of affiliation or distantiation varies according to one's environment, it seems safe to conclude that an aggregate of feelings toward one attitude or the other represents a basic and prevailing characteristic. A one-page inquiry (see Figure 2) was incorporated into the freshman survey in order to measure student feelings toward different groups and quantify these feelings in terms of group cohesion. The responses to this measure of the group cohesion variable by 1283 students were recoded according to whether they indicated relatedness or unrelatedness. (If the response was B, C, or F, the code was 1, indicating relatedness; if A, D, or E, -1 for unrelatedness.) The box score for each individual with obtained by adding the code numbers of the seven responses. The possible and actual range of the box scores, therefore, was -7 to $+7$.

People often feel differently with different groups and in different situations.

Which figure or figures in the boxes below best describe how you see yourself in relation to the different groups listed? (You may choose the same figure or different figures for your responses. Please mark one oval in each row.)

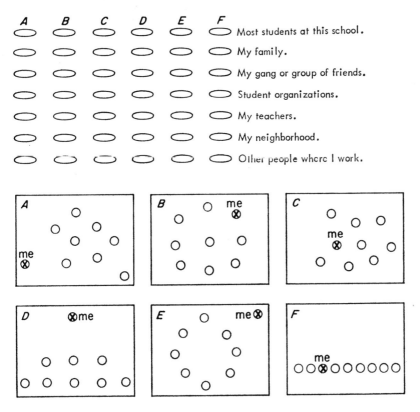

FIGURE 2: Self-perceptions in Different Groups and Situations.

A significant difference (F (2,1280) = 69.91, $p < .0005$) was found when these group cohesion scores were distributed over the functional potential groups. The low FP group had the lowest group cohesion score (mean = 0.511, SD = 3.888) and the high FP group had the highest group cohesion scores (mean = 3.934, SD = 2.510), while the students from the medium FP group had group cohesion scores falling in the middle here too (mean = 2.553,

SD = 2.695). When the group cohesion scores were examined over the three schools, a two-way analysis of variance resulted in a non-significant F ratio. The same nonsignificant results pertained to the number of units taken.(The group cohesion variable also was compared to attrition figures for the FP groups; these findings are reported in Chapter Fourteen.)

Summarily, then, an examination of the three variables described in this chapter in terms of selected independent variables reveals interesting results. In terms of the three school populations, students at Urban College indicate a higher school directedness score than students from the other two schools. However, no difference exists in terms of the impact of significant others scores. The group cohesion score was not tested in regard to the separate schools.

Although the three variables discussed in this chapter and functional potential scores are all derived from verbal statements that are contained in the same instrument. Therefore, generalization from their correlations must be more limited than they would be if behavioral evidence were available. Functional potential appears to be a better indicator of these three variables than individual schools. School directedness scores for the total population increase with the move from low to high on functional potential. Similarly, significant others and group cohesion scores are highest for those students who form the high functional potential group. These results point to the pervasiveness of feelings of closeness and suggest that perhaps they, as much as awareness of identity and other modes comprising functional potential, are fundamental dimensions that motivate people toward school and toward relationships with others—or, conversely, away from these. Perhaps, then, although pre-school experiences are essential to their determination, educational institutions need to be more deliberately direct themselves toward the development and encouragement of these characteristics.

Chapter 8

Students' Orientations

A circular figure depicting a model of the person was presented at the end of Chapter One. Here functional potential is seen as the core and other variables become the spokes around the rim. In addition to variables such as school directedness, impact of significant others, and group cohesion, which have already been discussed, orientations also are salient features of an individual. This chapter presents the rationale for as well as evidence supporting their usage.

Somewhere between the dynamics and manifestations of behavior is the general direction or inclination one's life assumes. An individual's orientation may be measured by the direction of libidinal flow, the involvement exhibited, and the energy focused on particular areas. In general, these indicators are directed toward one of five areas which I have categorized as ideas, esthetics, others, practical, and motor skills. (These categories roughly parallel types of people previously described by Eysenck, Fromm, Kretschmer, Jung,

Sheldon, Spranger, and Holland.) As in Werner's (1942) outline of cognitive structure, each orientation seems to originate as a rather undifferentiated core of attention which develops, intensifies, and expands to include other specialized features within narrower and more concentrated fields of emphasis.

Synthesizing several dimensions that are potentially insightful to both the individual and the outside observer, the orientations hinge on, but are not substitutes for, concepts that have a fairly long history—attitudes, values, needs, and, primarily, interests. Yet, while they are related to these other dimensions, the orientations are not substitutes for any one of them. They serve to focus several characteristics into a central construct in which the whole represents more than the sum of its parts.

The orientations lie somewhere between the motivating forces or dynamics of behavior and the actual behavioral manifestations demonstrated by the previously described modes. Just as functional potential is the superordinate mode subsuming several dimensions, the orientation category has several subsets. While a functional potential score is derived from each subcategory, however, no total orientation score is feasible. Rather, the five orientations are discrete variables; the relationships between the modes and the orientations should be perceived as parts of an integrated whole, with various needs, feelings, attitudes, and interests expressed at different points within the structure.

Just as the modes relate theoretical frameworks postulated by various behavioral scientists, the orientations relate to constructs defined in other theories of human functioning. They closely approximate Adler's (1930) "style of life" concept in which he maintains that there are various ways of working toward a universal goal. The particular life style exhibited by any individual is *the* principle by which he functions. One person, for example, may strive for superiority through muscular development; another, through intellectual attainments, but he learns, perceives, and retains that which best fits his particular style. Since feelings, attitudes, and apperceptions become fixed in the first years of life, Adler maintains it is practically impossible to change one's essential style after the formative period. New ways of expressing style may be acquired, but these are actually instances of the previously formulated basic style.

The orientations also relate to some ideas postulated by Jung (1923) in his classification of psychological types. Here two attitudes—introversion and extraversion—and four psychological functions—thinking, feeling, sensing, and intuiting—are described. Both introversion and extraversion are present in everyone, but only one is ordinarily dominant and conscious.

Similarly, the four fundamental psychological functions show varying degrees of intensity. Although every individual possesses all four functions, they are not necessarily equally well developed. In fact, unless the person is extremely well integrated and motivated, they are seldom developed to the same extent. Usually the superior function is more differentiated than the others and plays a prominent role in consciousness. The least differentiated of the four is called the inferior function; repressed and unconscious, it often expresses itself only in dreams and fantasies.

The four functions may be further described in the following way: *Thinking* is ideational and intellectual in nature, the way in which man tries to comprehend the nature of the world and himself; *feeling* is a value function, giving man his subjective experiences of pleasure and pain, of anger, fear, sorrow, joy, and love; *sensing* is a perceptual or reality function in which the senses act as the guides; *intuition* is perception by way of unconscious processes and subliminal contents. The intuitive man, for example, goes beyond facts, feelings, and ideas and constructs his own way of getting at the essence of reality. Hall and Lindzey (1957) provide an example that succinctly clarifies the nature of these four functions. "Suppose that a person is standing on the rim of the Grand Canyon of the Colorado river. If the feeling function predominates he will experience a sense of awe, grandeur, and breath-taking beauty. If he is controlled by the sensation function he will see the Canyon merely as it is or as a photograph might represent it. If the thinking function controls his ego he will try to understand the Canyon in terms of geological principles and theory. Finally, if the intuitive function prevails the spectator will tend to see the Grand Canyon as a mystery of nature possessing deep significance whose meaning is partially revealed or felt as a mystical experience" (p. 87).

The activities and functions interact in various ways: one system may compensate for the weakness of another; a system may oppose another system; or two or more systems may unite to form a synthetic whole. Compensation, for example, occurs when extraverted behavior is followed by a period of introversion. And compensation occurs between functions: a person who stresses thinking and intuition in his conscious life, has an active feeling-sensation unconscious. Jung maintains that if all four functions are equidistant on the circumference of a circle, the center of the circle will represent a synthesis of the four. In such cases, none is superior or inferior and there are no auxiliaries. Such a synthesis, with all functions fully differentiated, only occurs when the Self (Jung's central core) has become fully actualized

Having outlined the theoretical basis for orientation, a description of each should complete an understanding of their usefulness in further understanding the person. People who are oriented toward ideas are usually academic and prefer a general education curriculum. They choose academic courses and cite vocational goals that require theoretical, often scientific, approaches. Whether in or out of school, they are concerned with the pursuit of knowledge. They prefer to think through rather than to act out problems, and although complex and ambiguous situations may be sources of worry, they choose such concerns over nonideational experience. The person involved with ideas is related to the academic person in Clark and Trow's typology (1966), but he may or may not focus on vocational proficiency and social adaptness since, motivated by intellectual curiosity, he rejects basically social organizations for those of a political or intellectual bent. Accordingly, he is likely to respond affirmatively to items such as "Most courses are a real intellectual challenge" and "I would like to be a college instructor, lawyer, scientific researcher."

Esthetically-oriented individuals appreciate beauty for beauty's sake. They are generally individualistic, take unique approaches to even mundane situations, and frequently become emotionally involved with their school work. Many of these people tend to be creative in either a product sense or in the way they proceed through life. As a rule, however, they closely approximate Jung's (1933) sensation types, depending on and working through their senses, and for those whose esthetic orientation results in creative outputs, a considerable degree of intuition is usually involved. Chickering (1971) offers some insight into this type: "Encounters with wood, stone, clay, or paint, and the development of skills necessary for their management, offer potentials similar to those of athletics. Like the unequivocal achievements on the field, tangible and visible creations offer clear evidence of achievement and progress. And the creative process requires similar confrontations of emotions, enables similar legitimate expressions of feelings. . . . Experiences to develop skills in arts and crafts also interact with intellectual competence and the development of identity" (p. 30). In response to selected questions, the esthetically oriented person is inclined to state that he would like to be above average in such traits as artistic ability and creativity and, if his house were burning, he would rescue, in order, people, pets, and art objects.

Since the quest for self-knowledge is fundamental and information tends to be sifted through the person's perceptions of self, the others-oriented person may appear egocentric. Such concern with one's own experiences often eventually extends to a sincere interest in others, and the ostensibly self-involved person usually is compelled toward others. He may be, in spite of this involvement, either an introvert or extravert. In Holland's words, he is "responsible, humanistic, frequently religious, has both verbal and interpersonal skills . . . and prefers to solve problems through feelings and intrapersonal manipulations of others" (1966, p. 17).

Because the person who is aware of others must also have an interest in self, it is hypothesized that this orientation is tied to the modes of relatedness and identity, that the others-oriented person would think friendliness is desirable in the social environment and would indicate a desire to be popular and a leader.

Pragmatic types prefer occupations that require numerical abilities, are often concerned with power, leadership, and status, and are usually enterprising and expedient. Their orientation may be expressed in such vocations as salesman, business executive, or buyer (suggesting extratensive attitudes) or such introverted occupations as accountant, budget reviewer, or cost estimator. Students with this orientation, like Clark and Trow's vocational man, are going to college in order to make a career choice and would, for example, like to be holding down a good paying job in five years hence.

Motor-oriented individuals may operate at many levels and in many fields of interest (Roe, 1956), but they utilize the kinesthetic sense. In many respects, they resemble Holland's holistic individual, who "copes with his physical and social environment by selecting goals, values, and tasks that entail the objective, concrete evaluation and manipulation of things, tools, animals, and machines; and by avoiding goals, values, and tasks that require subjectivity, intellectualism, artistic expression, and social sensitivity and skill" (1966, p. 19). It would appear that "experiences encountered in athletics provoke reactions sharply relevant to the development of competence and sense of competence, and to the development of increased awareness of emotions and increased ability to manage them productively" (Chickering, 1962, p. 29). In response to certain items in the freshman survey, these students who expressed a motor orientation indicated possession of above average mechanical ability and a desire to be an athlete or use kinesthetics in their future occupations.

The five orientations are mosts accurately regarded as potentially useful speculations, and these brief sketches should suggest that it is a rare person whose orientation is entirely "pure." Each person, however, does show particular interests and special attitudes, and the degree to which he is involved in any one of these categories may tell us a good deal about the general orientation of his life.

Several questions follow: How do these orientations relate to the modes and to its integrating variable, functional potential? Do different people manifest different degrees of involvement in any or all five of the orientations? How do the orientations relate to designated academic majors for our junior college freshmen? Do they correlate with other personality or demographic characteristics? with the actual school attended by the respondents? The following presentation of data attempts to answer these questions.

Results: Orientations

The orientation scores were obtained by taking linear combinations of variables (items) from the freshman survey, which were independent of those used in computing the functional potential scores. The orientation scores—ideas, esthetics, others, practical, and motor—were then plotted for the students sampled. It was observed that the distribution of the motor orientation scores was not normal and that, except for the practical orientation scores, which approximated the normal distribution, the remaining orientation scores were highly skewed toward the lower possible scores. The orientation scores were divided into three equal intervals based on the range of scores possible. The χ^2 test for k independent samples was then used to test whether the frequencies of students in the three functional potential groups were the same as those for the three orientation levels. The results in Table 3 were obtained.

Orientations and Three Colleges

The orientations were also examined in terms of the three schools participating in the 3-D project. The results of these analyses are presented in Table 4.

In reviewing these data, it appears that the orientations are not good variables to discriminate among the three schools. Only esthetics and practical are of any importance, and in a practical sense the demonstrated differences are small. However, to prove that these are *not* good discriminating variables, a stepwise discrimination was performed with the order of entry of these variables as esthetics, practical, motor, others and lastly, ideas. These variables do not seem to classify with any accuracy.

In summary, the following conclusions were reached: Students scoring high on the ideas orientation tend to be those who (1) designate natural science, social science or humanities; natural science students score the highest, and engineering and technology students score the lowest; (2) like to plan their own work; (3) like to make policy decisions; (4) like to write reports; (5) like to do original research or writing; (6) like to keep records; (7) indicate a desire to instruct, counsel, or advise others; (8) like to make speeches or present reports; (9) like to organize operations; (10) like to attend meetings; (11) like to analyze data; (12) have fathers who are listed as Professional Type 1 (typically requiring a doctorate or advanced professional degree—such as architect or attorney); those who score the lowest on the ideas orientation had

Table 3.

ORIENTATIONS AND FUNCTIONAL POTENTIAL

IDEAS ORIENTATION LEVEL

F.P. Groups	N	Low	Middle	High
Low	170	88.6%	11.2%	0.0%
Medium	1271	64.8%	34.5%	0.7%
High	435	36.1%	59.8%	4.1%
N =	1876			

$$\chi^2 \ (4) = 188.35, \ p < .001$$

The number of students in the three functional potential groups is not the same for the three levels of the ideas orientation. Proceeding from the low to high FP groups, a higher proportion of students with ideas orientation is noted in the medium and high categories.

ESTHETICS ORIENTATION LEVEL

F.P. Groups	N	Low	Middle	High
Low	170	96.5%	3.5%	0.0%
Medium	1271	86.0%	13.5%	0.5%
High	435	77.9%	20.5%	1.6%
N =	1876			

$$\chi^2 \ (4) = 37.6, \ p < .001$$

The high functional potential group had a larger proportion of students in the higher esthetics orientation category. However, a high proportion of students in all functional potential groups belong to the low esthetics category.

OTHERS ORIENTATION LEVEL

F.P. Groups	N	Low	Middle	High
Low	169	81.8%	17.6%	0.6%
Medium	1268	49.8%	45.0%	5.2%
High	435	23.2%	61.4%	15.4%
N =	1876			

$$\chi^2 (4) = 209.56, \, p < .001$$

The number of students in the three functional potential groups is not the same for the three levels of the others orientation.

PRACTICAL ORIENTATION LEVEL

F.P. Groups	N	Low	Middle	High
Low	169	41.4%	55.0%	3.6%
Medium	1268	17.1%	72.4%	10.5%
High	435	9.7%	70.1%	20.2%
N =	1872			

$$\chi^2 (4) = 113.37, \, p < .001$$

A high proportion (96.4%) of students from the low F.P. group belong to the low and middle practical orientation categories. Ninety point three per cent of the students from the high FP group belong to the middle or high practical categories, while most of the students from the medium FP group were centered around the middle orientation category.

MOTOR ORIENTATION LEVEL

F.P. Groups	N	Low	Middle	High
Low	170	90.0%	10.0%	0.0%
Medium	1271	88.7%	10.1%	1.3%
High	435	84.4%	12.2%	3.4%
N =	1876			

$$\chi^2 (4) = 14.70, \, p < .01$$

Here again, a high percentage of students in all FP groups tend toward a low motor orientation score. The trend here is consistent with that noted for the previous four orientations: the low FP group had the highest proportion of students with a low motor orientation score, while the high FP group had the largest proportion with middle or high motor scores.

Table 4.

ORIENTATIONS AND THREE COLLEGES

IDEAS

	N	4.00 points or less	4.01– 8.00 points	8.01 points or more	Mean	S.D.
Urban	701	63.1%	35.4%	1.6%	3.87	2.00
Suburban	960	57.8%	40.0%	1.4%	4.13	1.91
Rural	215	62.3%	36.3%	1.4%	3.87	1.95

$N =$ 1876

$F(2,1873) = 3.95$, $p < .025$ from One way ANOVA

$\chi^2 (4) = 5.55$, not significant

By examining the means, it seems clear that the suburban students score higher in the ideas orientation than students at the other two schools. While this is statistically significant, however, practically there is no difference.

ESTHETICS

	N	2.00 points or less	2.01– 4.00 points	4.01 points or more	Mean	S.D.
Urban	701	89.9%	10.0%	0.1%	1.14	0.94
Suburban	960	80.8%	17.9%	1.3%	1.50	1.11
Rural	215	88.4%	11.2%	0.5%	1.26	0.99

$N =$ 1876

$F(2,1873) = 2464$, $p < .0005$ from One way ANOVA

$\chi^2 (4) = 30.65$, $p < .001$

As with the ideas orientation, the distributional characteristics of this orientation are a fair approximation to the normal curve. A higher percentage of suburban students scored three or more points on the esthetics orientation when compared with the other schools in our sample population.

OTHERS

	N	3.00 points or less	3.01– 6.00 points	6.01 points or more	Mean	S.D.
Urban	701	49.4%	43.7%	7.0%	3.45	1.82
Suburban	960	45.2%	47.6%	7.2%	3.66	1.79
Rural	215	43.3%	49.3%	7.4%	3.57	1.91

N = 1876

F (2,1873) = 2.48, not significant from One way ANOVA

χ^2 (4) = 3.94, not significant

There was no difference shown among the schools in the others orientation variable.

PRACTICAL

	N	2.5 points or less	2.51– 5.00 points	5.01 points or more	Mean	S.D.
Urban	701	18.8%	69.8%	11.4%	3.86	1.40
Suburban	960	15.7%	71.1%	13.1%	4.01	1.34
Rural	215	23.3%	67.0%	9.8%	3.67	1.52

N = 1876

F (2,1873) = 6.07, p < .005 from One way ANOVA

χ^2 (4) = 8.88, not significant

This variable was the most normal of all the five orientations. Although further contrasts would need to be run to statistically evaluate where the differences are, one could assume that the chief contributor is the lower practical orientation of Rural College students and the tendency of students from the Suburban school toward a higher practical orientation.

Table 4 (Cont.).

ORIENTATIONS AND THREE COLLEGES

MOTOR

	N	2.00 points or less	2.01– 4.00 points	4.01 points or more
Urban	701	88.7%	9.7%	1.6%
Suburban	920	88.0%	10.3%	1.7%
Rural	215	83.7%	14.4%	1.9%
N =	1876			

χ^2 (4) = 4.15, not significant

There is no difference among students from the three colleges in regard to their motor orientation.

fathers who were public officials, supervisors, small business proprietors, or farm owners; (13) expect to be Professional Type 1's; those who scored the lowest on the ideas orientation indicate a desire to become a public official, supervisor, small business proprietor, or a farm owner.

Students scoring high on esthetic orientation tend to be those who (1) are enrolled in the Suburban College; (2) indicate humanities and art majors; (3) express a desire to plan own work; (4) indicate a desire to make policy decisions; (5) show a desire to do original research or writing; (6) indicate a desire to instruct, counsel, or advise others score higher on esthetics orientation; (7) express a desire to take things easy; (8) be classified as white (no significant differences among other ethnic designations); (9) have fathers who do not fall into the semi-skilled or general laborer group and have fathers who are Professional 2; (teacher, accountant), Professional 1; salesman, or skilled clerical.

Students high in the others orientation tend to be those who (1) express desire to supervise others; (2) indicate a desire to make policy decisions; (3) show a desire to follow the directions of a boss they like; (4) express an interest in writing reports; (5) desire to do original research and writing; (6) show a desire to keep records;

(7) desire to counsel, instruct, and advise others; (8) show a desire to make speeches and present reports; (9) indicate a desire to organize operations; (10) indicate a desire to attend meetings; (11) indicate a desire to analyze data; (12) *not* indicate a desire to "take it easy"; (13) have fathers who are a Professional 1; those students whose fathers are small business proprietors or farmers; salesmen or skilled clerical; semi-skilled or general laborers, score the lowest on the others orientation; (14) expect to become public officials or supervisors score the highest on the others orientation while those students who expect to run small businesses, own farms, or become general laborers score lowest on the others orientation; (15) positively relate with most students at their schools; (16) indicate a desire to relate with student organizations.

Students scoring high on practical orientation tend to be those who (1) indicate a desire to supervise others; (2) indicate a desire to follow directions of one's boss; (3) indicate a desire to do original research or writing; (4) show an interest in keeping records; (5) indicate a desire to instruct, counsel, and advise others; (6) desire to attend meetings; (7) indicate a desire to analyze data; (8) do *not* indicate a desire to "take it easy"; (9) have mothers whose occupations are Professional 1 or 2, manager, or executive while students whose mothers are public officials or supervisors score the lowest in practical orientation; (10) expect to be public officials, supervisors, or salesmen; (11) are white; among the other races, orientals have the lowest practical orientation scores; (12) indicate positive relationships with other people where they work; the big difference is among those who score in the upper one-third of the practical orientations interval—i.e. a much higher percentage of students who scored 5 or more points on the practical orientation relate (positively) to people where they work than (negatively) those who indicate no sense of relatedness.

Students who score high on motor orientation tend to be those who (1) do not indicate the humanities and business administration and those who do, indicate engineering and technology as majors; (2) indicate a desire to supervise others; (3) indicate no interest in doing original research and writing; (4) indicate a desire to "take it easy."

These data suggest that, aside from their rather consistent

and expected relationships to certain occupational expectations as well as to other selected variables, the orientations also seem to represent a degree of intensity or commitment. In general, high functional potential students appear more definite in their orientations. At the same time, the orientations are not good indicators of inter-school differences. Of the five groups in this category, esthetics and practical appear to discriminate best between schools, but it seems that a school cannot be identified by the orientations of its students. In fact, throughout the three schools, there was a diversified group of respondents for all five orientations. Thus, while it now seems that the orientations are not as good indicators of personality type as the modes comprising the functional potential groups, they do suggest idiosyncratic patterns.

Chapter 9

The Omnibus
Personality Inventory
and Functional Potential

Among techniques designed to measure traits other than the ability and achievement of students in higher education, the most widely known is the Omnibus Personality Inventory (OPI) (Heist and Yonge, 1962), an objective paper and pencil instrument that assesses intellectual activity and normal ego functioning. Used in a number of studies, the OPI is responsible for much of the information now available about college students. Because it provides a basis for understanding this special population and because it is easy to administer in group form, machine scoreable, and well standardized, it was given to the students involved in our project immediately after they had completed the freshman survey. Information gained from responses to the OPI was used in three ways: to obtain an independent measure of similarities and differences among students in the three colleges; to assess changes in these same students between the beginning (September) and end (June) of their thirteenth year; and to measure, by comparison, the validity of the functional potential scores of this population.

This chapter briefly describes the OPI and its fourteen scales, discusses related research on two- and four-year college students, and compares responses to this instrument with selected demographic variables and functional potential scores for our 3-D students.

Omnibus Personality Inventory

The Omnibus Personality Inventory was developed at the Center for Research and Development in Higher Education at the University of California, Berkeley, as a research tool for assessing the "selected attitudes, values, and interests [of college students], chiefly relevant in the areas of normal ego-functioning and intellectual activity. Almost all dimensions [were] included . . . either for their particular relevance to academic activity or for their general importance to academic activity or for their general importance in understanding and differentiating among the students in an educational context" (1968, p. 1).

The OPI's Form F (used in the 3-D Project) consists of 385 true or false items which are divided into fourteen categories, or scales. This multiphasic technique takes into consideration such variables as previous experiences, the home and family situation, developmental patterns, and the possibility of changes in an individual's perceptions. A characteristic is considered applicable on most of the fourteen scales of Form F if the standard score is at least 60 (84th percentile), while a standard score above 70 suggests relatively accurate characterization. These scores are based on norms derived from 7,283 college freshmen (3,540 men and 3,743 women) from thirty-seven diverse institutions of higher education, including four junior colleges.

Thinking Introversion (TI). This scale measures the tendency toward academic activities and abstract, reflective thought. Persons with high TI scores appear interested in the broad range of ideas typically expressed in literature, art, and philosophy. Their thinking is less dominated by immediate situations, conditions, or accepted ideas than the thinking of low scorers who, conversely, prefer action and practical ideas over abstraction.

Theoretical Orientation (TO). These items reflect a tendency toward the scientific, logical, or critical thinking which is more restrictive than TI. High scorers are characterized by a rational and critical approach to problems; they enjoy performance tasks involving restructuring.

Estheticism (Es). This scale measures interest in artistic matters and activities as well as sensitivity to esthetic stimulation. High scorers may enjoy, for example, poetry, paintings, sculpture, or architecture; collecting prints; or reading about artistic and literary achievements. Conversely, low scorers do not dream about having time for painting or other artistic activities, would not want to be actors or actresses, and do not make friends with sensitive and artistic people nor read about literary achievements.

Complexity (Co). Flexible and experimental approaches are reflected here. High scorers are tolerant of ambiguity and uncertainty. They appreciate novel situations, like to take chances on things without knowing whether they will work out, and prefer complexity and diversity to simplicity and routine. Believing that there is more than one right answer to most questions, they are apt to search for the novel solution. Low scorers do not like the unpredictable; they prefer regulations and conservative, straightforward reasoning.

Autonomy (Au). This scale measures liberal, nonauthoritarian thinking and independence. High scorers are tolerant of viewpoints other than their own and maintain the importance of individual rights. They tend to be mature, independent of authority, nonjudgmental, intellectually and politically liberal, and realistic. Most low scorers feel that parents are generally right, that only a callous person does not think of parents in terms of love or gratitude, and that rebellious young people get over their ideas and settle down as they mature.

Religious Orientation (RO). High scorers are skeptical of and tend to reject most conventional religious beliefs and practices. Those scoring around the mean manifest a moderate view of religious beliefs and practices, while low scorers indicate strong religious commitment or orthodoxy. (The direction of scoring this scale, indicating that low scorers tend toward a religious orientation, correlates with TI, TO, Es and Co.)

Social Extroversion (SE). This scale reflects the preferred style of relating in social contexts. High scorers display interest in being with people, are cordial to strangers, and seek such social activities as parties and large gatherings. Low scorers do not enjoy large parties or crowds and prefer to work alone. The social introvert (very low scorer) tends to withdraw from social responsibilities and contacts.

Impulse Expression (IE). A general readiness to seek gratification and express impulses—either in conscious thought or overt actions—is measured by this scale. Very high scorers report frequent feelings of rebelliousness and aggression and high scorers attest to active imagination, value feelings and sensual reactions, and often act spontaneously. On the other hand, low scorers tend to be conventional in outlook, dress, opinions, and actions.

Personal Integration (PI). This scale assesses admitted responses to attitudes and behaviors that frequently characterize emotionally disturbed or socially alienated persons. High scorers deny feelings of having done wrong, being misunderstood by others, or experiencing barriers between themselves and others. Low scorers admit to strange and peculiar thoughts, feel useless and "no good," and often experience feelings of such urgency that they can think of little else. They intentionally avoid people, experience hostile and aggressive feelings, and feel isolated, lonely, and rejected.

Anxiety Level (AL). Persons scoring high on this scale deny anxiety feelings or symptoms and do not admit to worry or nervousness. Low scorers worry, are often restless, and are inclined to take things hard. While they *claim* to be happy most of the time, they are, in fact, generally high-strung, tense, often experience difficult adjustment to social environments, and have a poor opinion of self. Here the emphasis on denial is most important. (Note that on this scale a *high* score suggests a *low* anxiety level and a *low* score, a *high* level of anxiety).

Altruism (Am). This score measures degrees of affiliation, trust in others, and ethical relations. High scorers tend to be affiliative and strongly concerned with social issues. Low scorers are more interested in ideas than in facts and tend not to consider the feelings and welfare of others.

Practical Outlook (PO). High PO scorers believe that the best theories have direct applications. They prefer factual test questions to those requiring the analysis and synthesis of data and they believe that intelligent leadership must maintain the established order. Ideas rather than facts appeal to the low scorers, who enjoy philosophical problems and do not believe that most questions have only one right answer.

Masculinity-Femininity (MF). This scale assesses some attitudinal differences between college men and women. High scorers tend to deny esthetic interests and admit to few adjustment problems or feelings of anxiety or inadequacy. They tend to be more interested in scientific matters and less social than low scorers, who admit to greater emotionality and sensitivity and enjoy the arts, literature, and poetry.

Response Bias (RB). The final scale measures the response to test-taking items. High scorers respond similarly to students explicitly asked to make a good impression. They state that they enjoy solving geometric or philosophical problems and that they feel close to people, while low scorers express restlessness and difficulties in their relationships with others and may make conscious efforts to leave a bad impression.

Community College Students and the OPI

Since its initial development as a research technique, the OPI has been used by a large number of colleges and universities to assess their student bodies and to predict student performance. Yet, in spite of its popularity among people who study college populations, the OPI is mentioned rarely in the junior college literature. Considering the general paucity of nondemographic research on community college students, however, this is not surprising. I have cited here a few of the limited projects which do include OPI data on the junior college student as a basis for comparison with the 3-D project.

The longitudinal SCOPE project (School to College: Opportunities for Post-secondary Education), directed by Tillery (1963), followed nearly 90,000 high school students as they moved into work, marriage, and various types of post-secondary schooling. A 31-item scale derived from the OPI, which emphasized "intellectual disposition," was used to differentiate groups of young people who enter various colleges—junior college, four-year colleges and universities—from those who did not enter college in the fall following their high school graduation. Analyzing the data generated by this study, Cross notes that while the special intellectual-predisposition scale of the OPI is tentative, it does differentiate between young people who do or do not enter college and between those who attend junior or senior colleges. Students in four-year colleges, for example, "tended to score in the top third, whereas those not entering college tended to make the lowest scores. Junior college students were more evenly distributed across the score groups. But as a group they showed less interest in the intellectual attitudes sampled by the scale than senior college students, and more interest than . . . those who did not attend college" (Cross, 1968, p. 29). The greatest differences between those students who selected junior colleges and those choosing state universities occurred on the OPI/SCOPE scales measuring autonomy and authoritarianism. Further data indicate "considerable differences between junior and senior college students on scales measuring intellectual interests and commitments" (Cross, 1968, p. 33).

Telford and Plant's (1963) study of a college's impact on the "non-intellectual functions" of its students is more definitive than the SCOPE study. In 1960, over 4,000 applicants to six California junior colleges responded to Rokeach's Dogmatism Scale (1960) and Allport, Vernon, Lindzey's *Study of Values* (1951)—inventories significantly correlating with specific OPI measures and thus included in this chapter. Two years later, the same instruments were administered to all subjects who could be reached by mail. This longitudinal sample was then classified into three subgroups: those who applied to but did not actually attend a community/junior college; those who attended college for one or two semesters; and those who attended for three or four semesters. Despite its limitations—such as considerable sampling loss—Telford and Plant's study suggests that students who attended junior colleges for three or four semesters changed no more than nonattenders. Although college attendance seems to have some effect on authoritarianism and dogmatism, even those who did not attend college showed tendencies over time toward greater flexibility on these dimensions.

Could it be that differences between college students and nonstudents reflect developmental differences rather than more pervasive characteristics? One of the implications of Telford and Plant's study is that college students do mature more quickly than nonstudents in some ways but that they do not have a monopoly on such development.

Rose and Elton (1970) compared the OPI scores of students transferring from two- and four-year colleges to the University of Kentucky. Scores of the two groups on dimensions relating to scholarly orientation, nonconformity and masculinity/femininity were highly similar and indicated no justification for orientation programs designed exclusively for students transferring from junior colleges to the university.

Taking a somewhat different slant, Tillery (1971) compared 612 students at a University of California campus with 418 students at a junior college. Although much diversity was found within each institution, a higher proportion of junior college than university freshmen indicate little interest in abstract thinking, little originality, and greater tendencies "toward conventional and rigid thinking. The difference is even more severe when junior college women are compared with their peers at Berkeley. Forty-five percent of the Berkeley women were rated as having high intellectual disposition, but only nineteen percent of the junior college women were so rated" (Tillery, 1971, p. 199).

Few measures used in Tillery's investigation more clearly differentiated the two institutional groups of men and women than did the OPI scales measuring authoritarianism. On the average, university students were less authoritarian (thus implicitly, more socially mature) than their two-year college counterparts, with the difference being most evident among women students.

Among investigations of junior college students alone, only a few reports utilize OPI data. One exception is a study by Steward (ED 01150), who examined subjects enrolled in trade and vocational courses. Studying noncognitive variables such as sources of life satisfaction (job, marriage, family, leisure, religion), risk-taking attitudes, impulse expression, estheticism, and abstraction, Steward found that vocational students seemed quite different from junior college students in nonvocational programs and from students in four-year colleges and universities. However, as a group, individuals in vocational programs did not appear to be unable to complete an academic course of study.

In another study, Cohen and Brawer (1970) hypothesized that junior college freshmen would exhibit less heterogeneity on certain OPI scales than the norm groups. Significant discrepancies were found between the junior college students and the normative sample on nine OPI scales—TI, TO, Es, RO, SE, IE, PI, Am, and RB. The means of all scales were lower for the junior college population than for the normative group, with the exception of RO and IE, which were significantly higher than the mean for the normative sample. Because the Response Bias scale reflects a tendency to make a good impression, the low mean scores of the junior college students on this scale point to the validity of the thirteen other scales in accurately reflecting the responses. The symmetrical distribution and wide range of scores suggest heterogeneous tendencies on eleven scales, while negative skewness on TI and PO and positive skewness on RB imply a slight homogeneity.

When these same junior college students are compared with a sample of University of California freshmen, some scales do seem to discriminate considerably. For example, while Estheticism is not significantly different for the two populations, Complexity is significantly higher for the junior college group. On the Au scale, University of California freshmen were considerably higher than the norm group and higher yet than the junior college sample, although no significant difference existed between the normative group and the junior college sample. As with the normative sample, junior college students were lower on PI, AL, Am, MF and RB and higher on IE, suggesting greater tendencies toward impulsivity. On the MF scale, where the University of California freshmen scored significantly higher than the norm group, the junior college students were significantly lower than the University freshmen but not different from the normative sample.

A statistic that indicates the degree of homogeneity of a distribution is the *coefficient of variation*. Although it is seldom appropriate for psychological tests because it implies an absolute zero point, this statistic may be employed to compare distributions of scores on the same test. With CV as a measure of comparison, the junior college sample appears to be somewhat more homogeneous (i.e., has a lower CV) than the norm group on the scales Co, Au, RO, IE, and PO. On none of the scales does the junior college sample have a substantially higher CV than the norm group—indicating greater heterogeneity. In fact, the junior college sample shows more homogeneity on the scales Co, RO, IE, and PO.

Sex differences in the OPI responses of this group were also noted. The mean scores of females were higher than those of males on scales TI, Es, Co, Au, SE, and Am. Male mean scores were higher on scales RO, IE, PO, and IO.

The OPI and 3-D Students

Let us now consider some of the characteristics of the 3-D students who responded to both the freshman survey and the OPI. The rest of this chapter presents profiles of pre-test (Fall, 1969) and post-test (June, 1970) scores; a comparison of OPI responses according to special subsets; and, finally, OPI scores analyzed in terms of the three functional potential groups.

Student responses for the OPI were analyzed using Biomedical Computer Program 07D (BMD07D, Dixon, 1968). The histograms given by this program demonstrated that the OPI variables were approximately normally distributed. Means and standard deviations were computed for each group as well as for the combined group. Finally, the analysis of variance technique was used to test the null hypothesis that the samples obtained were from populations with the same mean, that is, $u_1 = u_2 \ldots = uk$. To determine the significance of each test, the F statistic obtained was compared with values of the F distribution, with the appropriate degrees of freedom and the corresponding p-value recorded. Tests yielding p-values less than 0.05 were judged to be significant. The various profiles are presented in Figures 3 and 4.

Any theory of personality must undergo constant testing and retesting until it is either accepted—in whole or in part—or rejected. One way to test its validity is to compare it with other efforts purporting to measure similar characteristics. The instruments used in the 3-D study were selected not solely to establish concurrent validity but to obtain as much information as possible about the re-

Urban	TI	TO	Es	Co	Au	RO	SE
Mean	43.7	44.5	48.7	48.2	44.3	49.9	45.4
S.D.	7.0	7.7	8.0	7.5	7.4	6.4	7.6
Suburban							
Mean	42.7	43.7	46.8	49.5	47.9	50.9	45.1
S.D.	8.7	9.2	8.9	9.6	9.1	7.8	9.5
Rural							
Mean	42.9	42.3	47.6	48.8	45.7	49.1	42.9
S.D.	9.3	8.9	9.1	9.2	8.6	7.7	9.5
One-way Analysis							
F	2.7	5.0	9.3	3.7	34.0	6.9	6.4
P	n.s.	<.01	<.0005	<.025	<.0005	<.005	<.005

Urban	IE	PI	AL	Am	PO	MF	RB
Mean	54.6	45.6	45.7	42.0	55.9	49.5	46.1
S.D.	9.0	8.5	8.3	8.1	7.2	7.6	9.0
Suburban							
Mean	55.1	47.2	47.7	43.3	51.6	48.7	43.7
S.D.	10.8	10.0	9.6	10.8	9.8	8.7	9.5
Rural							
Mean	53.5	44.5	45.5	42.2	51.9	46.8	42.2
S.D.	10.6	8.6	8.8	9.8	8.7	9.9	9.1
One-way Analysis							
F	2.0	9.5	11.7	3.8	52.0	7.0	18.6
P	n.s.	<.0005	<.0005	<.025	<.0005	<.001	<.0005

FIGURE 3.   Pre-test OPI Scores for Students at Three Junior Colleges

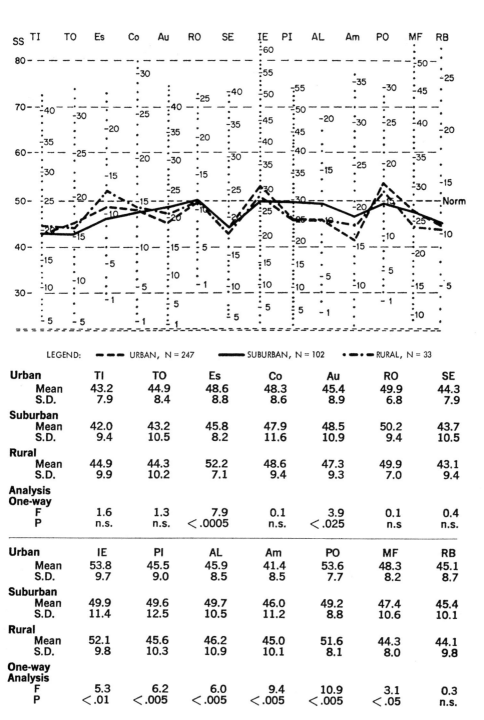

LEGEND: ━ ━ ━ URBAN, N = 247   ▬▬▬ SUBURBAN, N = 102   •━•━ RURAL, N = 33

Urban	TI	TO	Es	Co	Au	RO	SE
Mean	43.2	44.9	48.6	48.3	45.4	49.9	44.3
S.D.	7.9	8.4	8.8	8.6	8.9	6.8	7.9
Suburban							
Mean	42.0	43.2	45.8	47.9	48.5	50.2	43.7
S.D.	9.4	10.5	8.2	11.6	10.9	9.4	10.5
Rural							
Mean	44.9	44.3	52.2	48.6	47.3	49.9	43.1
S.D.	9.9	10.2	7.1	9.4	9.3	7.0	9.4
Analysis One-way							
F	1.6	1.3	7.9	0.1	3.9	0.1	0.4
P	n.s.	n.s.	$<.0005$	n.s.	$<.025$	n.s	n.s.

Urban	IE	PI	AL	Am	PO	MF	RB
Mean	53.8	45.5	45.9	41.4	53.6	48.3	45.1
S.D.	9.7	9.0	8.5	8.5	7.7	8.2	8.7
Suburban							
Mean	49.9	49.6	49.7	46.0	49.2	47.4	45.4
S.D.	11.4	12.5	10.5	11.2	8.8	10.6	10.1
Rural							
Mean	52.1	45.6	46.2	45.0	51.6	44.3	44.1
S.D.	9.8	10.3	10.9	10.1	8.1	8.0	9.8
One-way Analysis							
F	5.3	6.2	6.0	9.4	10.9	3.1	0.3
P	$<.01$	$<.005$	$<.005$	$<.005$	$<.005$	$<.05$	n.s.

FIGURE 4. Post-test OPI Scores for Students at Three Junior Colleges

spondents. However, in the course of analyzing the data, some interesting relationships were found between responses to the Freshman Survey and to the OPI.

The OPI is a paper and pencil test, designed to measure certain cognitive and affective characteristics of college students. Explicitly committed to assessing ego functioning in its respondents, the Freshman Survey (from which the functional potential scores are derived) is also a paper and pencil inventory. Unlike the OPI, however, it was developed especially for community college students. Items in the Survey deal with experiences, feelings, values, attitudes, interests regarding the respondent's early life, school, and future plans.

Despite some rather obvious differences between these two instruments, it was considered useful to compare the OPI and the functional potential (FP) scores derived from summing the modes (see Chapter 4). Several questions occurred in the course of this comparison: Is there any relation between FP and the OPI? Does this relationship hold for most test scores? Do changes occur in test-retests of either or both these assessment devices?

A study of the three FP groups (high, medium, and low) in relation to OPI profiles shows some interesting results. Although scores for the 3-D subjects are generally lower than for the established norm group representing several colleges throughout the country, the patterns seem to support the validity of functional potential. Consistently, the high FP group is closer to the mean except on scales measuring Impulse Expression and Practical Orientation. Consistently, too, the profiles of the medium and low groups are similar to, but lower than the profiles of the high group. These results seem to corroborate our point that the modes, organized to form functional potential, represent various degrees of functioning and that the higher the FP total, the closer it is to the norm of the OPI.

Because there seems to be considerable consistency when the three FP groups are compared with OPI profiles, OPI scores and different variables are presented here only as a total group. In Figures 5 and 6, these OPI patterns are compared individually in special subsets (pre-OPI, post-OPI) as well as in scores by FP groups. The classifications parallel those that were used in other analyses of these Freshman Survey data.

A significant relationship between the three FP groups and the OPI profiles exists in all but one of the fourteen OPI scales. It is interesting to note that OPI responses for all three FP groups fall beneath norms on twelve out of fourteen scales. Further, in that the high FP group is closest to the norm and the low group is farthest from it, the OPI patterns for the subjects in this study appear consistent.

Regarding pre-test and post-test results, the discrepant sample sizes point to the need for caution in interpretation. It does appear, however, that there is a general movement upward for those who responded to the second OPI. Interestingly, on the OPI Practical Outlook (PO) scale, the low FP group did not change from the first test to the second. For subjects in the medium FP group, however, PO showed a significant decrease ($p < .005$), moving closer to the OPI norm group. On the Autonomy (Au) scale, subjects in the medium FP group showed a significant increase ($p < .001$). For the high FP group, Au again moved up significantly ($p < .05$), while PO decreased, though not at a statistically significant level.

For further comparison among the three FP groups, certain demographic information and OPI responses were obtained. Comparisons of the three groups in terms of school attended and sex point to only minor differences. Comparisons of the FP scores of students in different age groups, however, show that a greater number of subjects in the subset 18 years and younger were in the high group. Comparisons on the basis of proposed academic majors indicate that more subjects designating a natural science major tend to fall in the high FP group than do other major designates, while business administration, engineering/technology, and education majors had more subjects in the low group. This suggests more certainty and, very possibly, more goal-directedness on the part of younger students who choose to major in the natural sciences.

The comparison of OPI with Freshman Survey items suggests two points in particular. First, the functional potential approach to assessment seems to be a valid way of measuring ego processes. Its construct validity was supported by comparison with the OPI. Second, if this population is representative of students in other community colleges, then these institutions must find nontraditional ways of dealing with their students if they expect to enhance devel-

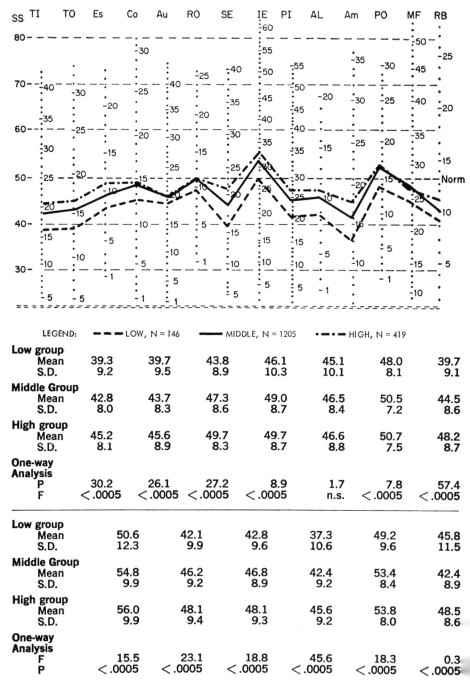

LEGEND: — — — LOW, N = 146   ———— MIDDLE, N = 1205   •—•—• HIGH, N = 419

Low group

Mean	39.3	39.7	43.8	46.1	45.1	48.0	39.7
S.D.	9.2	9.5	8.9	10.3	10.1	8.1	9.1

Middle Group

Mean	42.8	43.7	47.3	49.0	46.5	50.5	44.5
S.D.	8.0	8.3	8.6	8.7	8.4	7.2	8.6

High group

Mean	45.2	45.6	49.7	49.7	46.6	50.7	48.2
S.D.	8.1	8.9	8.3	8.7	8.8	7.5	8.7

One-way Analysis

P	30.2	26.1	27.2	8.9	1.7	7.8	57.4
F	<.0005	<.0005	<.0005	<.0005	n.s.	<.0005	<.0005

Low group

Mean	50.6	42.1	42.8	37.3	49.2	45.8
S.D.	12.3	9.9	9.6	10.6	9.6	11.5

Middle Group

Mean	54.8	46.2	46.8	42.4	53.4	42.4
S.D.	9.9	9.2	8.9	9.2	8.4	8.9

High group

Mean	56.0	48.1	48.1	45.6	53.8	48.5
S.D.	9.9	9.4	9.3	9.2	8.0	8.6

One-way Analysis

F	15.5	23.1	18.8	45.6	18.3	0.3
P	<.0005	<.0005	<.0005	<.0005	<.0005	<.0005

FIGURE 5.   Pre-OPI Scores for Three Functional Potential Groups.

Profile chart with scales: SS TI TO Es Co Au RO SE IE PI AL Am PO MF RB

LEGEND: ■ ■ ■ LOW, N = 20   ■■■■ MIDDLE, N = 244   ●—●—■ HIGH, N = 89

	TI	TO	Es	Co	Au	RO	SE
Low group							
Mean	41.7	42.4	47.4	45.6	45.5	49.0	41.6
S.D.	8.0	10.0	8.7	10.6	9.2	5.9	8.0
Middle Group							
Mean	42.5	44.0	47.5	48.2	46.8	50.1	43.0
S.D.	8.4	9.2	8.6	9.2	9.6	7.6	8.6
High group							
Mean	44.9	45.9	50.2	49.0	46.4	50.0	47.9
S.D.	8.6	9.1	8.2	9.6	8.7	7.9	9.1
One-way Analysis							
F	3.0	1.9	3.2	1.1	0.2	0.2	11.3
P	$<.05$	n.s.	$<.05$	n.s.	n.s.	n.s.	$<.0005$

	IE	PI	AL	Am	PO	MF	RB
Low group							
Mean	50.2	44.5	45.1	39.2	51.5	45.4	
S.D.	11.3	10.8	9.2	8.2	9.1	5.5	
Middle group							
Mean	52.3	46.9	47.2	42.7	52.0	48.3	
S.D.	0.9	10.3	9.6	9.5	8.2	9.9	
High group							
Mean	54.4	47.3	47.6	44.7	53.7	47.6	
S.D.	10.8	10.3	9.4	10.4	7.7	8.9	
One-way Analysis							
F	1.9	0.6	0.6	3.0	1.6	1.1	
P	n.s.	n.s.	n.s.	$<.05$	n.s.	n.s.	

FIGURE 6.   Post-OPI Scores for Three Functional Potential Groups.

opment. With the exception of the Impulse Expression and Practical Outlook scales, the 3-D sample consistently fell below the OPI norm group representing several thousand freshmen in colleges throughout the country. The highs on these two scales and the lows on the other OPI scales accentuate the need for substantial changes in school programs.

Chapter 10

Reflection
of Values

For years, fiction writers and philosophers alike have concerned themselves with attitudes and values. In spite of the popularity of these concepts as sources for human speculation, however, the precise study of man's beliefs is of recent origin, developing as it did out of two overlapping approaches to human appraisal—the individual, or psychophilosophical, and the sociopolitical, or group. While some psychologists were engrossed with such concrete questions as the rates and paths of nerve impulses and the presence or absence of imageless thought, others—particularly the personologists—were concerned with psychological symptomology and with the specific determinants underlying human behavior. When many psychologists were ignoring—or, at best, minimizing—the study of motivation, others took a different slant, viewing dynamics as important keys to human understanding.

Freud and McDougall were the first to consider motivational processes both seriously and systematically. Their emphasis on the dynamics underlying human behavior stimulated a new line of inquiry about the person's relationships to himself and to others. Subsequently, during the 1920s and 1930s, other people became engaged in the orderly study of belief systems—Murphy and Likert (1938), for example, who presented a combination of autobiographical and quantitative data, stressing the role of values as determinants of behavior. Much of Allport's work on values stemmed from Spranger's original *Lebensformen* (1928), which postulated the existence of six distinct and separate ideal types of subjective evaluation. Although Spranger's theory did not in any way imply that any given person belongs exclusively to one type, it did provide a definite schema within which to classify individual behavior and to emphasize the indispensability of man's belief systems in the psychology of personality. Today, few people would argue those points.

Despite this growing interest, however, only a handful of the earlier behavioral scientists were as concerned with the deliberate examination of values as was Allport. Among these few were Jung, Murray, Thomas and Znaniecki, and, somewhat later, Rogers. For Jung, values were seen as measures of intensity that represented the amount of psychic energy invested in elements of the personality. When a person places a high value on a particular feeling or idea, a considerable force is directed by that idea or feeling to instigate behavior, as in the case where "truth" is valued and a great deal of energy is thus expended toward its search. Jung's (1923) method of categorizing the attitudes of introversion/extraversion and the four functions of thinking, feeling, sensing, and intuition parallels other typologies geared to the classification of values.

Murray saw values as adjuncts of his need/press rationale rather than as separate dimensions of the human personality. He argued that because needs always operate in the service of some value or with the intent of inducing some end-state, no analysis of motives should fail to consider values. And since both experience and observation suggest that every "kind of action has an effect . . . which can be best defined in terms of some valued entities, . . . the naming of the valued entity in conjunction with the named activity should contribute a good deal to our understanding of dynamics of behavior" (1938, p. 288). Whereas Murray tied values to his need/press theory, Rogers (1969) related them to his view of the self's structure, to the formulation of the "I" or the "me."

Values accrue to the self-picture through direct environmental experiences as well as through adaptations from others. And experiences—both positive and negative—determine the selection and perpetuation of values.

This interest in attitudes and values as psychological representations of the influences of society and culture is consistent with the emphasis of Thomas and Znaniecki, who, as long ago as 1918, proposed the central task of social psychology to be the study of social attitudes. In their now classic studies of the Polish peasant in America (1927), they were first to operationally describe the concept of attitude. Following upon these pioneering efforts, many behavioral scientists have joined forces with those in other disciplines who attest to the importance of social attitudes in the assessment of human functioning.

Whatever the disciplinary boundary or the particular approach taken toward understanding people, goals, attitudes, and beliefs are important constructs. They cover the gamut of human activity—social, economic, psychological, educational, cross-cultural—and they concern people who are interested in many facets of human functioning. In fact, one can argue that the management of society can be rational only with total consensus on national goals and with relatively clear notions about the achievement of those goals. Just as emphatically, it can be asserted that consensus on national goals is possible—at least for now—only on the most general levels—for example, "We want the United States to remain an independent nation." Consensus on specific goals is dependent on individual value systems and, consequently, is considerably more limited and more difficult to attain.

Drawing in large measure on an earlier publication (Brawer, 1971), this chapter first presents definitions, measurement techniques, and Rokeach's approach to value assessment. The second part of the discussion presents a statistical analysis of the responses of the 3-D population to the Rokeach Value Scales—in terms of selected variables, student/faculty comparisons, and functional potential groups.

While most people will agree that belief systems have an important part in the total personality configuration, the confusion in defining these and associated concepts (attitudes, values, goals) makes it difficult to relate and compare studies in this area. To clarify some of this confusion Barton (1962) defines values "as general and stable dispositions of individuals, verbalized by them or inferred by the researcher, involving preference or a sense of obligation" (p. S-69). Specifically, he offers the following distinctions. Values may be seen as attributes of people or attributes of objects; they may be understood in terms of individual standards. Values may be explicit or implicit; implicit values may be inferred through either behavior or verbalization or both. Values are not always simple preferences. Barton cites Kluckhohn's distinction between "desired" and "desirable": "Even if a value remains implicit [there is] . . . an undertone of the desirable—not just the desired. The desirable is what is felt or thought proper to want" (1951, p. 396). Furthermore, the general value structure incorporates specific attitudes which, although related to, are less fixed than the central structure. One's esthetic values, for example, would include attitudes specific to sculpture, graphics, and the theatre which may be modified by experience and exposure but will remain consistent with the larger value structure.

Given an operational definition, however, the variables of any values system must be admitted. Smith (1963), for example, points out the importance of isolating the dominant value: "Since there are different values and some scale of importance must exist among them, we shall have to look for . . . the dominant value, introducing a measure of order and coherence into the whole. Though all values are, by their very nature, of importance to the self, some are more important than others and the most important will at the same time be most revelatory of the nature of the person" (p. 358).

Popular tendencies to place all values on one level, to lump them together under a common heading, and to examine them all together, obscure the fact that behind every situation involving values stands a person who is making the critical response. That individual can be better understood if the life he has selected and the values he holds have been determined. Although different people frequently indicate a common value, that value may not occupy the same position for all. One person, for instance, acknowledges tolerance because of its ethical implications, while another values it in order to further some purely selfish end. Unless both dominant and auxiliary values are recognized, understanding is decidedly limited. This recognition applies particularly to value disposition among various populations—cultural, generational, occupational—but it also suggests that individually determined values may be perceived in terms of hierarchical systems, a point that bears directly on the rationale and assessment schemes developed by Rokeach (1960, 1968, 1969) and discussed later in this chapter.

In spite of such difficulties as I have mentioned, attitudes and values are too important to be left unexamined. Central to any discussion of values assessment is the work of Allport and his colleagues, whose *Study of Values* (first published in 1931 and later revised as the *Allport-Vernon-Lindzey Scale,* 1951) is the first systematic approach to such an investigation. Their forced-choice technique measures the relative (rather than the absolute) importance to the individual of the six values summarized in Spranger's (1928) "types of men."

Other approaches to measuring attitudes and values include Morris's *Ways-to-Live* questionnaire (1956); the *Minnesota Teacher Attitude Inventory* (Cook, Leeds, and Callis, 1951); Gordon's *Survey of Interpersonal Values* (1960); and the *Attitude-Interest Analysis Test,* developed by Terman and Miles (1936). Barton (1962) reports on techniques devised by Kluckhohn and Strodtbeck (1961), Goldsen and others (1960), Stouffer and Toby (1966), and others.

Attempts to measure other variables sometimes disclose their relation to the individual's belief system. Adorno and others, for example, found, in their studies of *The Authoritarian Personality* (1950) that people with strongly ethnocentric belief systems and particular values and attitudes tended to be extremely authoritarian and to have the biases typically associated with fascism. Such studies are evidence, of course, of the role that values play in behavior and other manifestations of individual personality.

Definitions are as dependent on the interpretations assigned to them as on their clarity. And interpretations depend on the individual's frame of reference—a condition that goes well beyond any one issue at any one point in time. In order to understand how certain constructs are employed, it is important to adopt a phenomenological approach and to attempt to uncover the thinking and feeling of the subject because the person's general operational framework or life style may provide important clues to his behavior whether he is a college student or part of the nonacademic population.

Values and the College Student

In his appraisal of American college students, Jacob (1957) examined both their actual behavior choices and professed values structure. He defined values as those standards for decision-making which are normally identifiable from verbal statement or overt conduct. Data were acquired from student responses to contemporary value patterns; their college experiences, curriculums, instructors, and special teaching methods; and information regarding the development of particular values in certain institutions. Jacob could not attribute the impact of college on students to any particular factor. When student values were found to change in college—and there were some substantial changes—change did not appear due to the formal educational process but to other interactions. And the few institutions identified as most influential in changing values had their own prevailing atmospheres with strongly committed instructors who were both accessible and sensitive to students. The differential effects on values seemed attributable to institutional goals set by the faculty members and to the questions of values and attitudes raised by either the subject matter or the instructor. But in general these were rather singular cases that did not reflect the whole of higher education.

The overall impressions of failure conveyed by this report prompted a flurry of research and stimulated intense interest in the belief systems of the undergraduate college student and his teachers.

Much has happened in American society since 1957, when Jacob first issued his report. The general lethargy that marked the typical undergraduate student in the late 1950s and 1960s, has been replaced by active concerns about the relevance of education to their lives. Taken as a whole, students seem to be less interested in possessions, tend less to separate their academic lives from the rest of the world. Questions of goals and values are now more secular and tied to society as a whole rather than to either religious or academic programs.

For many institutions, the traditional academic goal is still to furnish the student with a broad general education and an appreciation of ideas. Other goals, however, transcend the merely educational. Vocational preparation and social development have assumed increasing significance in the curriculum, and the "ideal" college student of today is not only intellectually competent but also professionally and/or vocationally trained and socially adept—even adamant—in meeting the demands of the world. Equally important, as institutions that have evolved in society for the socialization of its members, schools are being increasingly seen as agencies of personal development. Merely proclaiming education in terms of intellectual and cognitive growth is hardly sufficient. As Sanford maintains, true education must be liberating and differentiating, and if the educational process has been successful, its participants must be different from—rather than mirror images of—others. Colleges must distinguish education from indoctrination, citing as their goal "the maximum development of the individual, bringing forth as much of his potential as possible, and setting in motion a process that will continue throughout his lifetime. This goal implies a development of certain qualities in a person which exist independently of any specialized skill or knowledge, qualities which are favorable to leading a rich, productive life . . . and to . . . performing effectively as a citizen in a democratic society" (Sanford, 1966, pp. 41–42).

Unfortunately, research in the community/junior college almost always follows the patterns of research established by the senior colleges and universities. This is as true of the study of belief systems as it is of other important human dimensions. Only recently have researchers and other interested educators concerned themselves with the value constellations of community college faculty or students. Some results of this interest are Blai's (1972, ED 061 945) report on the values and perceptions of private and public community college personnel, Park's (1971) examination of faculty values, and Brawer's (1971) comparison of student-faculty values in terms of the generation gap. Moore (1971) who compared students scoring low in value change and those ranking high on two (September and June) administrations of the Allport-Vernon-Lindzey Scale (1960) and such variables as scholastic aptitude, study habits, and parental education.

Abbas (1968) compared interpersonal values in three populations—junior college students enrolled in a terminal course, junior college transfer students, and university students—and found that university students scored lower on conformity and higher on leadership than the junior college students. Although Abbas suggested that junior college students tend to score higher on conformity because they live at home, it may be that the university atmosphere attracts the nonconformist. Perhaps this is why there has been generally less activism on the community college campuses than at residential colleges and universities.

Generation Gaps

Although the "generation gap" has existed in fact since there were first two generations, it was never so vigorously (and, to some, alarmingly) expressed as in the Free Speech Movement at Berkeley in 1964. The reaction to this unexpected uprising and its off-spring was predictable, given the nature of those most immediately threatened. Research on the cause, symptomatology, and cure for the congenital and suddenly virulent epidemic proliferated. Differences in the values of students and the older generation were only one of several hypothetical causes. The chasm between youth and adulthood—whether quiescent or raging—is nevertheless as real as that between their values. And with or without the stimulus of open hostility it seems worthwhile to examine changing behavior and the frictions between a population undergoing such change and that which is more or less stabilized.

In this vein, two different views are expressed by Feuer (1969), who suggests that the "emotional rebellion" of students in the 1960s was triggered by disillusionment with the older generation values, and by Keniston (1968), who sees activists as committed youths, concerned with the rights of others rather than their personal disillusionments. In both cases, however, differences between youth and adulthood might reflect fundamental differences in attitudes and values. This point, and the existence of attitudinal gaps, is corroborated by Morris's (1956) finding that older respondents to a life-orientation inquiry valued "enjoyment" less and showed more social restraint and self-control than younger respondents. While both young and old men were found to maintain high levels of aspiration and responsiveness to socially determined failure, older men decreased their aspiration level after experiencing success and appeared to conform more closely to group norms than did the younger men (Davis, 1969). The experiences of aging result in a rejection of such youth-oriented dominant values as science and technology and a lessened sense of disillusionment (Ludwig and Eichhorn, 1967).

The disparities demonstrated by youth's apparent lack of commitment to adult values and traditional roles are extended by behavioral scientists who note that numbers of young people also seem to be alienated from their parents' conceptions of adulthood, dissatisfied with traditional public life, and disaffiliated from many of the traditional institutions of our changing society. While Keniston (1968) relates this alienation to the "beat generation," it characterizes many young people for whom the phrase has little more significance than "flapper." Even those young adults who are involved in their studies and, at least ostensibly, are preparing for "establishment" vocations and professions, frequently view the world with great skepticism, if not mistrust.

Conversely, of course, many adults find it equally difficult to understand the young. Their confusion is particularly marked in regard to the Protestant ethic. In the past, praise was earned with economic accomplishments and task fulfillment, but today, when production often outweighs need, the emphasis is on individual fulfillment or self-actualization. The focus on leisure time, shortened work weeks, and alternate vocational patterns and the deemphasis of material goods suggests concurrent shifts in scholastic and vocational and avocational pursuits.

As far as college students are concerned, of course, the nonpeers with whom they most frequently interact are their teachers; thus several studies compare student and faculty attitudes. Blai (1970) selected ninety-five items from an inventory developed by Hadden (1969) and found that forty-two attitudes were shared by a majority of students from a private junior college and Hadden's college seniors. Other differences are apparent when the compatibility of student-faculty goals is examined. For example, although faculties establish student goals, many studies suggest that the student's peer group exerts a greater influence than his teachers (Bushnell, 1962; Feldman and Newcomb, 1969; Freedman, 1956; Newcomb, 1962; Sanford, 1962; Thielens, 1966). On the other hand, student and faculty attitudes may differ only by degree.

Terminal and Instrumental Values

Rokeach's (1968, 1969) Terminal and Instrumental Values Scales provide an especially interesting and operationally feasible means of examining individual value structures. Because of their importance to this discussion of values and college personnel, the scales are described in some detail.

Behind Rokeach's approach are the following assumptions: every person who has undergone some process of socialization has acquired certain beliefs about behavioral processes or end states of existence which he considers socially and personally desirable; values may be held in common, but interpretations of their importance differ among individuals; individual belief systems can be understood best if approached phenomenologically. He defines beliefs as predispositions that have cognitive, affective, and behavioral components and that, when activated, result in preferential responses. These responses may be toward others who take a position vis-a-vis the attitude, object, or situation; or toward the maintenance or preservation of attitudes. Attitudes—whether they describe, evaluate, or advocate action toward an object or a situation—are relatively enduring organizations of interrelated beliefs, consisting of interconnected assertions that certain things are desirable or undesirable (Rokeach, 1968, p. 16).

Values, on the other hand, are identified with types of conduct and end-states of existence. Extending the works of Kluckhohn (1957), Smith (1963), and Williams (1968), Rokeach maintains that "having a value" means that one consistently believes in and prefers a behavior, goal, or end-state. Once internalized, values are criteria by which the person justifies actions, develops and maintains attitudes "toward relevant objects and situations," exercises moral judgment, and compares himself with others (1968). Because all of anyone's values cannot be, and obviously are not, of equal significance to him, a value system is the individual's hierarchical ordering of beliefs.

Rokeach further distinguishes between terminal values and instrumental values. Both are based on the assumptions that "variations in value systems are, broadly speaking, a function of antecedent cultural and social experience, on the one hand, and personality factors on the other"; that value differences are "associated with differences in subcultural membership, sex, religion, age, race, ethnic identification, life style, socioeconomic status, child-rearing practices, intelligence, authoritarianism, and the like" (Rokeach and Parker, 1970, p. 98).

Terminal values represent beliefs that the person strives to maintain as personally and socially worthwhile (for example, a world at peace, wisdom, mature love). On the other hand, instrumental values determine the way he conducts himself to achieve these goals. They are similar to what some psychologists call "traits" or "modes of behavior."

Although the hierarchies in which values are conceptualized suggest a rank ordering along a continuum of importance or dominance, all values, whatever the ordering, fall into one category or the other—terminal or instrumental. When certain values conflict, the individual's idiosyncratic structure determines the value he assigns to a particular situation. In a conflict between the terminal values of self-fulfillment and prestige, as a case in point, or between two or more instrumental values, the person's own belief system reconciles the conflict by establishing primacy or dominance.

Rokeach measures values by presenting the subject with an alphabetically arranged list of eighteen terminal values and another of eighteen instrumental values. The subject is asked to rank the values on each list in order of importance to himself. The terminal values were distilled from several hundred terms gathered from various sources, and the instrumental values were selected from a compilation of 555 positively and negatively evaluated behavioral traits. (Those selected are positive by definition.) Because both scales consist of socially desirable values, the task of ranking seems difficult to many respondents and the reliability of the ordering process has been questioned. Rokeach maintains, however, that the order imposed by the respondent comes primarily from within and is not inherent in the structure of the stimulus material. In this sense, the value scales are similar to such projective techniques as the Rorschach and the Thematic Apperception Test. The two scales are presented in Table 5 as they appear in Form E.

Table 5.

INSTRUMENTAL VALUES	TERMINAL VALUES
Ambitious (hard-working, aspiring)	A comfortable life (a prosperous life)
Broadminded (open-minded)	Equality (brotherhood, equal opportunity for all)
Capable (competent, effective)	An exciting life (a stimulating, active life)
Cheerful (lighthearted, joyful)	Family security (taking care of loved ones)
Clean (neat, tidy)	Freedom (independence, free choice)
Courageous (standing up for your beliefs)	Happiness (contentedness)
Forgiving (willing to pardon others)	Inner harmony (freedom from inner conflict)
Helpful (working for the welfare of others)	Mature love (sexual and spiritual intimacy)
Honest (sincere, truthful)	National security (protection from attack)
Imaginative (daring, creative)	Pleasure (an enjoyable, leisurely life)
Obedient (dutiful, respectful)	True friendship (close companionship)
Polite (courteous, well-mannered)	Wisdom (a mature understanding of life)
Responsible (dependable, reliable)	A world at peace (free of war and conflict)
Self-controlled (restrained, self-disciplined)	A world of beauty (beauty of nature and the arts)

SOURCE: Permission to reprint these two lists of value has been graciously given by Milton Rokeach.

Rokeach Scales and the 3-D Project

The terminal and instrumental values scales were incorporated in the freshman and staff surveys developed for the 3-D project. Student and faculty responses were analyzed according to the following statistical methods. For each case (role affiliation, sex, age, major), the sample was separated into appropriate groups (e.g., male and female students). Then, for the eighteen values considered in each scale, the median response of each group was computed as well as the median response for the total sample. These medians were computed using the standard technique for grouped data (Nic, Bent, and Hull, 1970, p. 273) to determine if the groups represented samples from populations with the same median. Once the medians had been computed for all eighteen values in both scales, they were ranked.

Of the eighteen possibilities, even though only five terminal values were consistently ranked by students and staff or differed by only one point, some notable differences became apparent. For example, *sense of accomplishment* varies 10 points from a median ranking of 12 for the students to 2 for the staff; and *comfortable life*, rated 4 by the students and 13 by the staff, shows a difference of 9 points. Seven-point differences occurred for *inner harmony*, ranked 11 by students and 4 by the staff, and *world at peace*, which was rated 7 by students and 14 by the staff. Other differences are evident in Table 6, as are the appropriate degrees of significance.

The ranking of values by both groups shows that, in one sense, the students seem more inner-oriented than the staff. Students value *happiness, freedom, mature love, comfortable life.* (Whether the last implies freedom for themselves as individuals or for the population as a whole, we do not know.) On the other hand, and apart from their primary value of *freedom*, the staff stressed *self-respect* and *sense of accomplishment*. The value *inner harmony*, which is important for the staff, was ranked lower by the students. Other differences were noted but do not emphasize the inner/outer interpretations assigned the values ranked as dominant.

Results of instrumental value ratings for the total population of staffs are presented in Table 7.

In support of the notion that values reflect generation gaps, considerable differences are evident when the median rankings for the two groups are compared. In fact, only the top and bottom values appear exactly the same, although several values differed by only one or two points. A most interesting result occurred with the value *ambitious*—ranked third by the students and thirteenth by the staff.

Table 6.
MEDIAN TEST COMPARISON OF STUDENT AND STAFF IN ORDERING OF TERMINAL VALUES

Terminal Value	Student N = 1545		Staff N = 180		Total N = 1725		Median Test Degrees of Freedom: 1	
	Median	Rank	Median	Rank	Median	Rank	χ^2	p-value
Comfortable Life	6.94	4	11.69	13	7.41	6	69.91	< .001
Equality	8.53	10	9.53	11	8.64	10	7.06	< .01
An Exciting Life	10.04	13	9.13	10	9.98	13	1.74	< .20
Family Security	6.98	5	7.19	6	7.00	4	0.00	< .975
Freedom	6.04	2	6.50	3	6.08	2	1.05	< .40
Happiness	4.93	1	7.36	7	5.12	1	3927	< .001
Inner Harmony	9.81	11	6.86	4	9.46	11	58.67	< .001
Mature Love	6.26	3	7.73	8	6.40	3	12.62	< .001
National Security	13.71	17	15.20	17	13.94	16	43.21	< .001
Pleasure	11.20	14	13.77	16	11.51	14	56.00	< .001
Salvation	13.67	15	17.07	18	14.13	18	68.55	< .001
Self-Respect	7.39	6	5.04	1	7.10	5	41.85	< .001
Sense of Accomplishment	9.92	12	5.27	2	9.52	12	114.88	< .001
Social Recognition	14.15	18	12.95	15	14.02	17	11.84	< .001
True Friendship	8.49	9	7.93	9	8.43	8	2.34	< .20
Wisdom	8.40	8	6.97	5	8.24	7	15.15	< .001
World at Peace	7.95	7	12.78	14	8.63	9	121.34	< .001
World of Beauty	13.69	16	10.55	12	13.36	15	54.83	< .001

Table 7.

MEDIAN TEST COMPARISON OF STUDENT AND STAFF IN ORDERING OF INSTRUMENTAL VALUES

Instrumental Value	Student N = 1304		Staff N = 183		Total N = 1487		Median Test Degrees of Freedom: 1	
	Median	Rank	Median	Rank	Median	Rank	χ^2	p-value
Ambitious	6.19	3	9.97	13	6.69	3	45.91	< .001
Broadminded	7.94	6	7.03	4	7.77	5	6.06	< .025
Capable	9.23	11	7.00	3	8.97	9	28.76	< .001
Cheerful	8.79	8	10.80	15	9.13	10	21.00	< .001
Clean	9.20	10	14.42	17	9.90	12	131.80	< .001
Courageous	11.35	14	8.17	6	11.03	14	33.54	< .001
Forgiving	9.27	12	10.03	14	9.41	11	4.08	< .05
Helpful	8.96	9	8.55	8	8.88	8	0.60	< .90
Honest	4.67	1	4.50	1	4.66	1	0.06	< .80
Imaginative	12.57	17	9.70	12	12.25	17	44.89	< .001
Independent	7.84	5	8.25	7	7.90	6	1.02	< .40
Intellectual	10.48	13	9.17	10	10.23	13	15.46	< .001
Logical	11.73	16	9.22	11	11.34	15	47.03	< .001
Loving	5.93	2	7.33	5	6.08	2	11.41	< .001
Obedient	14.29	18	16.89	18	14.75	18	119.97	< .001
Polite	11.43	15	14.34	16	11.90	16	57.76	< .001
Responsible	7.36	4	5.82	2	7.12	4	32.92	< .001
Self-Controlled	8.60	7	9.10	9	8.64	7	0.17	< .70

One wonders about such a decided difference here, especially since many instructors at all educational levels may often suggest that their students lack motivation and ambition.

Although no particular constellation of student values appears in these data, the staff's responses appear to reflect the Protestant ethic, to which many of them possibly adhere. *Honest, responsible,* and *capable* all sound as if one were dedicated to the concept of a good day's work for value received. A question might be asked about the low ranks assigned to *obedient* and *polite* and an answer possibly gleaned by looking at the value *independent,* ranked fairly high by each group. For both staff and students, these findings are consistent with Rokeach's (1970) report of religious groups; and the students' de-emphasis on *clean, obedient,* and *polite* seems to parallel the values of "non-believers" who "put relatively less emphasis . . . on such Boy-Scout values as being *clean, obedient,* and *polite*" (1970, p. 35).

Age. Tables 8 through 11 give terminal and instrumental values for the "older" and "younger" age groups, with student values indicated in Tables 8 and 9 and faculty values in Tables 10 and 11.

In considering these results, one should note the small number of students in the sample who were 23 years or older and the extremely large number who were 22 or younger. Since such discrepancies in sample size undoubtedly affect results, interpretations are tentative. Although statistically significant differences ($p = <.01$) were found between these two groups on three values, sufficient similarity exists to indicate that age differences are not nearly so great as the differences between students and staff when combined as a whole, regardless of age. The differences between the *role* of the staff member and the *role* of the student might constitute more important differences. When these same age groups were compared, similar results hold for the instrumental values, with no significant differences noted. Here again, however, differences in sample sizes preclude much of a conclusion.

Tables 11 and 12 show the terminal and instrumental values for the faculties of the three schools. Among staff members, who were divided into two age groups (younger than and older than 39 years), the existing differences seem not nearly so great as those

Table 8.
Median Test Comparison of Two Student Age Groups in Ordering of Terminal Values

Terminal Value	22 or younger $N = 1422$		23 or older $N = 123$		Total $N = 1545$		Median Test Degrees of Freedom: 1	
	Median	Rank	Median	Rank	Median	Rank	χ^2	p-value
Comfortable Life	6.84	4	8.00	9	6.94	4	1.78	$< .20$
Equality	8.50	9	8.77	10	8.53	10	0.26	$< .70$
An Exciting Life	9.99	11	10.40	13	10.04	13	0.18	$< .70$
Family Security	7.18	5	3.61	1	6.98	5	19.20	$< .001$
Freedom	5.98	2	6.50	5	6.04	2	0.48	$< .50$
Happiness	4.91	1	5.14	2	4.93	1	0.55	$< .50$
Inner Harmony	9.99	12	7.36	7	9.81	11	9.64	$< .005$
Mature Love	6.25	3	6.30	4	6.26	3	0.00	—
National Security	13.81	17	12.13	14	13.71	17	5.05	$< .025$
Pleasure	11.67	14	12.83	15	11.20	14	5.60	$< .025$
Salvation	13.65	16	13.90	16	13.67	15	0.02	$< .90$
Self-Respect	7.50	6	5.70	3	7.39	6	4.34	$< .05$
Sense of Accomplishment	10.00	13	7.50	8	9.92	12	4.37	$< .05$
Social Recognition	14.15	18	14.08	17	14.15	18	0.00	$< .975$
True Friendship	8.43	8	9.10	11	8.49	9	1.28	$< .30$
Wisdom	8.51	10	7.32	6	8.40	8	4.40	$< .05$
World at Peace	7.73	7	9.58	12	7.95	7	7.35	$< .01$
World of Beauty	13.57	15	15.05	18	13.69	16	3.80	$< .10$

Table 9.
MEDIAN TEST COMPARISON OF TWO STUDENT AGE GROUPS IN ORDERING OF INSTRUMENTAL VALUES

Instrumental Value	22 or younger $N=1206$		23 or older $N=98$		Total $N=1304$		Median Test Degrees of Freedom: 1	
	Median	Rank	Median	Rank	Median	Rank	χ^2	p-value
Ambitious	6.22	3	5.80	2	6.19	3	0.06	< .80
Broadminded	7.99	6	7.25	5	7.94	6	0.35	< .70
Capable	9.29	12	8.56	9	9.23	11	1.00	< .50
Cheerful	8.66	8	9.89	11	8.79	8	2.20	< .20
Clean	9.12	10	10.50	12	9.20	10	1.75	< .20
Courageous	11.38	14	10.63	14	11.35	14	0.11	< .80
Forgiving	9.16	11	10.50	12	9.27	12	1.39	< .30
Helpful	8.98	9	8.25	7	8.96	9	0.56	< .50
Honest	4.68	1	4.50	1	4.67	1	0.01	< .90
Imaginative	12.59	17	12.29	17	12.57	17	0.04	< .90
Independent	7.73	5	8.76	10	7.84	5	2.36	< .20
Intellectual	10.67	13	8.50	8	10.48	13	4.79	< .05
Logical	11.77	16	11.25	16	11.73	16	0.17	< .70
Loving	5.83	2	7.00	4	5.93	2	3.25	< .10
Obedient	14.31	18	13.63	18	14.29	18	0.05	< .90
Polite	11.45	15	11.08	15	11.43	15	0.06	< .90
Responsible	7.40	4	6.50	3	7.36	4	0.52	< .50
Self-Controlled	8.65	7	7.92	6	8.60	7	0.42	< .70

Table 10.
MEDIAN TEST COMPARISON OF TWO STAFF AGE GROUPS IN ORDERING OF TERMINAL VALUES

Terminal Value	39 or younger N = 85		40 or older N = 95		Total N = 180		Median Test Degrees of Freedom: 1	
	Median	Rank	Median	Rank	Median	Rank	χ^2	p-value
Comfortable Life	10.70	12	12.67	14	11.69	13	1.74	< .20
Equality	10.00	11	8.64	10	9.53	11	2.72	< .10
An Exciting Life	7.70	9	10.83	12	9.13	10	6.48	< .025
Family Security	8.10	10	6.28	4	7.19	6	1.38	< .30
Freedom	7.50	8	5.42	3	6.50	3	5.70	< .025
Happiness	7.10	5	7.50	7	7.36	7	0.02	< .80
Inner Harmony	6.30	4	7.08	6	6.86	4	0.98	< .70
Mature Love	5.67	3	8.50	8.5	7.73	8	8.73	< .005
National Security	15.95	17	14.41	17	15.20	17	6.98	< .01
Pleasure	13.21	15	14.13	16	13.77	16	0.74	< .40
Salvation	17.36	18	16.90	18	17.07	18	0.95	< .40
Self-Respect	5.14	1	4.92	1	5.04	1	0.04	< .90
Sense of Accomplishment	5.17	2	5.32	2	5.27	2	0.00	< .975
Social Recognition	12.50	14	13.30	15	12.95	15	0.95	< .40
True Friendship	7.36	6	8.50	8.5	7.93	9	0.98	< .40
Wisdom	7.39	7	6.50	5	6.97	5	1.26	< .30
World at Peace	13.23	16	12.17	13	12.78	14	1.97	< .20
World of Beauty	11.50	13	10.07	11	10.55	12	2.72	< .10

Table 11.
MEDIAN TEST COMPARISON OF TWO STAFF AGE GROUPS IN ORDERING OF INSTRUMENTAL VALUES

Instrumental Value	39 or younger N = 89		40 or older N = 94		Total N = 183		Median Test Degrees of Freedom: 1	
	Median	Rank	Median	Rank	Median	Rank	χ^2	p-value
Ambitious	9.64	11	10.15	13	9.97	13	0.40	< .60
Broadminded	7.64	6	6.50	4	7.03	4	2.32	< .20
Capable	7.50	5	6.35	3	7.00	3	1.17	< .30
Cheerful	11.30	15	10.25	14	10.80	15	0.46	< .50
Clean	14.00	16	14.62	17	14.42	17	0.27	< .70
Courageous	9.90	13.5	7.19	5	8.17	6	7.40	< .01
Forgiving	9.10	9	10.86	15	10.03	14	2.99	< .10
Helpful	9.14	10	7.50	6	8.55	8	3.44	< .10
Honest	4.36	1	4.58	1	4.50	1	0.00	< .95
Imaginative	9.90	13.5	9.50	10.5	9.70	12	0.05	< .90
Independent	7.10	4	8.81	9	8.25	7	1.25	< .30
Intellectual	8.75	7	9.55	12	9.17	10	0.69	< .50
Logical	8.88	8	9.50	10.5	9.22	11	0.28	< .60
Loving	6.17	3	8.57	8	7.33	5	4.62	< .05
Obedient	17.27	18	16.68	18	16.89	18	0.54	< .50
Polite	14.21	17	14.37	16	14.34	16	0.00	< .95
Responsible	6.06	2	5.20	2	5.82	2	2.08	< .20
Self-Controlled	9.70	12	8.29	7	9.10	9	0.26	< .70

pertaining to the combined student and staff populations. On the whole, little can be said about differences here in terminal values, the only statistically significant differences ($p < .01$) being two ranked near the middle—*mature love* and *national security.* When instrumental values responses by the combined faculties were divided into the same age groups, more similarities than differences became evident. Indeed, whatever differences pertained were not nearly so great as the differences between students and staff. Again, roles seem more important than age differences in determining values.

Sex. Differences were also indicated for the subjects divided according to sex (Tables 12 and 13). In these combined student-staff comparisons, males and females agreed on their top value—*happiness*—but differed in regard to their second and third choices. One of the greatest differences occurred with the value *comfortable life,* ranked third highest by males and eleventh by females. This corroborates the suggestion made earlier that the hierarchical ordering of values may reflect the male's sense of financial responsibility toward his family, whether existent or intended. Although significant differences were found for ten values, no particular pattern appeared to show inner or outer value orientations as in the comparison of students and faculty as a whole. For the combined groups (male students and staff versus female students and staff), traditional values, roles, and self-images also might account for the responses.

Majors. The terminal and instrumental values for the designated major of students were also analyzed. Few differences were apparent among students in any one of the following categories: business administration, engineering/technology, humanities/arts, languages, mathematics, science, social science, other, don't know, or education. In fact, among respondents in these fields, only four values showed statistically significant differences ($p = < .01$). It is difficult to infer any pattern here because the various majors seem to neutralize whatever differences do exist. For example, whereas business administration majors value most a *comfortable life,* language majors rank it only thirteenth. However, the median rankings show that differences among respondents are perhaps not so large. In a sense, the students' designation of top values supports the gen-

Table 12.
MEDIAN TEST COMPARISON OF COMBINED MALE STUDENTS AND STAFF AND COMBINED FEMALE STUDENTS AND STAFF IN ORDERING OF TERMINAL VALUES

Terminal Value	Male $N = 967$		Female $N = 758$		Total $N = 1725$		Median Test Degrees of Freedom: 1	
	Median	Rank	Median	Rank	Median	Rank	χ^2	p-value
Comfortable Life	5.91	3	9.09	11	7.41	6	108.88	< .001
Equality	9.11	11	8.06	7	8.64	10	16.32	< .001
An Exciting Life	8.47	8	11.29	13	9.98	13	79.80	< .001
Family Security	6.92	5	7.05	5	7.00	4	1.74	< .20
Freedom	5.49	2	6.82	4	6.08	2	26.10	< .001
Happiness	5.20	1	5.04	1	5.12	1	2.35	< .20
Inner Harmony	10.07	13	8.47	9	9.46	11	31.97	< .001
Mature Love	6.53	4	6.22	3	6.40	3	1.42	< .30
National Security	13.99	17	13.83	17	13.94	16	1.64	< .30
Pleasure	10.52	14	12.54	14	11.51	14	74.94	< .001
Salvation	14.50	18	13.59	16	14.13	18	6.43	< .025
Self-Respect	7.82	6	6.02	2	7.10	5	54.55	< .001
A Sense of Accomplishment	9.50	12	9.55	12	9.52	12	0.02	< .90
Social Recognition	13.65	16	14.51	18	14.02	17	19.08	< .001
True Friendship	8.38	7	8.50	10	8.43	8	0.22	< .70
Wisdom	8.58	9	7.77	6	8.24	7	10.77	< .005
A World at Peace	9.02	10	8.07	8	8.63	9	6.97	< .01
A World of Beauty	13.50	15	13.22	15	13.36	15	1.32	< .30

Table 13.

MEDIAN TEST COMPARISON OF COMBINED MALE STUDENTS AND STAFF AND COMBINED FEMALE STUDENTS AND STAFF IN ORDERING OF INSTRUMENTAL VALUES

Instrumental Value	Male $N = 837$ Median	Male Rank	Female $N = 650$ Median	Female Rank	Total $N = 1487$ Median	Total Rank	Median Test Degrees of Freedom: 1 χ^2	p-value
Ambitious	5.33	2	8.14	6	6.69	3	66.11	< .001
Broadminded	7.97	6	7.47	4	7.77	5	2.45	< .20
Capable	8.74	8	9.18	11	8.97	9	3.95	< .05
Cheerful	9.85	10	8.22	7	9.13	10	22.65	< .001
Clean	10.73	15	8.83	10	9.90	12	35.96	< .001
Courageous	10.50	14	11.72	14	11.03	14	16.91	< .001
Forgiving	10.32	13	8.23	8	9.41	11	34.82	< .001
Helpful	9.46	9	7.98	5	8.88	8	37.46	< .001
Honest	5.29	1	4.10	1	4.66	1	23.14	< .001
Imaginative	11.82	16	12.88	17	12.25	17	18.83	< .001
Independent	7.56	5	8.50	9	7.90	6	6.27	< .025
Intellectual	9.87	11	10.66	13	10.23	13	4.38	< .05
Logical	10.29	12	12.71	16	11.34	15	64.28	< .001
Loving	6.75	3	5.27	2	6.08	2	20.37	< .001
Obedient	14.71	18	14.79	18	14.75	18	0.15	< .70
Polite	11.83	17	11.99	15	11.90	16	0.15	< .70
Responsible	6.90	4	7.30	3	7.12	4	1.28	< .30
Self-Controlled	8.25	7	9.41	12	8.64	7	8.50	< .005

eral stereotypes of the fields, although their least important values do not seem consistent with the typical image.

Considerably fewer students than in any of the other major groups designated a language major; thus, these findings are minimal. Greater differences were found with the mathematics and natural science samples. The social science majors were similar to other groups, especially in the values deemed least important. Perhaps other differences would be found if natural science and engineering majors were considered as one group and humanities and social science majors as another.

In regard to the students' ordering of instrumental values, significant differences appeared in the three values *clean, imaginative,* and *obedient.* However, where differences occurred between two groups, the combined groups so neutralize most of these that they appear less important.

On the terminal and instrumental value scales, faculty members in different teaching fields showed few differences when compared with differences that might be found if only one or two groups were examined—as with natural science and mathematics instructors versus social science/humanities faculty. In this case, as with the students divided into majors, it is suggested that the reader look at the tables in terms of the specific population that interests him most—for example, he might note that the value *self-respect* is consistently high for all groups whereas *happiness, true friendship,* and *world at peace* vary considerably. Here faculty disparities are often so small that it is difficult to draw any inferences from them.

Values and Functional Potential. Values of students in the three functional potential groups were also studied. (No similar analyses were made for the staff values.) For these particular variables, however, the functional potential data appear far less interesting than do other results of the value ordering.

The statistical approach used in these analyses was the same as that reported for the student and staff comparisons. The sample was separated into appropriate groups (e.g., male and female students) for each case. Using the standard technique for grouped data (Nic, Bent, and Hull, 1970, p. 273), the groups' median responses were computed for each of the values, as well as the median re-

Table 14.
Terminal Values
STRATIFICATION VARIABLE: FUNCTIONAL POTENTIAL

Value	LOW Median	LOW Rank	MIDDLE Median	MIDDLE Rank	HIGH Median	HIGH Rank	MEDIAN TEST Chi Sq	p-value DF = 2
	Sample Size: 84		Sample Size: 1063		Sample Size: 400			
Comfortable Life	5.57	3	6.77	4	7.70	6	4.3750	n.s.
Equality	7.00	6	8.50	9	8.73	10	1.2608	n.s.
An Exciting Life	9.57	11	10.04	12	10.17	13	1.0302	n.s.
Family Security	6.50	4	7.10	5	6.71	5	1.0851	n.s.
Freedom	4.89	1	5.96	2	6.50	3	1.1636	n.s.
Happiness	5.33	2	4.94	1	4.79	1	1.5287	n.s.
Inner Harmony	9.86	12	9.93	11	9.33	12	0.0088	n.s.
Mature Love	7.25	7	6.13	3	6.44	2	4.4156	n.s.
National Security	13.05	16	13.69	16	13.88	16	2.2443	n.s.
Pleasure	10.57	13	10.91	14	11.91	14	0.5751	n.s.
Salvation	13.56	17	13.81	17	13.32	15	0.0065	n.s.
Self-Respect	8.00	8	7.53	6	6.67	4	2.6323	n.s.
Sense of Accomplishment	10.65	14	10.13	13	9.13	11	1.2021	n.s.
Social Recognition	14.73	18	14.17	18	13.95	17	2.2018	n.s.
True Friendship	9.05	9	8.58	10	8.02	8	2.2664	n.s.
Wisdom	9.50	10	8.43	8	8.00	7	2.3609	n.s.
World at Peace	6.92	5	7.78	7	8.57	9	1.2794	n.s.
World of Beauty	11.82	15	13.65	15	14.16	18	10.1459	p < .01

Table 15.
Instrumental Values
STRATIFICATION VARIABLE: FUNCTIONAL POTENTIAL

Value	LOW		MIDDLE		HIGH		MEDIAN TEST	
	Median	Rank	Median	Rank	Median	Rank	Chi Sq	p-value
	Sample Size: 72		Sample Size: 895		Sample Size: 341			$DF = 2$
Ambitious	5.75	2	6.41	3	5.32	2	0.0282	n.s.
Broadminded	7.50	6	7.94	6	7.91	5	0.1812	n.s.
Capable	7.50	6	9.33	12	9.13	8	2.3847	n.s.
Cheerful	9.88	12	8.44	7	9.50	9	1.5967	n.s.
Clean	6.94	5	8.96	10	10.17	12	4.2946	n.s.
Courageous	10.50	14	11.18	14	11.94	16	0.0135	n.s.
Forgiving	10.13	13	9.09	11	9.61	10	1.8392	n.s.
Helpful	8.06	9	8.81	9	9.69	11	1.9821	n.s.
Honest	6.14	3	4.58	1	4.47	1	9.0404	$p < .02$
Imaginative	12.08	16	12.69	17	12.23	17	0.7774	n.s.
Independent	5.50	1	7.79	5	8.12	6	0.9696	n.s.
Intellectual	7.67	8	10.80	13	10.19	13	7.7115	$p < .05$
Logical	12.50	17	11.67	16	11.65	15	2.4646	n.s.
Loving	6.75	4	6.04	2	5.50	3	0.9116	n.s.
Obedient	15.12	18	14.21	18	14.21	18	8.9043	$p < .02$
Polite	10.50	14	11.54	15	11.34	14	0.8910	n.s.
Responsible	8.50	10	7.31	4	7.36	4	1.5057	n.s.
Self-Controlled	9.00	11	8.57	8	8.56	7	0.2000	n.s.

sponse for the total sample. Once the medians had been computed for all values, they were ranked (see Tables 14 and 15).

Although no abundance of significant χ^2's is evident, in many cases directional changes going from low to high functional potential are demonstrated. For the terminal values, no major differences are noted. The single exception here is the relative importance of the *world of beauty* value, to which the low and medium FP groups gave higher rankings than did the high FP group. On the instrumental value scale, significant differences were noted for three values—*honest, intellectual, obedient.* The low FP groups ranked *honest* and *obedient* lower than the other two groups and ranked *intellectual* higher.

In this study of the value systems of students and staff in three California junior colleges, the *role* of student or teacher seems to affect the person's value system more than any other variable—sex, designated major, age, or functional potential. Thus, the so-called generation gap seems not well-documented by our data.

Chapter 11

Dropouts
and Persisters

Educators, psychologists, and behavioral scientists in general have long been interested in the phenomenon of premature withdrawal from school. After it became mandatory for students to remain in public school until the age of sixteen, concern with this problem shifted to higher education and is widespread enough to account for much of the current literature on student populations. In fact, so many reports attest to the popularity of this issue that even in 1966, Knoell could state that studies of the college dropout would soon rival in sheer numbers the many studies on predicting success in college. The phrase has its own positive—and often negative—connotations for "well-propagandized parents who now equate learning solely with the number of school years completed" (Gross, 1969).

The construct—dropout or stopout—provides a comparatively clear-cut, either/or situation, one that can be readily assessed as an objective dependent variable. However, the ease of assigning a designation and the plethora of material available in the literature do not necessarily imply that the phenomenon is clearly understood. Despite the data regarding demographic, financial, and sociological concomitancies of attrition, there is a strong tendency to assign blame. "Motivational difficulties," for example, may sound respectable on paper and provide some justification for an act which students, parents, and educators perceive as failure, but such labels only serve to obscure the issues.

What are the concomitants of dropout? Do people who fail to complete two or four or eight years of post-secondary education fare any worse (or any better) than those who attain associate or baccalaureate or graduate degrees? Questions still remain regarding the characteristics that might differentiate students who drop out from students who complete college. Early withdrawal is tied up with a multiplicity of related dimensions—problems of economics for school, community, and students; sociological concerns; selection proceedings; academic preparation; and goal orientation. They also involve concerns with environmental press (Astin, 1964; Murray, 1938; Pace, 1966; Stern, Stein, Bloom, 1963) and all the area of personality assessment and ego functioning. When a student leaves school before he completes his course work or designated program, is it because the schools failed to meet his expectations? Is it because, initially, it was unrealistic for him to enter that particular institution? Are less adaptive students likely to drop out if expectations and realities are disparate? Or do many dropouts represent the most talented and independent students (Suczek and Alpert, 1966)? What are, in fact, the students' expectations? What are the realities of the community college and do these "realities" vary from one institution to another? Finally, is there a relation between ego strength or functional potential and the attrition patterns of college freshmen?

The perspectives from which student dropout has been surveyed provide some tentative information. For example, while economic and social conditions certainly contribute to attrition, there is no evidence that either of these variables is the primary cause. But conclusions seem remote when investigators are confronted by the varied and complex factors involved. Assuming that the problem must be analyzed from the student's perspective—although one might choose another approach—there are such variables as peer and parental influence, personality, and educational background. Even the identification of key variables may depend on the rationale and instruments from which the data are drawn.

If the dropout phenomenon continues to be a critical issue, our present level of understanding, must be elevated rapidly. Unfortunately, it has made little progress since Knoell, in 1966, observed that the research "has tended to be microcosmic in nature, rather than macrocosmic" (p. 68).

Related Studies

According to Knoell (1966), in junior colleges attrition is exceedingly high after only one year, and many of the students in a transfer program do not enter state institutions. Although most colleges tabulate data about persistence, these reports are seldom circulated. Some studies, most often demographic, are found in *Research in Education,* the monthly journal of educational abstracts, some are published in monograph or book form, but few are reported in either the educational or psychological literature. And in the few instances when information on junior college students is reported, it is usually as a peripheral note in a study of four-year-college and university students.

Recent data suggest that —assuming completion of the baccalaureate within four years is the indicator of persistence—53 percent of all students entering four-year colleges or universities can be called dropouts (Astin, 1972). In the participating junior colleges, dropout rates are somewhat higher—61.6 percent of the entering students dropping out before completing their programs. Higher rates at two-year colleges—although lower than Astin had expected—were attributed to the lower level of matriculation and the poorer academic preparation of the entering students. However, nearly half of the withdrawals surveyed by Bossen and Bennett (1970) eventually returned to school, implying that attrition rates in junior college may not be as high as originally estimated if the definition of attrition is altered. Again, problems of inconsistent definition and ambiguous criteria crop up—problems compounded by other variables that are sometimes conflicting. Time limits or other controlling variables must be added if dropout is to be distinguished from stopout.

In an attempt to relate selected variables to attrition data from one junior college, Cohen and Brawer (1970) defined dropouts as students who failed to complete their first college semester, did not enroll for a second semester, or did not transfer to another college. Persisters did complete their first semester and either reenrolled or transferred to another institution. Since several assumptions basic to this investigation seem appropriate for related research on the college dropout, they are designated here.

(1) There is a need for basic research to isolate personality dimensions so that the potential school dropout may be identified.

(2) Characteristics that differentiate students with high dropout potential from students with high persistence potential must be identified and compared so that academic procedures can be developed and evaluated (Kubie, 1960).

(3) Academic attrition cannot be viewed solely in terms of the student, no matter how thorough the analysis may be. The issue is a multifaceted one that requires investigation of the student interacting with other members of the college milieu—peers, faculty, administrative forces—and with the college environment itself.

(4) Despite many efforts to isolate and understand characteristics of the "good" teacher, student withdrawal rates typically are not related to teacher personalities, abilities, or goal orientations.

(5) Because a high dropout rate may eventually affect faculty morale, withdrawal rates have implications for faculty members. Especially in the teaching of introductory courses to college freshmen, a circular effect can take place—students become disenchanted with faculty members and faculty become disenchanted with students (Iffert, 1964).

(6) Lack of experimentation with action programs designed specifically to reduce attrition is apparent.

(7) A need exists for analysis of institutional organizational characteristics that might affect attrition rates.

(8) The question of college attrition requires continual in-depth investigation, as well as the implementation of relevant re-

search findings. While all dimensions of the phenomenon can hardly be encompassed in a single project with limited populations, suggestions from other studies should be entertained in any new research.

(9) "Although the term 'college dropout' has become a bad word in the popular press and the American hometown, . . . the possibilities of both loss and benefits should be considered" (Ford and Urban, 1966, p. 83). Perhaps dropout is not a negative term; indeed, the dropout may be exhibiting different strengths from those of his fellow students.

(10) "Early identification of the potential dropout may lead to clearly defined goals and efficient use of resources. Programs may be especially tailored to answer the specific needs of different students enrolled for varying periods of time and various purposes. Identification of problems associated with the dropout may also lead to evaluation of what is learned in the schools, by whom, and to what ends" (Cohen and Brawer, 1970, pp. 19–20).

In order to learn whether certain personality, ability, or demographic characteristics differentiate college dropouts from persisters, three instruments were administered to freshmen entering a California community college: the Omnibus Personality Inventory (Heist and Yonge, 1962), the Adaptive-Flexibility (A-F) Inventory (Brawer, 1967), and a short biographical questionnaire (Cohen and Brawer, 1970). At the end of what would have been their first college semester, dropouts tended to be enrolled for fewer than twelve units, whereas persisters were enrolled for twelve units or more ($\chi^2 = 20.03$, $p < .01$); to be employed more time outside school than were persisters ($\chi^2 = 20.05$, $p < .01$); and to have attended more schools prior to the tenth grade than did persisters ($\chi^2 = 12.65$, $p < .01$). The mothers of dropouts tended to have less education than those of persisters, with more mothers of dropouts failing to complete high school ($\chi^2 = 12.93$, $p < .05$).

In regard to the A-F Inventory, a technique designed to assess ego strength in the functioning adolescent or adult, the mean score for the persisters (4.35) was slightly higher than for the dropouts (4.28), but the difference was not significant.

Omnibus Personality Inventory data were tabulated after one and after two semesters. The mean for first-semester dropouts on the Thinking Introversion (TI) scale was significantly higher than the second-semester dropouts' mean ($t = 2.28$, $p < .05$), and was higher on the Estheticism (Es) scale ($t = 2.41$, $p < .05$). On the Interest Orientation (IO) scale, the mean for second-semester dropouts was higher than that for the first-semester dropouts ($t = 2.24$, $p < .05$).

Certain implications stem from these findings. Since nonpersisters tended to be enrolled for fewer than the twelve units typically considered a minimal load for a full-time junior college student, less commitment to school is implied. Hence, possibly, when conditions within the college become unpleasant or impinge on other activities—for example, jobs—the noncommitted are more inclined to leave school than are students who seem dedicated to a full program. Also suggested by the fact that dropouts reported more time spent in outside employment than that reported by persisters—and consistent with much of the literature on the college dropout—is that withdrawal may be related to financial pressures. Such employment may well reflect financial need, but since this variable was not definitely established for this sample, its influence is tenuous. Financial conditions may be related to attrition but not necessarily always.

Family mobility also is an influential predeterminator in that the nonpersisters of this sample attended more schools prior to the tenth grade than did persisters. There is an implication of early family instability as well as a pattern of noncompletion that, once established, may tend to persist in various forms when students react to different situations. Another instance of the influential role of family patterns on school persistence is the finding that mothers of dropouts were less likely than mothers of persisters to have completed high school.

Attrition and the 3-D Project

With respect to attrition figures for the students in the 3-D project, there are several questions to be considered. Is any one of the three sample schools—Urban, Suburban, or Rural—more likely to have higher or lower retention figures than the other two? Does attrition correlate with other demographic variables characterizing this student population? Does it correlate with functional potential?

These questions are addressed in the remaining section of this chapter. In some cases, the data were reported for a nine-month period—that is, after two college semester courses were completed. In other cases, both the one-year/two-semester (June 1, 1970) and the two-year/four-semester (June, 1971) periods were used to provide figures regarding attrition, program completion (as measured by obtaining the AA degree), and/or transfer to another institution.

Drop/Persist and Functional Potential. The χ^2 test for independent samples was used to test the hypothesis that the proportion of students who dropped out of junior college within the first year (two semesters) was the same for the three functional potential groups. While 31.3 percent of the 1,271 students in the medium FP group and 43.5 percent of the 170 students in the low FP group had dropped, only 26.2 percent of the 435 high FP students had done so. This resulted in a χ^2 (2) = 17.09 ($p < .001$). As one moves from low to high functional potential, the proportion of students who dropped out within their first year decreases.

Examination of dropout data for all three schools after two years by means of the k sample χ^2 test of homogeneity gave a χ^2 (4) = 13.01 ($p < .025$) with respect to both dropout and functional potential group. Of the 1,876 students in the total sample, 47 percent had dropped, 42.2 percent persisted and 10.8 percent were of unknown status. There were 170 in the low FP group; of these, 55.3 percent dropped, 34.1 percent persisted, and 10.9 percent were unknown. For the 435 students in the high group, 41.2 percent dropped, 48.5 percent persisted, and 10.3 percent were unknown.

Excluding the above unknowns, a χ^2 test was performed and resulted in a χ^2 (2) = 12.88 ($p < .005$). This indicates a definite statistical relationship between functional potential and persistence in college. The proportion of each group who persisted increases with an increase in functional potential group from low to high. This relationship is strongest in the Suburban school; the other two schools had the same tendency but to a lesser extent.

Using the two year data to determine whether each functional potential group had a similar dropout experience, the k sample χ^2 test of homogeneity was then applied to each school separately. For the Urban and Rural colleges, there was an increasing trend in the proportion never dropping out and functional potential levels. Thirty-eight point six of the low FP group, 46.2 percent of the medium, and 51.2 percent of the high FP groups did not drop out from the Urban college, while 37.5 percent low, 51.0 percent medium and 62.5 percent high FP groups persisted in the Rural college. However, these trends were not statistically significant.

Among the Suburban college students, a definite increasing statistical trend existed between the proportion not dropping out of college and the functional potential groups. The percent of persisters were 37.9 percent, 45.4 percent, and 54.2 percent for the low, medium, and high groups respectively. This trend was demonstrated by χ^2 (2) = 7.55 ($p < .025$). Thus, differences were suggested among the three functional potential groups.

Drop/persist comparisons for the first- and second-year periods reinforced what most administrators and faculty already know—that the highest attrition occurs in the first year of college. In this particular study, early dropout is more common for students in the low functional potential group than for those in the high or medium groups. Forty-three and five-tenths percent of the low FP group dropped during their first year, 31.3 percent of the medium group, and 26.2 percent of the high group. These figures compared to a 61.8 percent drop in the low group by the end of the second year, 53.8 percent of the medium group, and 45.9 percent of the high group. One-year dropout data by school, exclusive of functional potential, were also examined by the χ^2 test of homogeneity. The Urban and Rural schools had 66.0 percent and 62.3 percent persistence among 701 and 215 students. On the other hand, the Suburban school had a 72.2 percent persistence rate among 960 students. This lead to a χ^2 (2) = 11.79 ($p < .01$), suggesting a significant difference among the three schools.

Drop/Stay/Unknown. Examination of the data after two years led to a χ^2 (2) = 1.49 (not significant). This revealed that with respect to dropout/persistence, all three schools had a similar experience, with about half of the known cases dropping and the other half of the known cases staying. For all three categories, a χ^2 (4) = 105.44 ($p < .001$) resulted. The Rural school had an equal number of students in each category, while the Urban and Suburban schools had many fewer unknowns.

The evidence suggests that the dropout rate is related to factors other than curricula, grading systems, methods of instruction, and so forth. However, the Urban school seems to do a better job of retaining its students than the Suburban school, which had a higher number in the High functional potential group and thus should have had a higher number of persisters. The Rural school seems to have more of the extremes. Within the first academic year, the Rural school had a large number of dropouts; but of those in this sample who did stay in school, a higher percentage received their associate degree after four semesters. Perhaps at this school, the "rule of the medium"—that schools attend chiefly to the average or middle student—does not apply. Indeed, it might be inferred that the Rural college makes less effort to hold its first-semester students; but if a student does persist during this initial term, he has a better chance of finishing his program than do students from either of the other two colleges in our sample population.

Dropout/Persist and Other Variables. Degrees and information about institutional transfers are other dependent variables that provide information about students and their colleges. For those students who persisted in college, the three 3-D institutions were quite different. The Urban school had the lowest percentage (17 percent) of students receiving the AA degree, while the Rural school had the highest percentage (74 percent). The Suburban school had about 24 percent receiving degrees. Thus, in this respect the Urban and Suburban schools are quite distinct from the Rural school ($\chi^2 = 104.9$ with 2 d.f., $p = < .0001$).

Now in School? With respect to attendance in school at the time of the follow-up assessment (end of two years), the Urban and Suburban schools were similar in that no dropouts were re-enrolled. In contrast, the Rural school had about 4 percent of their previous dropouts re-enrolled—an in/out phenomenon currently giving rise to the term *stopout,* which may be a better indicator of status than the term *dropout.*

Among the persisting group, the Suburban school had 75.4 percent of 319 students enrolled; the Urban and Rural schools had 83 percent and 241 and 64 students still remaining. A χ^2 (2) = 6.59 ($p < .05$) shows that these percentages differ among the three schools. From this information, it would seem that it takes some students more than two years to complete their programs. This extended time may be due to the stopout phenomenon previously noted, to the fact that some students take only a few school units, or to both factors.

Transfer? If one considers the number of dropouts from higher education rather than from a particular institution, attrition figures decrease markedly. This applies to both the Urban and Suburban colleges, where dropouts had similar institutional transfer experiences, and about 25 percent transferred. These results for the Urban and Suburban schools seem to indicate that the persisting group had a higher proportion transferring. In contrast to the dropout group, this increase ranged from about 10 percent for the Urban college to about 20 percent for the Suburban college. The Rural school had an insufficient number of cases (2) for comparison. However, like other information reported for the two-year period, the data in these cases may not be reliable because cumulative records had to be examined. In some cases these records were incomplete, and in others the information was ambiguous.

Transfer Where? With respect to school transfers among dropouts, Suburban college tended to have a higher proportion (63 percent) transferring to four-year institutions than the Urban college (50 percent). Again because of an insufficient number of cases, comparison for the Rural school was not possible. In comparison to the dropout group, a higher proportion of persisters at both the Urban and Suburban schools transferred to other institutions. This increase for both schools was approximately 25 percent. Again, the Rural school had an insufficient number of cases.

Group Cohesion and Drop/Persist. Group cohesion is a measure of relatedness to specific reference groups—peers, faculty, family, and the like. The analysis of variance was used to test whether group cohesion would relate to dropout within the first year. The group cohesion scores of the 398 dropouts had a Mean = 2.523 whereas the 885 who did not drop had a Mean = 2.982 (significant at the .01 level), thus suggesting that group cohesion scores are not the same for both dropouts and persisters.

Crucial Issues

Hidden in most studies of attrition is the assumption that persistence in school has a value of its own. If persistence is not a value, why is there such concern with the dropout? The issue stems from the belief that a college education is so undeniably desirable that any individual who fails to complete college is either misguided or inadequate. (Note how a value judgment is built into ". . . who fails to complete college." Why not ". . . who elects an alternative"?) For well over forty years, college attrition rates have remained much the same (Iffert, 1957), averaging approximately 50 percent. This is, of course, in spite of "stay-in-school" campaigns and threats of unemployment, and it seems unlikely that the redundant information supplied by so many studies of background data and selected student traits will alter this figure. Findings from most studies are inconclusive (Eckland, 1964; Pervin, Reik and Dalrymple, 1966; Mitchell and Moorehead, 1968; Panos and Astin, 1968), and organizational changes in the schools have not reduced the dropout rate.

Because the simplest measure of academic output is the number of students emerging from the system and because our society attaches special importance to the certification of its people, dropout is considered important as a way of viewing educational systems. Students who exit prematurely, before completing a standard cycle, are seen as dropouts or failures, depending on whether they have left voluntarily or have been rejected by the sorting mechanism of the system. Granted that the nonpersisters are not a total loss—that they do carry something useful away—"the important point is that societies and educational systems themselves make a sharp distinction between finished and unfinished products" (Coombs 1968, p. 65). The system's problem is that it judges itself by its output, and its output is the number of students who have *completed* a program. The individual's problem is that "in a society where educational attainments—symbolized by certificates and degrees—are closely linked to preferred categories of employment and to social status, the student who finishes has much more promising career prospects. The one who drops out or fails, on the other hand, burns important bridges to the future. . . . When the dropout rate is high, the managers of such a system can be tormented by a sense of guilt suspecting that they may have been the hand that cut off the dropout's future chance" (Coombs, 1968, pp. 65, 69).

In a selective system, specified percentages of students are pushed out—usually by examination—at various stages. In an open system, every person is given a chance and students must drop out if they are to leave. If students are prevented from deselecting themselves in high school, the process becomes "the dropout problem" at the junior college level. If junior colleges screened entering students, many young people would be denied the right of further education. If the staff encouraged dropout—for example, by assigning failing marks—the failures would have to accept the faculty judgment that "You're just not college material." If the schools accepted the responsibility for graduating all students, the dropout problem would be passed on to the four-year college.

Cohen and Brawer (1970) suggest that this ludicrous situation is the result of erroneous premises. A system that judges its worth by its finished products and a society that views certification as evidence of knowledge are the causes of the dropout problem. Instead of viewing students as the "input" and "output" of an educational factory, Laurits (1967) suggests that we need to view the school as a "field of force" and the students as "the charged particles which enter the field" at certain velocity and spin, each headed in a certain direction. Rather than a mass to be shaped, the student is a dynamic individual who reacts to and is influenced by the force field of education.

In light of these arguments, it seems clear that educators must ask new questions. Should the open-access policy change our negative attitude about dropout? Do we weaken ourselves in this mass exodus of people from institutions of higher education or is this just another feature of the kind of selectivity that apparently exists in a democracy which pledges itself to active education but simultaneously encourages passive (and sometimes not so passive) rebellion? If our basic trust in America today is to educate all who desire education through the fourteenth year, and in view of both the open-door policy of many junior colleges and some universities and the great diversity in certain dimensions of entering freshmen, is it reasonable to expect that attrition rates can be lowered? Much remains to be understood and to be done.

The very studies that swell the literature also serve to compound our confusion about attrition—its causes, the purposes it serves or fails to serve, and related social-economic-political questions. At this point, our knowledge of the dropout phenomenon is so clouded by value judgments and indecision about the future responsibility of higher education that we cannot ascertain the nature or extent of the problem. We have only a limited amount of knowledge about an issue that many people perceive to be a major problem of education today.

Despite this pessimistic view, some of the information now available is worth summarizing. For example, the family's influence on persistence/withdrawal in school appears to be a major consideration—whether in terms of the number of books in the home, the educational levels attained by the mother or by both parents, the socioeconomic status as measured by vocation or profession, the mobility patterns as reflected in the number of schools attended. Peer influence has also been isolated as a possible predictor of persistence in schooling, although less so than the ubiquitous GPA or tests of academic achievement administered previous to enrollment.

For the community college freshmen engaged in the 3-D Project, some differential results stand out as particularly interesting. The influence of the school seems to be less important than might be expected. While only three schools were engaged in this study and thus it is impossible to extend findings to a larger number of institutions, some diversity among these three schools is undoubtedly pervasive. However, Lombardi (1971) may be right in pointing to many similarities which are due merely to the fact that the schools are all junior colleges, even though the differences in geographical area, population, age, size, and a few other dimensions do suggest some heterogeneity. Yet, the attrition rates in these three schools—urban, suburban, and rural—are much the same. Some interschool differences did prevail—for example, the initial drop rate in the rural school exceeded those rates in the other schools, but the rates after two years and four semesters were amazingly similar. And of the differences still remaining, few were statistically significant.

The variable called group cohesion, or box scores, also provides a different approach to separating out the potential withdrawal. Simply stated, if an individual is not able to relate to other groups and other individuals, it is likely that he cannot see himself in a school situation when attendance is not forced. It is possible to be fairly isolated and still participate minimally when required to by a compulsory school attendance law that deems everyone in this country must attend school until he is sixteen years old or the unwritten "law" of high school completion. Whatever the hold, when the isolated or alienated individual is offered a choice of continuing or not continuing his schooling, he may succumb to the easiest alternative—to enter college because other choices (get a job, go on welfare) are less desirable. But when confronted with an alternative to persisting in college when he does not care about it, he may find it easier to withdraw than to continue. The basically isolated person may be encouraged to react in particular ways, but when left to his own devices in a situation that he cares little about in the first place, he may not persist.

As for ego strength, developmental level, maturity—however one defines the dimensions that I have described as functional potential—this variable does seem to bear watching as a predictor of college dropout. In most cases, the first-year dropout tended to be in the low functional potential group. Students constituting the high functional potential group were less likely to withdraw than were those in either the low or medium groups. Further investigation is needed to substantiate the notion that dropout is inversely related to functional potential, but the idea is notable and worth pursuing. Perhaps in the concept of ego functioning we can also find important predictors of persistence or premature withdrawal from school, and perhaps these predictors will aid in the development of programs that help to develop the individual in new ways.

Chapter 12

Implementing
the Theory

Facts and figures, rationales and theories, hypotheses to be accepted or rejected—what do they all mean? What does the functional potential concept hold for our understanding of college students? Given people and social institutions as they are, few major changes can or will be made in educational institutions within a period of a few months or a year. Yet, with enough time, or enough pressure, or enough enlightenment—whatever it takes—the data we gather and the ideas we advance eventually may be implemented in new programs, new curriculums, new approaches to helping people grow. How can college deans and counselors; institutional researchers; psychologists; and just those who would understand others, use the material presented in this context to facilitate educational planning and encourage personal development in the college students of tomorrow?

Ideas presented throughout this book provide some tentative directions. Most of these are based on certain assumptions that seem more and more appropriate as we advance in our understanding of human behavior—as, for example, that the study of man is a fascinating business but it must not start forever anew anymore than it must always refer back to Genesis. We are in a fortunate position with so much readily available literature from which to choose. And choose we can, freely taking and building on those theories that fit our own perceptions of human functioning or the way we like to look at people, born out of both experience and intuition, and ignoring those ideas that do not fit.

I have mentioned the necessity for a holistic approach to looking at the person—whether self or others. Thus, while independent variables are of interest and may even provide new information, their interpretation demands an amalgamation of many dimensions. Whatever notions are examined, whatever hypotheses tested, they become most useful when they can fit into a totality, the gestalt of the person and the situation.

At the same time, one person's way of integrating the singular events and traits that characterize man as a functioning human being may be quite different from the approach taken by another. Thus, in order to understand the individual—whether he be parent or spouse or sibling or child, student or instructor, peer or friend, political leader or the man on the street—a phenomenological approach is essential. It is important to get into the person's frame of reference—perhaps I should say, to *try* to adopt such a stance—since the task is a difficult one, at best, and one that may never be completely resolved. Even the attempt is significant, however, because it allows the type of perceptual view that makes for sensitive and accurate understanding.

Other assumptions prevail. We generally accept the notions, for example, that grade point averages and demographic data and scores on achievement tests do not tell the whole story about the way in which the college student of today functions; that cognitive dimensions tell us some things about the person but cannot explain everything, nor can they validly predict future behavior; that the person is part mind, but he is also feeling and psyche, conation and body. To look at any individual along singular dimensions is too narrow, too limiting. One's feelings are as important in guiding behavior as one's thinking—indeed, in a given situation, the person may act impulsively on sheer emotions rather than thinking out his actions and thereby utilizing different types of input. So often mind and body do not speak to each other, let alone work together.

Colleges now serve the so-called non-traditional student who, in another day, would not have thought about entering college and may be the first in his family to consider higher education as a rung on the ladder so often referred to as upper mobility. This is the student who Cross (1971) describes as typically less able, less well prepared to meet the challenges of the usual kinds of colleges, and thus, more in need of different types of educational experiences that are more meaningful to him and more relevant to his life. I concur with Cross's (1971) statement that there is a "New Student," especially in the community college, for whom traditional placement measures are inadequate if not inapplicable. Assessment methods must be designed for a developmental curriculum based on realistic views of these students' aptitudes, potentials, and goals, as well as accurate knowledge of the vocational opportunities they will encounter after college. The "traditional" student, too, must be evaluated in more than intellectual terms.

Over the years, many techniques have been developed. Based on numerous theoretical considerations for appraising human beings, these range from informal, often intuitive, approaches to projective devices to systematic and objective tests. In this book, I have presented one model that appears to have promise for implementation in educational institutions, whether these be community colleges, four-year colleges, multiversities, or alternative forms of education yet to be developed. This scheme is based on precise notions of functioning in the "normal" adolescent and adult. I have reported responses to a paper-and-pencil multivariant inventory—the freshman survey—as they relate to such variables as life styles or orientations, values, demographic information, future outlook, and family history. Primarily, though, the inventory responses have been interpreted in terms of functional potential—the core dimension described here as a way of appraising the person in a holistic, psychodynamic sense. While community college freshmen were the subjects for the 3-D project, I believe that other populations can serve equally well. These include students at different community colleges throughout the country and students at other types of postsecondary institutions as well as college faculty and other staff members—even the public at large. I think that limitations in the use of functional potential as the primary variable would be determined by age rather than occupational role, and I expect that most functioning older adolescents and adults could be assessed in the same way that we have evaluated our 1876 freshmen.

Functional potential indicates the ideal rather than the typical. In order to be effective and practical in the ways that I envision the concept to be, the approach to its assessment must be standardized on much wider populations and must prove to have both concurrent and predictive validity; the question of concurrence has been minimally dealt with in the chapter on the Omnibus Personality Inventory. Since a theory or an approach cannot be either proven or disputed over a short span of time with a limited number of respondents, much still remains to be done. For now, what can we say about functional potential as a way of looking at people? How does it compare with other methods of appraisal? Following are some conclusions:

(1) Functional potential is presented here as a new way of assessing individual development and ego functioning in community college freshmen. It appears to be a feasible approach that can be used with other populations operating in various situations.

(2) From the responses to two inventories—the Omnibus Personality Inventory and the freshman survey—a sizeable amount of information is now available about some 1,800 students enrolled as freshmen in three diverse but proximate community colleges.

(3) Functional potential, derived from selected responses to the freshman survey, appears to cut across many of the barriers commonly erected between people and across several variables by which they might be characterized. These include religion, ethnic background, and marital status.

(4) Functional potential appears to cut across schools. While the Suburban school had fewer students in the low functional potential group and a greater number of students in the high group, the other two schools in our sample claimed the same functional potential distribution among their students.

(5) Functional potential appears to be an accurate means

by which to predict completion of a school program. More students in the low functional group dropped out of school than did those in the other two groups.

(6) Most students in our three-college sample appear to fall below the norm for the Omnibus Personality Inventory (established on thirty-seven colleges and universities throughout the country, including four junior colleges). The higher the functional potential score earned by the student, however, the closer he is to the OPI norm.

(7) Functional potential seems to have concurrent validity with the Omnibus Personality Inventory, the two techniques showing a high correlation.

The rationale for functional potential was based on certain hypotheses that have been tried and tested and retested—hypotheses that draw heavily on theories of development, maturity, and ego strength. The construct is also founded on certain ideas about individual differences in many prescribed dimensions—an interesting phenomenon. If everyone were the same on a preponderant number of traits, if institutions were filled with homogeneous populations, how dull our lives would be. Man and the social institutions that he erects in order to enhance his own functioning are the better for the differences existing within him and them. This diversity is perceptible in the variations in the people within institutions, not in the institutions themselves. Indeed, on the surface, a number of social establishments appear very similar. The diversity lies *within* the organization, rather than among them.

Murray's (1938) individual needs–environmental press theory is also relevant, not only for assessing people operating in prescribed situations but as a means of predicting behavior. Whatever the level of individual development, both the environment and the "significant others" in a person's life play important roles. While the student at the highest level of functional potential may be less susceptible to a negative environment because he has more inner resources on which to rely, he can be influenced by these externals. Similarly, the person in the middle group may be also influenced by his environment—in fact, he is more likely to be buffeted about by it, more likely to react to negative external forces than to follow his own inner sense. Looking at the same kind of nonsupportive, threatening environment, however, the low functional potential person is most at the mercy of these outside presses because his own resources are less well developed. If the climate is supportive, he functions fairly well. If it is less than positive, he may cope in one of three ways: He can turn to another situation—to "split," in contemporary vernacular—even though the initiative required by such an act requires a bit more flexibility than is usually seen at this level. Or, rather than move away, he can sink into a state of apathy—dealing with the negative forces through mere acquiescence. He becomes the Caspar Milquetoast of our society—passively accepting through emotional, if not actual physical, retreat and, possibly, resentful and angry inside. Finally, as the third possibility, the low functional potential person can cope by fighting, by attacking the institutions that confront him. While all people can deal with situations by moving toward, moving against, or moving away, the less flexibility, sense of direction, and ability to look beyond the present individuals have, the more likely they are to be at the mercy of the situations with which they are confronted. They have few alternatives from which to choose.

Let us now turn to an idealistic perspective: Perhaps in a Utopian world most people would function at the highest possible levels—would be actualized adults, well individuated, closely related to their innermost selves. Although every person would not be able to attain the highest degree of development possible, at least he would be operating at his *own* highest level. This would mean that in the earliest years of life, parents and parental surrogates would meet the child's basic needs for security. Each infant and young child would be cuddled and nurtured. All physiological and emotional needs would be met in an atmosphere of love and security. In Rorschach terminology, the person would be able to readily offer differentiated shading responses, indicating "an awareness of and acceptance of affectional needs experienced in terms of desire for approval, belongingness, and response from others," needs that are believed to be "essential for the establishment of deep and meaningful object relations; . . . [this] occurs only where the basic security needs have been reasonably well satisfied" (Klopfer, 1954, p. 273). With his early needs for security met, the well-functioning individual shows that "the need for affection has developed sufficiently well and is integrated well enough with the rest of the personality organization that it has a sensitive control function, assisting the individual in his interaction with other people without implying a vulnerable overdependency on response from others" (Klopfer, 1954, p. 292).

Because these early needs have been met, other things can follow—providing that the ensuing experiences were deep and broad enough to permit a variation in response. These experiences would, of course, have to include unsuccessful, even frustrating moments— things that don't work out as well as those that do. In this way, the person has the opportunity to try alternate courses, devise different ways of coping with situations, or, if no recourse is available, to retreat and perhaps become stronger for the unsuccessful encounters.

A sense of identity rather than amorphism derives from both early experiences and later demands. As the developing individual grows, he learns to expect a certain amount of continuity within himself and in those with whom he interacts—especially the "significant others" in his life. His identity may depend on a number of factors, but it is something that he has a role in developing, that he controls, and that he knows is his.

From these same experiences, flexibility rather than rigidity is allowed to develop, and, in turn, this flexibility permits a wide latitude of reactions—the ability to act impulsively or to control more archaic forces, to show emotions and yet act within a framework of reality. The balance shifts with the situation, a further indication of flexibility, and it is appropriate for the person and the conditions.

These developing characteristics include also a balance between dependence and independence, progression and regression. One is truly independent only when he can be dependent. The person who functions at a high level of functional potential is able to strike a balance between progression and regression. For the most part, he moves forward—as a child, growing physically as well as emotionally, and, as an adult, continuing to grow both intellectually and emotionally. However, moments of regression have their place, and occasionally the person must step back and let the unconscious lead him, even if the path goes to more primitive responses. Only if he feels sure of himself and knows who he is, can he afford to allow the primitive to take over when necessary, secure in the knowledge that he can bounce back whenever necessary to more realistic phases.

Relatedness stems from early experiences. The infant relates to the person who feeds and cuddles and cares for him. In Utopia, no person would lack these early experiences of warmth that allow trust and love to develop. Aloofness may temporarily color the person's response to a particular situation, but his basic reaction is one of feeling with or relating to the other person.

Now that the ideal has been described, how do we turn objective data into ways of dealing with people who function in that social system we call school? What do the data tell us? How can they help us devise different school curriculums to encourage development, both cognitive and emotional, in all students, the traditional as well as the new? If we know what we want, how do we go about getting it? And can it be achieved? The answers must be ambivalent—yes and no—perhaps and of course.

In response to such broad questions, general answers must necessarily be given. Simply and succinctly, to talk about college students as a group is like talking about aggregates of people (most have two legs, two arms, two eyes). We can only repeat what so many others have said: "In general, junior college students fall below the means for college-going populations." With the exception of a few dimensions, this statement seems applicable to OPI scores as well as achievement scores on such instruments as the SCAT and ACT Testing Battery.

Broad questions followed by equally broad responses, however, are no more appropriate to contemporary ways of looking at people than are antiquated and inaccurate stereotypes of various religious or ethnic groups. Again, people are people—and they differ in ways both obvious and subtle. Since community college students are people, too, to view them only as "generally below" their counterparts at other institutions of higher education reveals a myopia that is potentially debilitating, even destructive—both for these students and for society as a whole.

Looking at the OPI data—information derived from several hundred students considered representative of college freshmen throughout the nation in the late 1960s and early 1970s—we see that many students involved in the 3-D project do not look at all like their peers enrolled in other postsecondary institutions. Thus, it seems ridiculous to present to these people the courses and curriculums that appear to be rewarding for students in four-year colleges and universities. Some junior college freshmen—those with low functional potential—just cannot relate to typical and traditional college patterns; in fact, they can never fit the typical academic patterns. Their college experiences must be tailored to their own interests, abilities, and personal bents. Since change is particularly difficult for these people, colleges must find ways of adjusting to them. The reverse will not hold.

But the preponderant number of students in our sample fall into the middle group. This is the group with which the junior college must primarily deal. Here again, however, one wonders whether the typical college curriculums can mean much to these nontraditional students, students who hear a different drummer. The world is large and the stimuli complex, and as everyone else, our 3-D subjects need training in more than vocational skills. Still, theoretical abstractions, esthetic emphases, and experiences that demand independent action and autonomous thinking are not recognized by the large number of students who fall within this group. Again, the schools must change; and the students must be given opportunities to try out various directions. Specific vocational training is only part of the answer for part of the students. They must be offered experiences that foster their independence, encourage their flexibility, let them move—but always within a structure that allows them to know who they are, what they are about, and how they can most effectively function in the world they will encounter outside of school.

A third group of community college students are functioning at the high functional potential level. Their OPI responses are more like those of students in four-year colleges and universities. Whether or not these students are enrolled in transfer programs in community colleges, they appear to be more amenable to traditional college programs. They are more intellectually and esthetically oriented, more independent in their thinking. They are more tolerant of ambiguity and adapt a "live and let live" attitude toward religion. These are the students who are border-line in the sense that they could fit fairly well into either the university or the community college. For some instructors in the junior college, they are the pet students, the ones who "understand" their teachers, who are more likely to fit the expected patterns of college development.

Overall, the findings presented throughout this book suggest that measures of ego functioning can be used as the basis for adjusting schools to people, rather than trying to twist all students into traditional molds that apply to only relatively few. As Jencks (1972) points out, since we do not know what school environment makes a difference in student learning and since there is a strong suggestion that school alone accounts for little of the variability in cognitive and emotional growth, maybe the best we can hope for is that schools become more humane, more satisfying to all who spend portions of their lives in them—in short, more pleasant places to be.

The suggestions that follow are based on theses similar to that proposed by Jencks, as well as upon findings from the freshman survey responses. These indicate, in short, that most of the 3-D students test considerably lower on salient personality characteristics and intellectual disposition (OPI) than the established norm group and that they are at the middle or low functional potential groups. How can schools, then, provide environments that are pleasing, not harmful, and possibly helpful? How can they encourage students to develop to their highest potential—that long-touted, seldom-realized goal? If education is a dynamic force that directs social behavior, then it is necessary to view it according to two perspectives. These can be considered in terms of the concepts of *interaction* and *effect*.

It is not possible to consider people or groups or major institutions in isolation. The person must be seen functioning as a member of various groups, in terms of his own frame of reference and the reciprocal situations called interaction. We are a secular nation and cannot divorce ourselves from other people, the community, or the world as a whole. Such people as Kurt Lewin and Henry Murray have left a mark upon our way of viewing such interaction. Lewin, who was primarily concerned with group dynamics, emphasized the need for studying interaction processes, while Murray suggested an approach that considered both the person and his environment. His need-press rationale has become the basis for a considerable amount of work that looks at both the individual, with his needs, and the environment, with the pressures it places upon that individual.

Whether looking at elementary, secondary, or higher education, we need to think of students, faculty, and associated personnel as individuals, with their idiosyncratic desires and the sundry demands placed upon them, as well as people operating in reciprocal situations. The student is not completely acted upon by any teacher or teachers, but he interacts with them—at least this is what education ostensibly is all about. Similarly, the faculty cannot be viewed as a discrete body of associated members but as individuals, each of whom has an effect upon the people with whom he interacts. Any educational enterprise must be seen in terms of its personnel, and then that view must be extended to the community or society in which it is housed. One school may not have much effect on the city, but an aggregate of schools, affecting people in various ways, is bound to have some impact on society.

The second concept with which we are concerned here is that of effect. At one time one merely assumed that, because a person had some schooling, he was therefore "educated." Until 1957, when the Jacob report first suggested that schooling might not be influencing its students as society expected, our assumptions about the effects of education remained more or less unquestioned. A considerable amount of research concerned with problems of effect culminated in the late 1960s in the thesis that the most obvious result of education can be seen only in terms of observed behavioral change. Such a premise is predicated upon the notion that teaching is firmly interwoven with *learning*—that is, if no learning has ensued, teaching has not taken place.

In the last few decades, the community college has grown at an unprecedented rate and now enrolls a vast number of students. Efforts have only recently been made to evaluate this institution, however, and while some of these efforts have been well executed in terms of design and well founded on the basis of some— although limited—theoretical structures, most have compiled masses of data used to support optimistic expectations. These hardly form guidelines for institutional development. At this stage, it is important to look at the community college in terms of many variables.

Interaction and effect are two of the most salient, while others are founded in psychological and sociological theories that attempt to understand individual functioning and predict human behavior. Still different variables may be found in other disciplines.

Not so long ago, a high school education was considered to be a union card that would permit most people to enter a fair level of occupational endeavor. In recent years we have begun to consider the fact that even a bachelor's degree may be hardly sufficient if one is to have a variety of occupational choices open to him. And, for the next part of the twentieth century, the mean number of years of schooling will probably be thirteen or fourteen years. In thinking about the two-year college, we need also to think of education at other institutions that incorporate a thirteenth or fourteenth year. Accordingly we propose to center our attention on the two-year community college but to entertain the idea that the two-year college also duplicates many activities of university extension centers and, therefore, any attempt to look at these activities must be seen in a broad context of society and its social institutions.

Erikson (1963) defines the adolescent mind as "essentially a mind of moratorium, a psychosocial stage . . . an ideological mind" (pp. 262–263). Using this observation as a partial basis for interpreting the information gleaned from selected responses to the freshman survey, I would like to propose the Thirteenth Year for the community college freshman who needs time to explore in an unpressured environment. It differs from the typical first year of college in several respects, one of which is a revised time element. Instead of fitting programs into a span of several months, the idea of finite time would be eliminated or at least modified. Time, of course, cannot stand still, but what one does with it can—and does—vary considerably. The idea of breaking out of this time barrier is somewhat similar to the thesis developed by Arthur Cohen in *Dateline '79*. However, it differs in that the responsibility for this period is put on the shoulders of the student rather than the school.

In fact, the Thirteenth Year could be a few weeks or more than twelve months, but the time involved would be determined by the students. The student coming out of high school who falls into our high functional potential area might complete the Thirteenth Year in just one day. Another student might require a few weeks in a college setting where he could explore opportunities and better settle on who he is and where he is going. And still another person—the one with low functional potential—not sure of self, rather amorphous and without a firm sense of identity—might well require more than twelve months of his Thirteenth Year. In other words, time becomes fluid, and the individual himself determines how much time he needs. This decision requires some sense of responsibility and the ability to judge what is required, but during this Thirteenth Year the person will associate with others with whom he can talk and interact. He will get help in arriving at a decision at the appropriate time for him.

Beyond this difference in the concept of time, the notion of the Thirteenth Year has other aspects. For example, if the Thirteenth Year is to effectively resolve some of the problems in education today—dissatisfaction, irrelevance, attrition—we have to think about development from more than a cognitive standpoint. Development must be total—cognitive and affective. And to encourage such development, the environmental setting must be positive rather than punishing. Nonpunitive grading policies are a minimum requirement. Most people cannot develop into the self-actualized individuals we conceive of as being most integrated if they must continually battle forces that are negative and unrewarding. Let the Thirteenth Year be one in which the person can explore ideas and self in a climate of structured flexibility.

Structured flexibility? An oxymoron? It is feasible. How about an educational institution—a community college—that remains the same in terms of physical setting but throws away preregistration forms and registration regalia along with grades, curricular tracking, and course prerequisites? One that allows a person to enter a course or class or program, stay as long as he wants, and meet certain specified objectives or move on to something else before he fulfills them? One that believes that what turns one person on may not interest another, and that people must be given opportunities to choose from many courses and many media—autotutorial, structured lectures, self-study, audiovisual? Imagine one person walking into a course on Shakespeare and assuming the role of Hamlet or Lady Macbeth or King Lear in a formal production of the bard's work. Or another reading Shakespeare's sonnets alone but ingesting and enjoying them. Or still another who encounters the language and the style of the Shakespearean world and after an hour decides that it isn't for him. Alternatives would be there; it would be up to the students to find them.

The same flexibility could pertain to other programs—ranging from the most esoteric to vocational courses. College presidents and institutional planners need not revamp their programs completely but they do need to adopt different ways of thinking about them. They must allow students the privilege of making decisions. Some community college educators do pay particular attention to the humanizing, developmental aspects of their programs. But financial support patterns, legislation, district policies—bureaucratic rules in general—are not typically focused on individual student concerns. In order to counteract this lack of focus the educator must be especially attuned to the ways his college enhances or retards student development.

Earlier we talked about ego strength and the fact that various experiences both positive and negative can encourage its development. Functional potential is based on the notion that people can develop flexibility, a sense of identity, and heightened self-awareness if they have an environment that allows for the expression of these characteristics: a permissive setting with a clear-cut structure, an institutional administrative staff and faculty that believe students must be provided with opportunities to explore, to know. How different this environment is from the more rigid situation in which one must preenroll months ahead, meet specific requirements, do what everyone else does, and, perhaps, in order to cope at all, shrink back, drop out, or vehemently protest an educational situation that is unrelated, unfeeling, and inflexible.

One of the enigmas of twentieth-century society is that as schools increase in comprehensiveness, the individuals who attend those schools tend to specialize. Are we then seeing, in essence, a slightly altered version of Jung's theory of the opposites in the sense that an experience of one kind leads to the opposite behavior? And is that what we would choose for ourselves and for our children? If we are content with education today and man's place in society, then we accept the situation. If we believe that life could—should—must be different, then we think of various possibilities, directions, and alternatives.

I believe that the Thirteenth Year concept could work for every person at some critical phase of his life. It seems especially logical after the individual has finished high school and before he goes on to either college or the working world. For some people, however, a moratorium—a period wherein one can ponder past, present, and future directions—might be most appropriate at either an earlier or later time—even at that period which Jung describes as the second half of life.

The comprehensive community college may not be the educational structure that best accommodates a variety of people at varied stages of development. Perhaps institutional specialization is called for. Using the structure of personality presented in the concept of functional potential and the community college as our unit of analysis, three institutions seem warranted. The first is specialized, concentrating on technical programs that allow the student to move from the enunciation of a precise goal (to be a computer programmer, a paraprofessional technician) to sufficient expertise to implement his goal. The second institution is also specialized, but this school offers only transfer programs which guarantee the student who has mastered them direct entrance to that college which acts as the upper-division institution for this feeder community college. The programs it offers would parallel those offered by the four-year colleges and universities, and articulation between these institutions would be so clear that difficulties with prerequisites, comparable course requirements, and grades would be eliminated. The use of defined objectives in both the feeder college and the upper-division institutions would aid in easing the transition for students who complete the programs and do transfer—conceivably, a much larger proportion than is typically the case today.

In both cases, the institutions would not be comprehensive. They would not offer something for everyone because their leaders would have abandoned the belief that any one institution can be "all things to all people." These two community colleges would have declared their intentions and, based on defined notions of what they are and what they are supposed to be doing, would become expert technical schools or excellent transfer institutions. They would consider student emotional development as important as cognitive development and would see the total person. But because students attending these institutions would be fairly sure of themselves, operating at middle or high levels of functional potential, greater emphasis could be put on cognitive learning and less on providing facilities that encourage people to know themselves better.

The third community college would be built most heavily on the Thirteenth Year concept. Just how this idea would be implemented would vary with the institution, its previous effectiveness and its commitment to the total development of the student. This implementation would take time, thought, effort—and dedication. Only if an institution becomes dissatisfied with its old methods of operation, only if it decides that new times demand new techniques and new theories, will it want to make this effort.

Academic institutions must integrate into their curriculums the considerable knowledge now available about the diverse ways in which people function. They must replace comprehensiveness in words and intent by appropriate programs for aiding the person in his development. Only then will each individual become the well individuated, well integrated person he has the potential to be. Only then will society look at its people as people and be able to profit from their accurate and sensitive perceptions. I think the time has come. In fact, it is long overdue.

Appendix

List of Items
Included in Variables

Modes

Relatedness/Aloofness

HEADING

How close would you say you have been to your father? to your mother?

Which figure or figures in the boxes below best describe how you see yourself in relation to the different groups listed?

People feel about and relate to others in different ways. In the

STATEMENT

Extremely close
(Mother) (Father)
Quite close
(Mother) (Father)
Somewhat close
(Mother) (Father)

Most students at this school
My family
My gang or group of friends
Student organizations
My teachers
My neighborhood
Other people where I work

I feel most of the people I know mean what they say.

list below, mark all items that apply to the way you usually feel.

Why did you choose this college?

My parents wanted me to come to this school.

If your mother is working outside the home do you think she would prefer to

Continue to work
Stay at home

Basically, regardless of sex, which parent do you think you are more like?

Father
Mother

I felt especially proud of my mother, father, or other member of my family.

Often, sometimes

How do your parents react to your thinking?

They feel I am mistaken in my opinions but think that I will get over them.
They feel I am mistaken in my ideas and seriously doubt whether I will ever "return to the fold."
They take my ideas seriously and respect my differences as reasonable choices.

How much do you worry about choosing an occupation?

It bothers my folks more than it does me.

Identity/Amorphism

HEADING

STATEMENT

When I was 10

I felt especially proud of my mother, father, or other member of my family.

What do you think your college major will be?

States major

When did you decide on your college major?

6th grade or earlier
7th through 9th grade
In high school
After high school but before college

Pick three of the following occupations that appeal to you.

States occupation

How definite is your choice of major?

Very definite
Fairly definite, but still considering other possibilities
Have some idea but could use some help

Flexibility/Rigidity

HEADING

STATEMENT

Who should have the major responsibility for educational policies in junior college?

Board of Trustees
The administration (president, deans)
The faculty
The students
Others

What do you think will be characteristic of this campus? What would you like? If the statement describes a condition, event, etc., that you think will be true of this college, mark the T column. If you think it will not be true, mark the F column. If you would like a characteristic to be true, mark L, if not, mark NL.

Students are encouraged to criticize administrative policies and teaching practices. (L)
The school offers many opportunities for students to understand and criticize important works in art, music and drama. (L)
Students are actively concerned about national and international affairs. (L)
Many famous people are brought to the campus for lectures, concerts, student discussions. (L)

How do you see yourself when compared with the average college freshman? Rate yourself on each of the following traits.

Originality, creativity (Above Average)

Now, please choose 3 of the below traits on which you would like to be above average and mark the item.

Originality, creativity

If you have a goal in mind, how

Yes, but when I achieve this

do you feel about your chances to achieve it?

goal, I'll have to go on to another.

Independence/Dependence

HEADING

What do you think will be characteristic of this campus? What would you like? If the statement describes a condition, etc., that you think will be true of this college, mark the T column. If you think it will not be true mark the F column. If you would like a characteristic to be true, mark L, if not, mark NL.

STATEMENT

Many older students play an active role in helping new students adjust to campus life. (L)
The instructors go out of their way to help you. (L)
Students ask permission before doing something different from common policies or practices. (L)

If you were told that all classes and all work were canceled for the following day, how would you spend your time?
When I was 10

Feeling lost

I had or wished I had a dog, cat, or other animal I could cuddle and care for—often, sometimes.

Progression/Regression

HEADING

What do you think will be characteristic of this campus? What would you like? If the statement describes a condition, etc., that you think will be true to this college, mark the T column. If you think it will not be true mark the F column. If you would like a characteristic to be true, mark L, if not, mark NL.

STATEMENT

Students set high standards of achievement for themselves. (L)

What is your best guess that you will do any of the following?

Transfer to another college or university after obtaining an A.A. degree (Good chance)

How do you see yourself when

Ambition (Above Average)

compared with the average college freshman?

When compared with the average college freshman, what do you think your chances of future success will be?

Better

What would you like to be doing five years from now?

Preparing for a profession (e.g., law, medicine, academic requiring a doctorate)

How do you usually think and feel?

If I were to apply to another college, I'd choose one that I really want to go to even if my chances of getting in are uncertain.

In the list below, mark all items that apply to the way you usually feel.

I believe that if I work hard, things will work out for me.
I don't think things will ever work out right for me.

Delay of Gratification/Impulsive Expression

HEADING

STATEMENT

What would you like to be doing five years from now?

In graduate school
Preparing for a profession (law, medicine, academic requiring a doctorate)

How do you usually think and feel?

All too often the present is filled with unhappiness. It's only the future that counts. . . . Although we do not know what is happening we must plan ahead. . . . I find it hard to plan in advance.

People feel about and relate to others in different ways.

I believe that if I work hard, things will work out for me.

Orientations

Ideas

HEADING

STATEMENT

Facilities, procedures, policies, requirements, attitudes, etc., dif-

Most courses are a real intellectual challenge.

fer from one campus to another. What do you think will be characteristic of this campus? What would you like?

How do you see yourself when compared with the average college freshman?

Now, please choose the traits on which you would like to be above average and mark the items.

The question of a vocation or occupation is important to all of us. We would like to know your ideas about the kind of career or careers you might be considering.

Sometimes it seems important to have an idea of where you're going. What would you like to be doing five years from now?

If suddenly you were told that all classes and all work were canceled for the following day, how would you spend your time?

Look over each of the following items. In the first column, mark those items that represent the way you see yourself.

Now, please mark three items that represent the way you *would like* to be seen by others.

If your house or apartment were burning, what would be the first thing you'd rescue after people and pets?

Careful reasoning and clear logic are valued most highly in grading students papers, reports, or discussions.

Academic ability
Mathematical ability
Writing ability

Academic ability
Mathematical ability
Writing ability

College teaching
 (1st, 2nd, and 3rd choice)

Lawyer
 (1st, 2nd, and 3rd choice)

Scientific research work
 (1st, 2nd, and 3rd choice)

Preparing for a profession
 (e.g., law, medicine, academic requiring a doctorate)

Reading a novel

A creative individual
A brilliant student

A creative individual
A brilliant student

A pile of books
My class notes

Esthetics

HEADING

The college environment

STATEMENT

The school offers many opportunities for students to understand and criticize important works in art, music, drama.

How do you see yourself when compared with the average college freshman?

Originality, creativity
Artistic ability

Now please choose three of the below traits on which you would like to be above average.
Pick three of the following occupations that appeal to you.

Artistic ability
Originality, creativity

Artist, musician, actor, etc.
   (1st, 2nd, 3rd choice)

If your house or apartment were burning what would be the first *thing* you'd rescue after people and pets?

Art objects

Others

HEADING

Facilities, procedures, policies, requirements, attitudes, etc., differ from one campus to another. What do you think will be characteristics of this campus? What would you like?

STATEMENT

This school has a reputation for being friendly.

It's easy to get a group together for card games, singing, going to the movies, etc.

Students are actively concerned about national and international affairs.

What is your best guess that you will do any of the following?

Be elected to student office
   (Good chance)
Join a social club
   (Good chance)

How do you see yourself when compared with the average col-

Leadership ability
   (Above average)

lege freshman? Rate yourself on each of the following traits as you really think you are when compared with the average student of your own age.

Popularity
  (Above average)

Now, please choose three (3) of the below traits on which you would like to be above average.

Leadership ability
Popularity

The question of a vocation or occupation is important to all of us. We would like to know your ideas about the kind of career or careers you might be considering.

Doctor or dentist
  (1st, 2nd, 3rd choice)

Elementary school teaching
  (1st, 2nd, 3rd choice)

High school teaching
  (1st, 2nd, 3rd choice)

Minister, priest, rabbi
  (1st, 2nd, 3rd choice)

Nurse
  (1st, 2nd, 3rd choice)

Social worker
  (1st, 2nd, 3rd choice)

Sometimes it seems important to have an idea of where you're going. What would you like to be doing five years from now?

In politics

Look over each of the following items. In the first column, mark those items that represent the way you see yourself.

Most popular

In the second column, mark those that represent the way you think you appear to others.

Most popular

If your house or apartment were burning, what would be the first *thing* you'd rescue after people and pets?

Some pictures of friends and myself

People feel about and relate to others in different ways. In the list below, mark all items that apply to the way you usually feel.

I enjoy working in cooperation with others in a group undertaking.

Practical

HEADING

Please mark the oval in the T column (true or mostly true) for all items that you feel applied to your high school experiences and those that you feel will apply to this school.

What will characteristics of this campus be?

What is your best guess that you will do any of the following?

Pick *three* of the following occupations that appeal to you. Mark the appropriate oval to indicate that which is most appealing, second most, and third most appealing.

If you could do anything you wanted to do this year, which of the following most appeals?

Sometimes it seems important to have an idea of where you're going. What would you like to be doing five years from now?

STATEMENT

There are not enough good courses that mean good jobs.

Offers many really practical courses such as typing, report writing, etc.
Students are conscientious about taking good care of school facilities.

Select a major field
(Good chance)
(Some chance)

Make a career choice
(Good chance)
(Some chance)

Business (administration)
(1st, 2nd, and 3rd choice)

Business (bookkeeping, secretarial, etc.)
(1st, 2nd, and 3rd choice)

Owner of my own business
(1st, 2nd, and 3rd choice)

Sales
(1st, 2nd, and 3rd choice)

Working at a good paying job and saving money so that I could go to a different school

Holding down a good job with a steady income

People feel about and relate to others in different ways.

I believe that if I work hard, things will work out for me.

Motor

HEADING

STATEMENT

How do you see yourself when compared with the average college freshman?

Above average:
    Mechanical ability

Choose 3 traits on which you would like to be above average.

Mechanical ability

Pick 3 of the following occupations that appeal to you.

Farming

Forestry or conservation

Military career

Other medical (X-ray, etc.)

Technical

If suddenly you were told that all classes and all work were canceled for the following day, how would you spend your time?

Going for a walk or ride

Look over each of the following items, mark those items that represent the way you see yourself.

See myself: An athletic star

Would like: An athletic star

School Directedness

HEADING

STATEMENT

People attend college for many different reasons, some of which are listed.

Get training for a job, acquire skills
Get a basic general education and appreciation of ideas
Learn more about people
Learn more about community and world problems
Develop moral and ethical standards
Develop talents and creative abilities

	Attain a satisfactory emotional and social adjustment Other
Why did you choose this college?	I hope to get my grades up and enter a four-year college or university.
How many of your H.S. teachers and/or counselors affected your life in the way specified below?	Helped me work out financial problems
When people get in trouble in school, what do you think should happen to them?	It's none of my business. They should be expelled. Should see a counselor who can help them Should be given a warning and a second chance Their parents should take care of them. They should be allowed to express themselves as individuals in whatever way they see fit.
When did you definitely make up your mind to go to college?	I always assumed that I would go. While in elementary school In junior high school In high school After graduation from H.S. While I was in the military
Do you plan to transfer to another school? If yes, when?	Next semester After one year After two years Undecided
Applied to your H.S.	I think the school is generally good.
About this school?	There are not enough good courses that mean good jobs. The teachers don't know how to dig students.
Facilities, procedures, policies,	It's easy to get a group together

requirements, attitudes, etc., which are true or false about *this campus.*

for card games, singing, going to movies, etc.

Students are encouraged to criticize administrative policies and teaching practices.

The school offers many opportunities for students to understand and criticize important works in art, music, and drama.

Students are actively concerned about national and international affairs.

Many famous people are brought to the campus for lectures, concerts, student discussions.

Student publications never make fun of dignified people or institutions.

Most courses are a real intellectual challenge.

Students set high standards of achievement for themselves.

Most courses require intensive study and preparation out of class.

Would like to be a characteristic of this school.

Students are conscientious about taking good care of school property.

Students are expected to report any violation of rules and regulations.

Students ask permission before doing something different from common policies or practices.

Impact of Significant Others

Heading	Statement
Is this your first term enrolled in any college?	Yes No
How many units are you carrying?	11 or less 12 or more

Among your circle of friends in H.S., about how many went to college?

All, or nearly all
Most
About half
Very few
Have no idea

How must did you participate in various activities in H.S.?

Foreign student exchange

People attend college for many different reasons, some of which are listed below.

Be with friends

Why did you choose this college?

My best friend goes here.
I hope to get my grades up and enter a four-year college or university.
My parents wanted me to come to this school.
I like the social life associated with this campus.
Heard or read about this college in its catalogue or from radio, T.V., newspapers
Other

How many of your H.S. teachers and/or counselors affected your life in the way specified below?

Took an interest in me
Helped me to work out my educational plans
Helped me with my vocational plans
Helped me to understand my aptitudes and interests
Helped me with my personal problems
Helped me with my studies
Helped me to see the kind of person I would like to be

If you had complete choice in the matter, what kind of school would you most like to be attending?

State University
State college
This school
Another J.C.
A liberal arts school
A school in Europe
Technical or professional school

Do you plan to transfer to another school?	Yes No
Who should have the major responsibility for educational policies in the junior college?	Board of trustees The administration The faculty The students Others
All items which applied to your H.S.	The people who plan school programs don't know how we really feel. Schools are out of date. There is too much thinking involved and not enough feeling. People who rebel don't know how grateful they should be for the chance to go to school. There are not enough good courses that mean good jobs.
Facilities, procedures, policies, requirements, etc., this campus	Careful reasoning and clear logic are valued most highly in grading student papers, reports, or discussions.
What would you like?	Frequent tests are given in most courses.
	There is a recognized group of student leaders on this campus.
	Students are encouraged to criticize administrative policies and teaching practices.
	Students are actively concerned about national and international affairs.

Group Cohesiveness

Heading	Statement
People often feel differently with different groups and in different situations.	

Which figure or figures in the boxes below best describe how you see yourself in relation to the different groups listed.

Most students at this school
My family
My gang or group of friends
Student organizations
My teachers
My neighborhood
Other people where I work

Bibliography

ABBAS, R. D. *Interpersonal Values of the Junior College and University Student.* Columbia: NDEA Institute, University of Missouri, 1968. (ED 023 390)

ABE, C., AND OTHERS. *A Description of American College Freshmen.* Research Report 1. Iowa City: American College Testing Program, 1965.

Activity, Nov. 1970, *8* (4).

ADELSON, J. "The Teacher as a Model." In N. Sanford (Ed.), *The American College.* New York: Wiley, 1962.

ADLER, A. "Individual Psychology." In C. Murchison (Ed.), *Psychologies of 1930.* Worchester, Mass.: Clark University, 1930.

ADLER, A. *The Individual Psychology of Alfred Adler; A Systematic Presentation in Selections from His Writings.* H. L. Ansbacher and R. R. Ansbacher (Eds.). New York: Basic Books, 1956.

ADORNO, T. W., AND OTHERS. *The Authoritarian Personality.* New York: Harper and Row, 1950.

ALLEN, M. G. "The Development of Universal Criteria for the Measurement of the Health of a Society." *Journal of Social Psychology,* 1962, *57* (2), 363–382.

ALLPORT, G. W. "Attitudes." In C. C. Murchison (Ed.), *A Handbook of Social Psychology.* Worchester, Mass.: Clark University, 1935.

ALLPORT, G. W. *Personality: A Psychological Interpretation.* New York: Holt, Rinehart, and Winston, 1937.

ALLPORT, G. W. *Pattern and Growth in Personality.* New York: Holt, Rinehart, and Winston, 1961.

ALLPORT, G. W. *The Person in Psychology.* Boston: Beacon Press, 1968.

ALLPORT, G. W., AND ODBERT, H. S. "Trait-Names, a Psycho-Lexical Study." *Psychological Monographs,* 1936, *47* (1).

ALLPORT, G. W., AND VERNON, P. E. *Study of Values.* Boston: Houghton Mifflin, 1931.

ALLPORT, G. W., VERNON, P. E., AND LINDZEY, G. *Study of Values.* (3rd ed.) Boston: Houghton Mifflin, 1960.

American Association of Junior Colleges. *To Work in a Junior College.* Washington, D.C., 1966. (ED 032 886)

American College Testing Program. *The Two-Year College and Its Students: An Empirical Report.* Iowa City, Iowa, 1969. (ED 035 404)

ANDERSON, C. C., AND CÔTÉ, A. D. J. "Belief Dissonance as a Source of Disaffection Between Ethnic Groups." *Journal of Personality and Social Psychology,* 1966, *4,* 447–453.

ASTIN, A. W. "An Empirical Characterization of Higher Educational Institutions." *Journal of Educational Psychology,* 1962, *53,* 224–235.

ASTIN, A. W. "Personal and Environmental Factors Associated With College Drop-Outs Among High Aptitude Students." *Journal of Educational Psychology,* 1964, *55* (4), 219–227.

ASTIN, A. W. *Who Goes Where to College?* Chicago: Science Research Associates, 1965.

ASTIN, A. W., AND HOLLAND, J. L. "The Environmental Assessment Technique: A Way to Measure College Environments." *Journal of Educational Psychology,* 1961, *52* (6), 308–316.

BAIRD, L. L., RICHARDS, J. M., JR., AND SHEVEL, L. R. "A Description of Graduates of Two Year Colleges." Iowa City, Iowa: American College Testing Program, 1969. (ED 026 998)

BARRON, F. *Creativity and Psychological Health.* Princeton, N.J.: Van Nostrand, 1963.

BARRON, F. "An Ego Strength Scale Which Predicts Response to Psycho-Therapy." *Journal of Counseling Psychology,* 1953, *17,* 327–333.

BARRON, F. "Personal Soundness in University Graduate Students; An Experimental Study of Young Men in the Sciences and Professions." *Publications in Personality Assessment and Research #1*. Berkeley: University of California, 1954.

BARTON, A. H. "Measuring the Values of Individuals." *Religious Education*, 1962, *57* (4), 62–97.

BERDIE, R. F. "Validities of the Strong Vocational Interest Blank." In W. L. Layton (Ed.), *The Strong Vocational Interest Blank: Research and Uses*. Minneapolis: University of Minnesota, 1960.

BERDIE, R. F., AND HOOD, A. B. *Decisions for Tomorrow*. Minneapolis: University of Minnesota, 1965.

BETTELHEIM, B. *The Children of the Dream*. New York: Macmillan, 1969.

BINET, A. *L'Étude expérimentale de l'Intelligence*. Paris: Alfred Costes, 1902.

BLAI, B., JR. "Values and Attitudes of Harcum Students and Faculty-Staff." Bryn Mawr, Pa.: Office of Research, Harcum Junior College, 1970. (unpublished)

BLOOM, B. S. *Stability and Change in Human Characteristics*. New York: Wiley, 1964.

BLUM, G. S. "Revised Scoring System for Research Use of the Blacky Pictures." (unpublished)

BOLTON, C. D., AND KAMMEYER, K. C. W. *The University Student; a Study of Student Behavior and Values*. New Haven, Connecticut: College and University Press, 1967.

BOSSEN, D. A., AND BURNETT, C. W. "What Happens to the Withdrawal Student?" *Junior College Journal*, June–July 1970, *40* (9), 30–36.

BRAWER, F. B. "The Concept of Ego Strength and Its Measurement Through a Word Association Technique." University of California, Los Angeles, 1967. (unpublished)

BRAWER, F. B. *The Person: A Conceptual Synthesis*. ERIC Clearinghouse for Junior Colleges, Topical Paper #11. Los Angeles, University of California, 1970. (ED 037 219)

BRAWER, F. B. *Personality Characteristics of College and University Faculty*. ERIC Clearinghouse for Junior Colleges, Monograph #3. Washington, D.C.: American Association of Junior Colleges, 1968. (ED 026 048)

BRAWER, F. B. *Values and the Generation Gap*. ERIC Clearinghouse for Junior Colleges, monograph #11. Washington, D.C.: American Association of Junior Colleges, 1971. (ED 050 724)

BRAWER, F. B., AND COHEN, A. M. "Global and Sign Approaches to Rorschach Assessment of Beginning Teachers." *Journal of Projective Techniques,* Dec. 1966, *30* (6), 536–542.

BROWN, D. (Ed.) *Social Changes and the College Student.* Washington, D.C.: American Council on Education, 1960.

BUHLER, C. "Basic Theoretical Concepts of Humanistic Psychology." *American Psychologist,* Apr. 1971, *26* (4), 378–386.

BUROS, O. K. (Ed.) *Fifth Mental Measurements Yearbook.* Highland Park, N.J.: Gryphon Press, 1959.

BUROS, O. K. (Ed.) *Sixth Mental Measurements Yearbook.* Highland Park, N.J.: Gryphon Press, 1965.

BUSHNELL, J. "Student Culture at Vassar." In N. Sanford (Ed.), *The American College.* New York: Wiley, 1962.

CATLIN, R. "Ego Functioning and Regression in College Students." In D. L. Farnsworth and G. B. Blaine, Jr. (Eds.), *Counseling and the College Student.* Boston: Little, Brown, 1970.

CATTELL, J. MC B. "Mental Tests and Measurements." *Mind,* 1890, *15.*

CATTELL, R., SAUNDERS, D., AND STICE, G. *The Sixteen Personality Factor Questionnaire.* Champaign, Illinois: Institute of Personality and Ability Testing, 1949.

CHICKERING, A. W. *Education and Identity.* San Francisco: Jossey-Bass, 1971.

CHICKERING, A. W. "Institutional Objectives and Student Development in College." *Journal of Applied Behavioral Science,* 1967, *3* (3), 287–304.

CHICKERING, A. W. "Institutional Size and Student Development." Paper presented at the CAJC Conference on Factors Affecting Student Development in College, 1965.

CHRISTENSON, J. "Clinical Assessment of Ego Strength." *International Record of Medicine,* 1951, *164.*

Chronicle of Higher Education, Jan. 10, 1972a, *6* (14).

Chronicle of Higher Education, Feb. 14, 1972b, *6* (19).

CLARK, B. R. *The Open Door College: A Case Study.* New York: McGraw-Hill, 1960.

CLARK, B. R., AND TROW, M. "The Organizational Context." In T. M. Newcomb and E. K. Wilson (Eds.), *College Peer Groups: Problems and Prospects for Research.* Chicago: Adeline, 1966.

COHEN, A. M. *Dateline '79: Heretical Concepts for the Community College.* Beverly Hills, Calif.: Glencoe Press, 1969.

COHEN, A. M., AND BRAWER, F. B. "Adaptive Potential and First-Year

Teaching Success." *Journal of Teacher Education,* Summer 1967, *18* (2), 179–184.

COHEN, A. M., AND BRAWER, F. B. *Confronting Identity: The Community College Instructor.* Englewood Cliffs, N.J.: Prentice-Hall, 1972.

COHEN, A. M., AND BRAWER, F. B. *Focus on Learning—Preparing Teachers for the Two-Year College.* Los Angeles: University of California Junior College Leadership Program, 1968. (ED 019 939)

COHEN, A. M., AND BRAWER, F. B. *Measuring Faculty Performance.* ERIC Clearinghouse for Junior Colleges, Monograph #4. Washington, D.C.: American Association of Junior Colleges, 1969. (ED 031 222)

COHEN, A. M., AND BRAWER, F. B. *Student Characteristics: Personality and Dropout Propensity.* ERIC Clearinghouse for Junior Colleges, Monograph #9. Washington, D.C.: American Association of Junior Colleges, 1970. (ED 038 130)

COHEN, A. M., AND OTHERS. *A Constant Variable.* San Francisco: Jossey-Bass, 1971.

CONSTANTINOPLE, A. "An Ericksonian Measure of Personality Development in College Students." *Developmental Psychology,* 1969, *1* (4), 357–372.

COOK, W. W., LEEDS, C. H., AND CALLIS, R. *The Minnesota Teacher Attitude Inventory.* New York: Psychological Corp., 1951.

COOLEY, W. W. "Differences Among College Students." In J. C. Flanagan and W. W. Cooley (Eds.), *Project Talent: One-Year Follow-up Studies.* Pittsburgh: University of Pittsburgh, 1966.

COOMBS, P. H. *The World Educational Crisis; A Systems Analysis.* New York: Oxford University Press, 1968.

COOPER, L. B. "A Study in Freshman Elimination in One College." *Nation's Schools,* Sept. 1928, *2,* 25–29.

COX, R. D. "The Normal Personality: An Analysis of Rorschach and Thematic Apperception Test Responses of a Sweep of College Students." *Journal of Projective Techniques,* 1956, *20,* 70–77.

CREAGER, J. A., AND OTHERS. *National Norms for Entering College Freshmen.* Washington, D.C.: American Council on Education, 1969.

CROSS, K. P. "Access and Accommodation in Higher Education." *The Research Reporter,* 1971, *6* (2).

CROSS, K. P. *Beyond the Open Door.* San Francisco: Jossey-Bass, 1971.

CROSS, K. P. *The Junior College Student: A Research Description.*

Princeton, N.J.: Educational Testing Service, 1968. (ED 024 354)

CROSS, K. P. "Occupationally Oriented Students." *Junior College Research Review,* Nov. 1970, *5* (3). (ED 043 328)

DARLEY, J. G., AND HAGENAH, T. *Vocational Interest Measurements: Theory and Practice.* Minneapolis: University of Minnesota, 1955.

DAVIS, B. H. "American Association of University Professors." *Junior College Journal,* Dec. 1968–Jan. 1969, *39* (4), 11–16.

DAVIS, J. A. *Undergraduate Career Decisions: Correlates of Occupational Choice.* Chicago: Aldine, 1965.

DIENST, E. "On Alienation and Activism." *The Research Reporter,* 1972, *7* (1), 1–4.

DIXON, W. J. *Biomedical Computer Programs.* Los Angeles: University of California, 1968.

DOMAS, S. J., AND TIEDMAN, D. V. "Teacher Competence: An Annotated Bibliography." *Journal of Experimental Education,* Dec. 1950, *19,* 101–218.

DOUVAN, E., AND KAYE, C. "Motivational Factors in College Entrance." In N. Sanford (Ed.), *The American College.* New York: Wiley, 1962.

DRESSEL, P. L. "On Critical Thinking." In P. L. Dressel (Ed.), *Evaluation in the Basic College at Michigan State University.* (1st ed.) New York: Harper, 1958.

DRESSEL, P. L. "Liberal Arts Students Advised to Withdraw." *Journal of Higher Education,* Jan. 1943, *14,* 43–45.

ECKLAND, B. K. "College Dropouts Who Came Back." *Harvard Educational Review,* Summer 1964, *34* (3), 402–420.

ELTON, C. F., AND ROSE, H. A. "Male Occupational Constancy and Change: Its Prediction According to Holland's Theory." *Journal of Counseling Psychology,* Nov. 1970, *17* (6), 1–19.

EMMERICH, W. "Personality Development and Concepts of Structure." *Child Development,* 1968, *39,* 671–690.

ERIKSON, E. H. *Childhood and Society.* (2nd ed.) New York: Norton, 1963.

ERIKSON, E. H. "Growth and Crisis of the 'Healthy Personality.' " In M. J. E. Senn (Ed.), *Symposium on the Healthy Personality.* Supplement II. New York: Josiah Macy, Jr. Foundation, 1950.

ERIKSON, E. H. "Identity and the Life Cycle." *Psychological Issues, 1* (1), Monograph #1. New York: International Universities Press, 1959.

ERIKSON, E. H. *Insight and Responsibility*. (1st ed.) New York: Norton, 1964.

FADER, D. "Shaping an English Curriculum to Fit the Junior College Student." *Junior College Research Review,* June 1971, 5 (10). (ED 049 734)

FEDER, D. D. "Factors Which Affect Achievement and Its Prediction at the College Level." *Journal of the American Association of Collegiate Registrars,* 1940, *15* (2), 107–118.

FELDMAN, K. A., AND NEWCOMB, T. M. *The Impact of College on Students*. San Francisco, Jossey-Bass, 1969.

FEUER, L. S. "Conflict of Generations." *Saturday Review,* Jan. 18, 1969.

FISHMAN, J. A. "Some Socio-Psychological Theory for Selecting and Guiding College Students." In N. Sanford (Ed.), *The American College*. New York: Wiley, 1962.

FLACKS, R. *Deviant Subcultures on a College Campus*. Ann Arbor: University of Michigan, 1963.

FLANAGAN, J. C. "Stability of Career Plans." In W. W. Cooley and J. C. Flanagan (Eds.), *Project Talent: One-Year Follow-up Studies*. Pittsburgh: University of Pittsburgh, 1966.

FORD, D. H., AND URBAN, H. B. "College Dropouts: Successes or Failures?" In L. A. Pervin, L. E. Reik, and W. Dalrymple (Eds.), *The College Dropout and the Utilization of Talent*. Princeton, N.J.: Princeton University, 1966.

FREEDMAN, M. B. *The College Experience*. San Francisco: Jossey-Bass, 1967.

FREEDMAN, M. B. *Impact of College*. Washington, D.C.: Office of Education, U.S. Department of Health, Education and Welfare, 1960.

FREEDMAN, M. B. "The Passage Through College." *Journal of Social Issues,* 1956, *12*, 13–27.

FRIEDENBERG, E. Z. "The Revolt Against Democracy." *Change in Higher Education,* May–June 1969, *1* (3), 11–17.

FROMM, E. *Escape From Freedom*. New York: Farrar, Straus, and Giroux, 1941.

FROMM, E. *The Sane Society*. New York: Holt, Rinehart, and Winston, 1955.

GALTON, F. *Inquiries Into Human Faculty*. New York: Macmillan, 1883.

GARRISON, R. *Junior College Faculty: Issues and Problems*. Washington, D.C.: American Association of Junior Colleges, 1967.

GETZELS, J. W., AND JACKSON, P. W. *Creativity and Intelligence; Explorations With Gifted Students.* New York: Wiley, 1962.

GOLDSEN, R. K., AND OTHERS. *What College Students Think.* Princeton, N.J.: Van Nostrand, 1960.

GOLDSTEIN, K. *The Organism; a Holistic Approach to Biology Derived From Pathological Data in Man.* New York: American Book Co., 1939.

GOODLAD, J. L., KLEIN, M. F., AND ASSOCIATES. *Behind the Classroom Door.* Worthington, Ohio: Charles A. Jones Publishing, 1970.

GOODMAN, P. *Growing Up Absurd.* New York: Random House, 1960.

GORDON, L. V. *Survey of Interpersonal Values.* Chicago: Science Research Associates, 1960–63.

GREENBERGER, E., AND SØRENSON, A. B. "Toward A Concept of Psychosocial Maturity." Report #108. Baltimore, Md.: Center for Social Organization of Schools, Johns Hopkins University, 1971.

GREENBERGER, E., AND OTHERS. "Toward the Measurement of Psychosocial Maturity." Report #110. Baltimore, Md.: Center for Social Organization of Schools, Johns Hopkins University, 1971.

GROSS, M. L. "It's the Dropout Level, Not the Rate, That's Worrisome." *Los Angeles Times,* Mar. 14, 1969.

HAAN, N. "Proposed Model of Ego Functioning." *Psychological Monographs,* 1963, *77* (8), 1–23.

HADDEN, J. K. "The Private Generation." *Psychology Today,* Oct. 1969, 32–35.

HALL, C. S., AND LINDZEY, G. *Theories of Personality.* New York: Wiley, 1957.

HARLOW, H. F. "The Nature of Love." *The American Psychologist,* 1958, *13,* 673–685.

HARRIS, S. E. *A Statistical Portrait of Higher Education.* New York: McGraw Hill, 1972.

HARTMANN, H. *Ego Psychology and the Problem of Adaptation.* New York: International Universities Press, 1961.

HARVEY, O. J., HUNT, D. E., AND SCHRODER, H. M. *Conceptual Systems and Personality Organization.* New York: Wiley, 1961.

HATHAWAY, S. R., AND MEEHL, P. E. *An Atlas for the Clinical Use of the MMPI.* Minneapolis: University of Minnesota, 1951.

HEATH, C. W. *What People Are; a Study of Normal Young Men.* Cambridge, Mass.: Harvard University, 1945.

HEATH, D. H. *Explorations of Maturity: Studies of Mature and Immature College Men.* New York: Appleton-Century-Crofts, 1965,

HEATH, R. *The Reasonable Adventurer.* Pittsburgh: University of Pittsburgh, 1964.

HEATH, R. "The Reasonable Adventurer and Others." *Journal of Counseling Psychology,* 1959, 6 (1), 3–14.

HEIST, P. (Ed.) *The Creative College Student: An Unmet Challenge.* San Francisco: Jossey-Bass, 1968.

HEIST, P. "Creative Students: College Transients." In P. Heist (Ed.), *The Creative College Student.* San Francisco: Jossey-Bass, 1968.

HEIST, P., AND YONGE, G. *Omnibus Personality Inventory, Form F Manual.* New York: Psychological Corp., 1962.

HENDRIX, V. L. "Relationships Between Personnel Policies and Faculty Life Record Data in Public Junior Colleges." *California Journal of Educational Research,* May 1964, 15 (3), 150–157.

HINSIE, L. E., AND CAMPBELL, R. J. *Psychiatric Dictionary.* New York: Oxford University, 1960.

HODGKINSON, H. "The Next Decade." *The Research Reporter,* 1970, 5 (1).

HOLLAND, J. L. *The Psychology of Vocational Choice.* Waltham, Mass.: Blaisdell, 1966.

HOLLAND, J. L., AND RICHARDS, J. M., JR. *Academic and Non-Academic Accomplishment: Correlated or Uncorrelated?* Research Report #2. Iowa City, Iowa; American College Testing Program, 1965.

HORNEY, K. *Our Inner Conflicts; a Constructive Theory of Neurosis.* New York: Norton, 1945.

HOYT, D. P. *The Relationsship Between College Grades and Adult Achievement: A Review of the Literature.* Research Report #7. Iowa City, Iowa: American College Testing Program, 1965.

IFFERT, R. E. "Institutional Implications—Facilities, Faculties, Students." Paper presented at the Princeton University Conference, Oct. 8, 1964.

IFFERT, R. E. "Retention and Withdrawal of College Students." U.S. Department of Health, Education and Welfare, Bulletin 1958, #1. Washington, D.C.: U.S. Government Printing Office, 1957.

IFFERT, R. E. "What Ought Colleges and Universities Do About Student Mortality?" In G. K. Smith (Ed.), *Proceedings of the Ninth Annual National Conference on Higher Education* of the Association for Higher Education. From *Current Issues in Higher Education,* 1954, 170–180.

JACOB, P. E. *Changing Values in College: An Exploratory Study of the*

Impact of College Teaching. (1st ed.) New York: Harper, 1957.

JENCKS, C., AND RIESMAN, D. *The Academic Revolution.* (1st ed.) Garden City, N.Y.: Doubleday, 1968.

JUNG, C. G. *Psychological Types.* London: Routledge & Kegan Paul, 1923.

KATZ, J., AND OTHERS. *No Time For Youth: Growth and Constraint in College Students.* San Francisco: Jossey-Bass, 1968.

KELLY, M. F., AND CONNOLLY, J. *Orientation for Faculty in Junior Colleges.* ERIC Clearinghouse for Junior Colleges, Monograph #10. Washington, D.C.: American Association of Junior Colleges, 1970. (ED 043 323)

KENISTON, K. "Social Change and Youth in America." In K. Yamamoto (Ed.), *The College Student and His Culture.* Boston: Houghton Mifflin, 1968.

KING, S. H. *Personality Stability: Early Findings of the Harvard Student Study.* Paper presented at the American College Personnel Association Conference in Dallas, Texas, March 21, 1967.

KLAPP, O. *Collective Search for Identity.* New York: Holt, Rinehart & Winston, 1969.

KLOPFER, B., AND DAVIDSON, H. *The Rorschach Technique; an Introductory Manual.* New York: Harcourt Brace Jovanovich, 1962.

KLOPFER, B., CRUMPTON, E., AND GRAYSON, H. "Rating Scales for Ego Functioning Applicable to Diagnostic Testing." *Journal of Projective Techniques, 1958, 1.*

KLOPFER, B., AND OTHERS. *Developments in the Rorschach Technique.* Vol. I. Yonkers-on-Hudson, N.Y.: World Book Co., 1954.

KLOPFER, B., AND OTHERS. *Developments in the Rorschach Technique.* Vol. II. Yonkers-on-Hudson, N.Y.: World Book Co., 1956.

KLOPFER, B., AND OTHERS. Rorschach Prognostic Rating Scale. In B. Klopfer, *Developments in the Rorschach Technique,* Vol. 1. Yonkers-on-Hudson, N.Y.: World Book Co., 1954.

KLUCKHOHN, C. "Values and Value Orientations in the Theory of Action." In T. Parsons and E. A. Shils (Eds.), *Toward a General Theory of Action.* Cambridge, Mass.: Harvard University, 1954.

KLUCKHOHN, F. R., AND STRODTBECK, F. L. *Variations in Value Orientation.* Evanston, Ill.: Row, Peterson, 1961.

KNODE, J. C. *Foundations of an American Philosophy of Education.* New York: Van Nostrand, 1942.

KNOELL, D. M. "A Critical Review of Research on the College Dropout." In L. A. Pervin, L. E. Reik, and W. Dalrymple (Eds.), *The College Dropout and the Utilization of Talent*. Princeton, N.J.: Princeton University, 1966.

KOESTLER, A. *The Act of Creation*. New York: Macmillan, 1970.

KOHLBERG, L. "The Developmental Modes of Moral Thinking in the Years Ten to Sixteen." University of Chicago, 1958 (unpublished).

KRIS, E. "On Preconscious Mental Processes." In D. Rapaport (Ed.), *Organization and Pathology of Thought*. New York: Columbia University, 1951.

KRIS, E. *Psychoanalytic Explorations in Art*. New York: International Universities Press, 1952.

KROEBER, T. C. "Coping Functions of the Ego Mechanisms." In R. W. White (Ed.), *The Study of Lives*. New York: Atherton Press, 1963.

KUBIE, L. S. "The Ontogeny of the Dropout Problem." In L. A. Pervin, L. E. Reik, and W. Dalrymple (Eds.), *The College Dropout and the Utilization of Talent*. Princeton, N.J.: Princeton University, 1966.

KUDER, G. F. *Administrator's Manual, Kuder Preference Record, Vocational*, Form C. Chicago: Science Research Associates, 1960.

LAURITS, J. "Thoughts on the Evaluation of Teaching." *Educational Horizons*, Spring 1967, *45*, 87–97.

LEHMANN, I. J., AND DRESSEL, P. L. *Critical Thinking, Attitudes and Values in Higher Education; Final Report*. U.S. Office of Education Cooperative Research Project #590. East Lansing, Mich.: Michigan State University, 1962.

LIDZ, T. *The Person: His Development Throughout the Life Cycle*. New York: Basic Books, 1968.

LOEVINGER, J. "The Meaning and Measurement of Ego Development." *American Psychologist*, 1966, *21* (3), 195–206.

LOEVINGER, J., AND WESSLER, R. *Measuring Ego Development*. San Francisco: Jossey-Bass, 1970.

LOMBARDI, J. Personal communication, 1971.

LUDWIG, E. G., AND EICHHORN, R. L. "Age and Disillusionment: A Study of Value Changes Associated With Aging." *Journal of Gerontology*, February, 1967, *22* (1).

MC KEACHIE, W. J. "How Do Students Learn?" In R. M. Cooper (Ed.), *The Two Ends of the Log*. Minneapolis: University of Minnesota, 1958.

MC KEACHIE, W. J. "Procedures and Techniques of Teaching: A Survey of Experimental Studies." In N. Sanford (Ed.), *The American College,* New York: Wiley, 1962.

MC KEACHIE, W. J. "Student-Centered vs. Instructor-Centered Instruction." *Journal of Educational Psychology,* 1954, *45,* 143–150.

MC KEACHIE, W. J., AND OTHERS. "Student Affiliation Motives, Teacher Warmth, and Academic Achievement." *Journal of Personality and Social Psychology,* 1966, *4* (4), 457–461.

MAC KINNON, D. W. "The Nature and Nurture of Creative Talent." *American Psychologist,* 1962, *17* (7), 484–495.

MARLAND, S. P., JR. "A Year Ago This Week." Address to the National Press Club, Washington, D.C., Dec. 15, 1971.

MARTIN, W. B. *Conformity: Standards and Change in Higher Education.* (1st ed.) San Francisco: Jossey-Bass, 1969.

MARX, K. *Selected Writings in Sociology and Social Philosophy.* T. B. Bottomore and M. Rubel (Eds.); T. B. Bottomore (Trans.). London: Watts, 1956.

MASLOW, A. H. *Motivation and Personality.* (1st ed.) New York: Harper and Row, 1954.

MEDSKER, L. L., AND TILLERY, D. *Breaking the Access Barriers; a Profile of the Two-Year Colleges.* New York: McGraw-Hill, 1971.

MERTON, R. K., READER, G. G., AND KENDALL, P. L. (Eds.) *The Student-Physician: Introductory Studies in the Sociology of Medical Education.* Cambridge, Mass.: Harvard University, 1957.

METZ, J. R. "A Method for Measuring Aspects of Ego Strength." *Journal of Projective Techniques,* 1961, *25* (4).

MISCHEL, W. "Father-Absence and Delay of Gratification: Cross-Cultural Comparisons." *Journal of Abnormal and Social Psychology,* 1961, *63* (1), 116–124.

MISCHEL, W., AND METZNER, R. "Preference for Delayed Reward As a Function of Age, Intelligence, and Length of Delay Interval." *Journal of Abnormal and Social Psychology,* 1962, *64* (6), 425–431.

MITCHELL, J. A., AND MOOREHEAD, R. "A Study of Full-Time Students Who Discontinued Their Attendance at A.W.C. After Attending One or Both Semesters of the 1966–67 School Year." Yuma: Arizona Western College, 1968. (ED 024 360)

MOORE, W., JR. *Blind Man on a Freeway.* San Francisco: Jossey-Bass, 1971.

MORRIS, C. *Varieties of Human Value.* Chicago: University of Chicago Press, 1956.

MÜNSTERBERG, H. *On the Witness Stand.* New York: Doubleday, 1908.

MURPHY, G., AND LIKERT, R. *Public Opinion and the Individual: A Psychological Study of Standard Attitudes on Public Questions, With a Retest Five Years Later.* New York: Russell and Russell, 1967.

MURPHY, L. B. "Coping Devices and Defense Mechanisms in Relation to Autonomous Ego Functions." *Bulletin of the Menninger Clinic,* 1960, *24,* 144–153.

MURPHY, L. B., AND RAUSHENBUSH, E. (Eds.) *Achievement in the College Years; a Record of Intellectual and Personal Growth.* (1st ed.) New York: Harper and Row, 1960.

MURRAY, H. A., AND OTHERS (Eds.) *Explorations in Personality.* New York: Oxford University Press, 1938.

NEWCOMB, T. M. "Student Peer-Group Influence." In N. Sanford (Ed.), *The American College.* New York: Wiley, 1962.

NIC, N., BENT, D. H., AND HULL, C. H. *SPSS: Statistical Package for the Social Sciences.* New York: McGraw-Hill, 1970.

PACE, C. R. *CUES: College and University Environment Scales,* Technical Manual. (2nd ed.) Princeton, N.J.: Educational Testing Service, 1962.

PACE, C. R. "Methods of Describing College Cultures." In K. Yamamoto (Ed.), *The College Student and His Culture: An Analysis.* Boston: Houghton Mifflin, 1968.

PACE, C. R. "Perspectives on the Student and His College." In L. E. Dennis and J. P. Kauffman (Eds.), *The College and the Student.* Washington, D.C.: American Council on Education, 1966.

PACE, C. R. "University-Wide Studies in Evaluation of General Education at Syracuse University." In P. L. Dressel (Ed.), *Evaluation in General Education.* Dubuque, Iowa: Brown Co., 1954.

PACE, C. R., AND STERN, G. G. "An Approach to the Measurement of Psychological Characteristics of College Environments." *Journal of Educational Psychology,* 1958, *49* (5), 269–277.

PAETZ, C. G. "A Comparison of Perceived Educational Values of Community College Students, Their Parents, and Faculties in Five Oregon Community Colleges." University of Oregon, Eugene, 1966. (ED 016 477; not avail. EDRS)

PANOS, R. J., AND ASTIN, A. W. "Attrition Among College Students." ACE Research Reports, *2* (4). Washington, D.C.: American Council on Education, 1967.

PARK, Y. *Junior College Faculty: Their Values and Perceptions.* ERIC Clearinghouse for Junior Colleges, Monograph #12. Washington, D.C.: American Association of Junior Colleges, 1971. (ED 050 725)

PARK, Y. "The Junior College Staff: Values and Institutional Perceptions." University of California, Los Angeles, 1970. (unpublished)

PARKER, S., AND ROKEACH, M. *The Annals of the American Academy of Political and Social Science.* March 1970, *388,* 98–111.

PERVIN, L. A., REIK, L. E., AND DALRYMPLE, W. (Eds.), *The College Dropout and the Utilization of Talent.* Princeton, N.J.: Princeton University, 1966.

PIAGET, J. *The Psychology of Intelligence.* New York: Harcourt Brace Jovanovich, 1947.

PLANT, W. T. "Changes in Ethnocentrism Associated With a Four-Year College Education." *Journal of Educational Psychology,* 1958, *49* (3), 162–165.

PLANT, W. T. *Personality Changes Associated With a College Education.* U.S. Office of Education Cooperative Research Project #348. San Jose, Calif.: San Jose State College, 1962.

PLANT, W. T., AND TELFORD, C. W. "Changes in Personality for Groups Completing Different Amounts of College Over Two Years." *Genetic Psychology Monographs,* 1966, *74,* 3–36.

PRELINGER, E., AND OTHERS. *Rating Scales for Characterological Assessment.* New Haven, Conn.: Yale University, 1964.

PRICE, P. B., AND OTHERS. "Measurement of Physician Performance." *Journal of Medical Education,* 1964, *39,* 203–211.

RAPAPORT, D. "The Conceptual Model of Psychoanalysis." *Journal of Personality,* 1951, *20,* 56–81.

RIESMAN, D. "The Influence of Student Culture and Faculty Values in the American College." In G. Z. F. Bereday and J. A. Lauwerys (Eds.), *The Yearbook of Education, 1959.* London: Evans Bros., 1959.

RIESMAN, D. "The Jacob Report." *American Sociological Review,* 1958, *23* (6), 732–738.

ROE, A. *The Psychology of Occupations.* New York: Wiley, 1956.

ROGERS, C. R. *Client-Centered Therapy: Its Current Practice, Implication and Theory.* Boston: Houghton Mifflin, 1951.

ROGERS, C. R. *Freedom to Learn; a View of What Education Might Become.* Columbus, Ohio: Merrill, 1969.

ROGERS, C. R. *On Becoming a Person.* Boston: Houghton Mifflin, 1961.

ROKEACH, M. *The Open and Closed Mind: Investigations Into the Na-*

ture of Belief Systems and Personality Systems. New York: Basic Books, 1960.

ROKEACH, M. *Beliefs, Attitudes and Values.* San Francisco: Jossey-Bass, 1968.

ROKEACH, M. *The Measurement of Values and Value Systems.* East Lansing: Michigan State University, 1969.

ROKEACH, M. "Faith, Hope and Bigotry." *Psychology Today,* April 1970, 33–37.

ROKEACH, M., AND PARKER, S. "Values as Social Indicators of Poverty and Race Relations in America." *Annals of the American Academy of Political and Social Science,* March 1970.

RORSCHACH, H. *Psychodiagnostics.* P. Lemkau and B. Kronenberg (Trans.), (7th ed.) New York: Grune and Stratton, 1969.

ROWE, F. B. *Characteristics of Women's College Students.* SREB Research, Monograph #8. Atlanta, Ga.: Southern Regional Education Board, 1964.

SANFORD, N. (Ed.) *The American College: A Psychological and Social Interpretation of the Higher Learning.* New York: Wiley, 1962.

SANFORD, N. "Motivation of High Achievers." In O. David (Ed.), *The Education of Women.* Washington, D.C.: American Council on Education, 1959.

SANFORD, N. "Personality Development During the College Years." *Personnel and Guidance Journal,* Oct. 1956, *35* (2), 74–80.

SANFORD, N. *Self and Society: Social Change and Individual Development.* New York: Atherton Press, 1966.

SANFORD, N. *Where Colleges Fail: A Study of the Student as a Person.* San Francisco: Jossey-Bass, 1967.

SANFORD, N., WEBSTER, H., AND FREEDMAN, M. "Impulse Expression as a Variable of Personality." *Psychological Monographs,* 1957, *71* (11).

SCHAFER, R. "On the Psychoanalytic Study of Test Results." *Journal of Projective Techniques,* 1958, *17* (3), 335–339.

SCHOENFELDT, L. F. "Post High-School Education." In J. C. Flanagan and W. W. Cooley (Eds.), *Project Talent.* Pittsburgh: University of Pittsburgh, 1966.

SHIPE, D., AND LAZARE, S. "Two Measures of Delay Gratification: Age and Socioeconomic Status in Young Children." Ontario Institute for Studies in Education, Canada. *Psychological Abstracts,* 1969, *43* (2).

SHYBUT, J. "Delay of Gratification and Severity of Disturbance Among Hospitalized Psychiatric Patients." Dissertation Abstracts, 1966, 26 (11).

SMITH, M. B. "Personal Values in the Study of Lives." In R. W. White (Ed.), The Study of Lives. New York: Atherton Press, 1963.

SNYDER, B. R. "Adaptation, Education, Emotional Growth." In L. A. Pervin, L. E. Reik, and W. Dalrymple (Eds.), The College Dropout and the Utilization of Talent. Princeton, N.J.: Princeton University, 1966.

SPRANGER, E. Types of Men. P. J. W. Pigors (Trans.). Halle (Saale): M. Niemeyer, 1928.

STERN, G. G. "Environments for Learning." In N. Sanford (Ed.), The American College. New York: Wiley, 1962.

STERN, G. G., STEIN, M. I., AND BLOOM, B. S. Methods in Personality Assessment (rev. ed.). Glencoe, Ill.: Free Press, 1963.

STEWARD, L. H. "Characteristics of Junior College Students in Occupationally Oriented Curricula." School of Education Report #1966-1. Berkeley: University of California, 1966. (ED 011 450)

STOUFFER, S. A., AND OTHERS. Measurement and Prediction. New York: Wiley, 1966.

STRONG, E. K., JR. Vocational Interests of Men and Women. Stanford, Calif.: Stanford University, 1943.

SUCZEK, R. F., AND ALPERT, E. A. Personality Characteristics of College Dropouts. Cooperative Research Project No. 5-8232. Berkeley, Calif., University of California, 1966.

SULLIVAN, E. V., MC CULLOUGH, G., AND STAGER, M. "A Developmental Study of the Relationship Between Conceptual, Ego and Moral Development." Child Development, June 1970, 41 (2), 399–411.

SULLIVAN, H. S. The Interpersonal Theory of Psychiatry. H. S. Perry and M. L. Gawel (Eds.). (1st ed.) New York: Norton, 1953.

SUMMERSKILL, J. "Dropouts From College." In N. Sanford (Ed.), The American College. New York: Wiley, 1962.

SUPER, D. E., AND CRITES, J. O. Appraising Vocational Fitness by Means of Psychological Tests. (Rev. ed.) New York: Harper and Row, 1962.

SUSSMAN, L. Freshman Morale at M.I.T.: The Class of 1961. Cambridge, Mass.: Massachusetts Institute of Technology, 1960.

SYNGG, D., AND COMBS, A. W. Individual Behavior. New York: Harper and Row, 1949.

TELFORD, C. W., AND PLANT, W. T. *The Psychological Impact of the Public Two-Year College on Certain Non-Intellectual Functions.* Cooperative Research Project SAE 8646. San Jose, Calif.: San Jose State College, 1963. (ED 002 985)

TERMAN, L. M. "The Discovery and Encouragement of Exceptional Talent." *American Psychologist,* 1954, *9* (5), 221–230.

TERMAN, L. M., AND MILES, C. C. *Sex and Personality.* New York: McGraw-Hill, 1936.

THIELENS, W., JR. "The Structure of Faculty Influence: A Case Study of the Instructor's Role in Three Kinds of Change Among Columbia College Students." New York: Columbia University, 1966.

THISTLEWAITE, D. L. "College Press and Student Achievement." *Journal of Educational Psychology,* 1959, *50,* 183–191.

THOMAS, W. I., AND ZNANIECKI, F. *The Polish Peasant in Europe and America.* New York: A. A. Knopf, 1927.

TILLERY, D. "Differential Characteristics of Entering Freshman at the University of California and Their Peers at California Junior Colleges." University of California, Berkeley, 1964. (unpublished)

TILLERY, D. *School to College: Distribution and Differentiation of Youth.* Berkeley: University of California, 1971.

TOLOR, A., AND LE BLANC, R. F. "Personality Correlates of Alienation." *Journal of Consulting and Clinical Psychology,* 1971, *37* (3).

VERNON, P. E., AND ALLPORT, G. W. "A Test for Personal Values." *Journal of Abnormal and Social Psychology,* 1931, *26* (3), 231–248.

WARREN, J. R., AND HEIST, P. "Personality Attributes of Gifted College Students." *Science,* July 1960, *132,* 330–337.

WEBB, S. C., AND CROWDER, D. G. *The Psychological Needs of Emory College Students.* Research Memorandum #5-61. Atlanta, Ga.: Emory University, 1961.

WEBSTER, H., FREEDMAN, M. B., AND HEIST, P. "Personality Changes in College Students." In N. Sanford (Ed.), *The American College.* New York: Wiley, 1962.

WERNER, H. *Comparative Psychology of Mental Development.* (Rev. ed.) Chicago: Follett, 1948.

WERNER, H. "The Concept of Development From a Comparative and Organismic Point of View." In D. B. Harris (Ed.), *The Concept of Development; an Issue in the Study of Human Behavior.* Minneapolis: University of Minnesota, 1957.

WHIPPLE, G. M. *Manual of Mental and Physical Tests.* Baltimore: Warwick and York, 1910.

WHITE, R. W. *Lives in Progress: A Study of the Natural Growth of Personality.* New York: Dryden Press, 1952.

WIERGYNSKI, G. H. "A Student Declaration: 'Our Most Wrenching Problem. . . .' " *Fortune,* 1969.

WILIE, R. C. *The Self-Concept; a Critical Survey of Pertinent Research Literature.* Lincoln, Neb.: University of Nebraska, 1961.

WILLIAMS, R. M. "Values." In *International Encyclopedia of the Social Sciences.* New York: Macmillan, 1968.

WOLFE, D. *America's Resources of Specialized Talent.* New York: Harper and Row, 1954.

YAMAMOTO, K. (Ed.) *The College Student and His Culture: An Analysis.* Boston: Houghton Mifflin, 1968.

Index

225